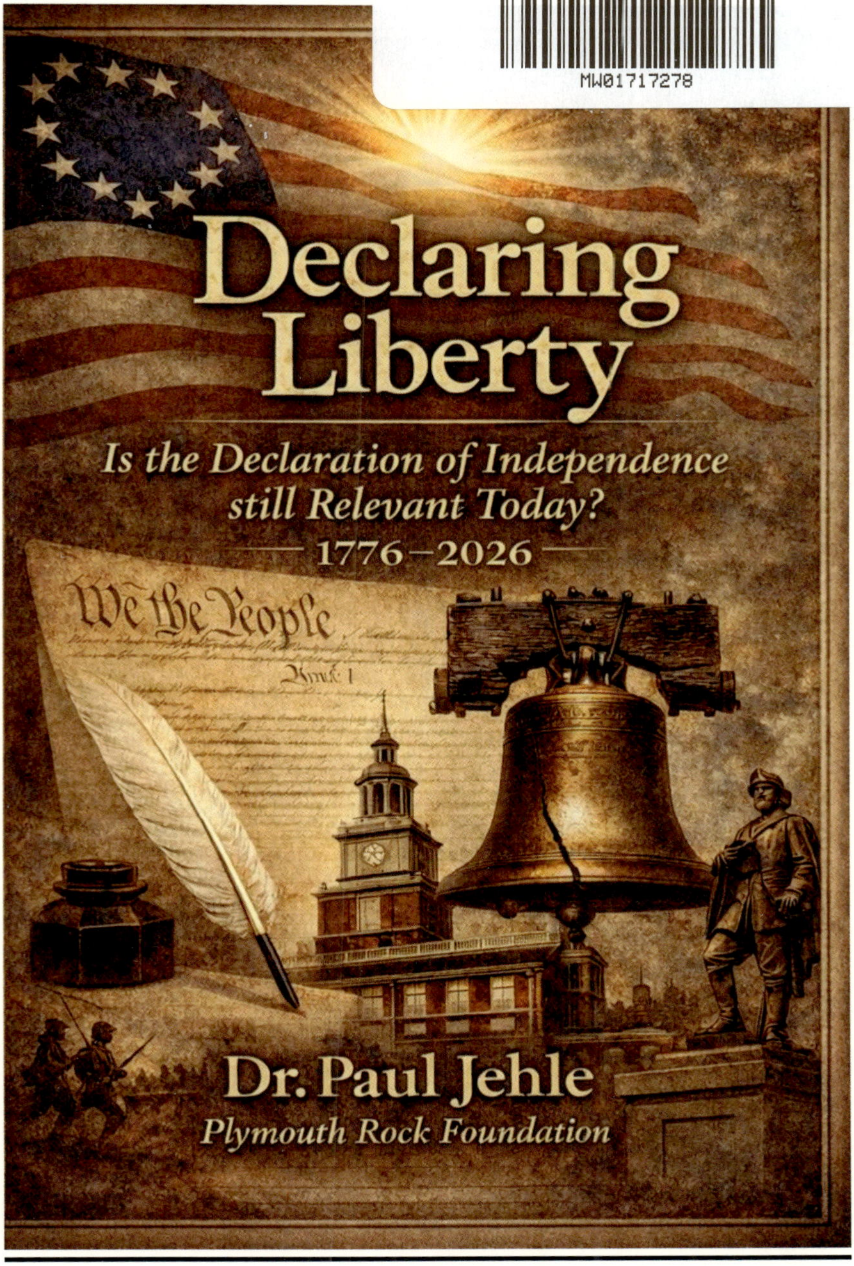
Declaring Liberty
Is the Declaration of Independence still Relevant Today?
1776–2026
We the People
Dr. Paul Jehle
Plymouth Rock Foundation

Bill

Declaring Liberty

Is the Declaration of Independence still Relevant Today?

Paul Jehle

Dr. Paul Jehle
Plymouth Rock Foundation
www.plymrock.org

Published by:
Brentwood Christian Press
PO Box 4773
Columbus, Georgia 31914-4773
(800) 334-8861

In Dedication from Paul and Charlene to
Our Children and Grandchildren

Jonathan and Rebecca Jehle
Judah, Noah, Eliana, Lydia

Asad and Shauna (Jehle) Moosa

That the blessings of liberty would be taught and understood by our Posterity

Table of Contents

What People are Saying about *Declaring Liberty*

A new Spiritual Awakening is here, and Paul Jehle's new book, *Declaring Liberty*, arrives at the perfect moment to guide a rising generation into why preserving our national liberties is not just a civic duty — it is a divine calling. Understanding the Christian roots of our nation's founding and the long struggle of the human race for religious and civil liberty is essential to understanding the future. It is also critical to our understanding of what our mission should be in this world. Without this knowledge, we risk confusion about our responsibilities. We are blind to the blessings of freedom that God has entrusted to us—and unaware of the critical role our stewardship of that liberty plays in the salvation of the world.

Long before President Reagan's 1989 Farewell Address called on Americans to educate future generations about the importance of preserving our freedom principles, Paul Jehle was already blazing this trail. We met Paul in 1981, and he had already spent five years researching the history of American Christian liberty. Now, with *Declaring Liberty*, Paul shares a treasure trove of insights on the Declaration of Independence and the freedom principles that shaped our nation—knowledge that is more vital today than ever. This is not just a book to read — it is a call to action. Master its teachings, share them with your children, and spread the message of liberty to everyone you meet. This book is a must-have to champion this mission!

Bob and Rose Weiner, FL, President and Founders of Weiner Ministries International and Maranatha Publications/WeinerMedia

Dr. Paul Jehle represents the present generation of 'founders' who are reviving the Declaration in this age. They are challenging American Christians to embrace and understand again the principles and power that free and ensure the happiness of nations. The Declaration must be retaught and relearned generationally or lost. In the present, the need is vital.

Thank you, Paul, for forwarding the gift of liberty through your lifelong work in proclaiming American Christian government and education.

Carole Adams, President
Foundation for American Christian Education, VA

During this 250th Anniversary, if there is one book every Christian should read regarding the Declaration of Independence, Paul Jehle's is my recommendation. In addition to explaining its origin and context, Jehle brings out almost every phrase of it and explains technical legal concepts in an accessible way for most people. He draws constantly from the Scripture and from history to teach the depth of the Declaration's ideas, while also making it relevant to modern issues such as racism, life, family rights, liberty, the place of resistance and fighting for liberty.

Mark Beliles, Ph.D. co-author of *America' Providential History, Contending for the Constitution*, and *Thomas Jefferon and the God Who Gave Us Liberty,* VA

I have known Dr. Paul Jehle since 1989 when I first interviewed him for a nationwide program, hosted by D. James Kennedy, on the Pilgrims. Paul Jehle is incredibly well-informed on what made America. He is a walking encyclopedia on America's Christian roots. Paul speaks and writes so well on the link between our God-given liberties, as found in the Bible, and the American experiment of self-rule under God. The whole American experiment began in a very real way in the cabin of the Mayflower when the Pilgrims wrote up the Mayflower Compact in 1620. Jumping ahead 150 years or so later, Samuel Adams, who called himself "the last of the Puritans," remarked, "Is not America already independent? Then why not declare it?" This book explains why they "declared it." I am happy to recommend this new book by Dr. Paul Jehle on the 250th anniversary of the Declaration of Independence, on the Biblical ideas that ultimately inspired its creation.

Dr. Jerry Newcombe, author, executive director of Providence Forum (of Coral Ridge Ministries), FL

Many are ignorant of the historical and theological foundations of our nation. In "*Declaring Liberty*", Dr. Jehle not only skillfully unearths the foundation of liberty, he also historically and theologically offers a blueprint to how that foundational document, rooted in Scriptural truths offers a clear way forward for any nation and its people, who are willing once again to declare in thought, and demonstrate in character, the principles that made a great reset in the world of its time.

I have known Dr. Jehle for more than 35 years. The principles that he taught regarding Biblical covenant, balanced church government and the joining of the generations, became the basis for our church preamble and constitution that has guided us as a church and Christian school for more than 30 years. This has included establishing a Christian University training leaders in many nations of the world. In the many years of our working together, Dr. Jehle has demonstrated a character that is articulate, careful, thoughtful, and humble. His insights are precious and offer hope and practical application to answer the Great Commission call to disciple nations.

I encourage you to not just read "*Declaring Liberty*" but study the truths and ponder how they might serve as an application to your role in the family, community, church and nation. "*Declaring Liberty*" should be required reading for schools, universities, religious and community leadership training.

Ronald L. Bernier, President, Master Builder Ministries, East Gate Christian Academy, Master Builder Christian International University, MA

In Declaring Liberty Paul Jehle has written a very important analysis of a familiar but often misunderstood document, the Declaration of Independence. With his expert knowledge of the Bible, history and Biblical principles of government, Paul carefully explains the many valuable truths detailed in this world changing document, and he connects the dots so we are enabled to restore our nation to its original Godly design. Today, we are in a national crisis as the forces of tyranny, cloaked in sheep's clothing, seek to bring us further into bondage. Those who eschew tyranny and love liberty will find much in Declaring Liberty to encourage them, and equip them to pass these truths down to the next generation.

Max Lyons, Ph.D. - The Biblical Thinker LLC, VA

Dr. Jehle is a brilliant historian and writer presenting incredibly thoughtful and thorough research and analysis of the Declaration of Independence. He demonstrates its relevance not just to the United States but to the world- recognizing the key principles held within it set a historic precedent that we can still learn from today.

Katherine Gallagher, CEO, GoStrategic, CA

Having had the privilege of attending Dr. Jehle's lectures for years. I have always admired his rare ability to marry rigorous historical credibility with profound spiritual insight. In Declaring Liberty, his extensive scholarship and theological insights converge to reveal the hidden dimensions of our nation's founding document.

Dr. Jehle challenges us to look beyond our contemporary cultural lens to rediscover the Framers' original intent and perspective, providing exquisite clarity on the meaning of liberty in the United States of America. He is particularly insightful on the subject of slavery and mistreatment of Native Americans, reconciling the vices of our past with the bold ideals of our heritage. Declaring Liberty is an illuminating guide for anyone seeking to better understand the charter set forth in 1776; it left me filled with awe at the vision and boldness of our nation's founders and a strengthened resolve to uphold this legacy. I give it my highest and most enthusiastic recommendation!

Russel Williams, Educator and U.S. Military Veteran, TX

I have known Dr. Paul Jehle for many years. He is an American Patriot and a historian of the highest degree. His love of God and this nation has driven him to write this book! The reputation of Dr. Jehle as a respectable community leader begins in Plymouth, MA, "America's Hometown", and transcends throughout the Commonwealth of Massachusetts, and beyond. "American Exceptionalism" is not because we are the smartest, strongest, or most informed people. President Ronald Reagan warned that "Freedom is never more than one generation away from extinction." The warning given in the Old Testament to the Israelites was to teach their children all that the Lord God Almighty had done for Israel. That warning is just as applicable to us today. We must heed that same warning by teaching our people all that God has done for the United States of America. We must NEVER forget; and this book is a good start!

Attorney James R. McMahon, III, Cape Cod, MA
Former Republican Candidate for Attorney General (2018, 2022)

I am honored to endorse Dr. Paul Jehle's enlightening book, Defending Liberty, a profound exploration of the foundational principles that shaped our nation. Having attended the New Testament Church where Dr. Jehle has served as Senior Pastor since 1988, I have witnessed firsthand his unwavering commitment to educating others about the historical and spiritual roots of American liberty.

In this book, Dr. Jehle meticulously examines the motivations that inspired our forefathers to declare independence from England. He presents a compelling argument that their quest was not merely for autonomy, but was a deep-seated conviction rooted in faith and the belief that all individuals are endowed by their Creator with unalienable rights: Life, Liberty, and the pursuit of Happiness.

I wholeheartedly recommend Defending Liberty as essential reading for anyone seeking to understand the true intentions of our nation's founders. Dr. Jehle's writing serves as a clarion call to appreciate the divine source of our freedoms, emphasizing that our success as a nation stems from our acknowledgment of these God-given rights. This book is a vital reminder of the principles that underpin our identity as Americans and the responsibility we have to uphold these truths for future generations.

Best regards, Vinny deMacedo, MA
State Representative 1999–2014; State Senator 2014–2019

Dr. Paul Jehle's treatise on the Declaration of Independence and our American Founding is a scholarly work, decades in the making, and centuries in its scope. Dr. Jehle skillfully addresses the background and issues that led ultimately to our "American Creation" two hundred and fifty years ago and offers us a rare insight into the hearts and minds of our Founding Fathers. This work is an uncommon combination, being simultaneously educational and inspirational, and answers the question as posed in its title with a resounding "Yes!" Readers who take the time to enjoy this work will gain a greater knowledge of the facts of our founding, but most importantly they will receive a greater understanding and appreciation of the "why" of our founding. I look forward to making a gift of this book to all my fellow Sheriffs here in the Commonwealth of Massachusetts, and to many other of my fellow elected officials.

Sheriff Joseph McDonald, Plymouth County, MA

For years I have had the distinct honor of knowing Dr. Paul Jehle and his work with the New Testament Church, both professionally, and as a friend. Paul is a beloved figure, and there is deep respect for him amongst his church members and in the community. After 30 years of a love of history, matched with a passion for studying the Bible, Paul has penned "Declaring Liberty." In this book, Paul eloquently depicts America's first 200 years through the eyes of the colonial Pastor. In his introduction, Paul said he hopes to inspire others to be the "salt and light" to the community where they live. I would suggest Dr. Paul Jehle is just that in our community. I hope that you will enjoy this book as much as I did.

Plymouth County District Attorney Timothy J. Cruz, MA

Dr. Paul Jehle is an inspiration who expresses the importance of preserving our God-given rights of life, liberty and the pursuit of happiness. By looking at the history of where we began and where we are he understands the importance of our Declaration. I strongly believe in protecting our rights and have put those words into action by enlisting in the military many years ago, then volunteering for service in Vietnam during the Easter offensive of 1972. Many people will remind us that "freedom is not free," unfortunately I have seen that firsthand. With no regrets I will give my life to support the oath that we all took to defend our freedoms at all costs. It is this dedication and commitment by many who serve and have served that will protect and preserve the rights provided by our Creator. A life given to protect others is a life well spent.

Denis M. Russell
Vietnam Veteran and Plymouth Post 1822 Commander, MA

The subtitle of Dr. Jehle's book, *Is the Declaration of Independence still Relevant Today?* inspires thought and discussion, that in today's society might cause heated debate. With so many people today pushing back on what and who we are as a country, this book will help the reader better realize the context in which our great country was born. As we continue to move away from our roots and our God toward a godless communist state, people need a reminder of who we are and how we got here. People need the facts behind the creation of this great nation before they so quickly try to demonize it and remake it into something that has been tried and failed many times in the past. I recommend that you read this book!

Marc Duphily, Public Servant, Carver, MA

I'm glad Paul Jehle has written another book. His writing is clear, powerful, and motivating. A committed father, husband and discipler of young men and women, Paul for years has helped produce the next generation of leaders. His knowledge of the foundation of this nation is always a thrill to hear him teach. He is certainly one of my favorite teachers. Not just for content, but his passion for the material is also highly motivating.

Paul is a man for this time, and I am honored to have worked with him for many decades and to strategically use in my work many of things that Paul is using in his. He is a man for today, and I can enthusiastically say, Paul, stick around, we really need you!

Dennis Peacocke, Founder of Strategic Christian Services and Global Council of Nations, CA

Preface

Having been a law professor for nearly half a century, I have observed that although almost every law school teaches constitutional law (note I said constitutional law, not the Constitution), few if any offer a course on the Declaration of Independence. Unsurprisingly, many assume the Declaration is merely an historic document that has no legal force today.

In fact, the Declaration is as foundational as the Constitution. The *United States Code Annotated* begins with the Declaration, the Articles of Confederation, the Constitution, and the Northwest Ordinance as the four organic laws of the United States. The Supreme Court frequently cites the Declaration as authority for its decisions.

The reason is simple: *The Declaration established our nation*. The Constitution established our government. The Gettysburg Address begins, "Four score and seven years ago, our fathers brought forth on this continent a new nation…" Eighty-seven years before 1863 is 1776, the year of the Declaration.

G.K. Chesterton said "America is the only nation in the world that is founded on a creed." That creed is found in the Declaration. The Declaration sets for the ideals upon which America is founded; the Constitution sets forth a practical mechanism for the realization and preservation of those ideals in a society of imperfect people like you and me. That's why the preamble to the Constitution is short and simple: The Declaration is the true preamble to the Constitution.

And yet, while most Americans vaguely recall that the Declaration separated us from England, they are largely ignorant of its contents. And that's why America has lost its moorings and is drifting unanchored in a wild sea.

America's 250th birthday, the anniversary of the Declaration, opens an opportunity, perhaps a last opportunity, for America to rediscover and return to the founding principles that made us a great nation.

And that's why Dr. Paul Jehle's book, *Declaring Liberty,* is the book of the year that is desperately needed today.

Pastor and historian Paul Jehle, President and Director of the Plymouth Rock Foundation, lives American history and makes it come alive for others. He writes with the same passion and dynamism with which he speaks, and his book is a concise but eloquent statement of why America was founded and what America is all about. But his supreme passion is for the Lord Jesus Christ and His Word. He loves America because our nation was founded upon principles consistent with His Word – principles many Americans have forgotten.

Dr. Jehle guides us through those turbulent but thrilling days of 1776 when the Continental Congress declared independence. Knowing that they must hang together or they would certainly hang separately, they placed their trust in the Supreme Judge of the world and pledged their lives, fortunes, and sacred honor. Jehle demonstrates convincingly that the God of the Declaration is not some generic deistic god but rather is the God the Bible. He relates the Declaration to the Magna Charta, the Mayflower Compact, and the Constitution, and he explains in clear and understandable language the meaning of key phrases such as "All men are created equal," "Life, liberty, and the pursuit of happiness," and "consent of the governed."

Declaring Liberty closes with the moving and sometimes heart wrenching stories of the signers of the Declaration and a ringing call to arms to Americans and freedom-loving people of all nations to rediscover and re-implement its ideals.

Suitable for the classroom but written in a style any layperson can understand, Paul Jehle's book will grip you from start to finish.

What better way to celebrate America's birthday than by learning about the founding of our nation? If you have time to read only one book about America this year, ***Declaring Liberty* is that book!**

Read it and then let's make America's birthday a re-birth of freedom!

Godspeed, Colonel John Eidsmoe, Lt. Colonel, USAF (Ret.)
Chaplain, (Colonel MS), Mississippi State Guard
Professor, Oak Brook College of Law and Govt Policy
Senior Counsel & Resident Scholar, Foundation for Moral Law

Introduction

This book has been in the making for more than three decades. The chapters are drawn from research and ideas that were delivered as orations and sermons at the New Testament Church in Plymouth, Massachusetts where I have served as Senior Pastor since 1988. Many of the orations were given at our annual Christian Heritage Sunday on the anniversary of the Declaration of Independence.

My wife, Charlene, and I first visited the church in September of 1975, and soon joined thereafter. We served as Sunday school teachers and soon I began to teach Bible studies, serve as youth pastor, and then help begin the New Testament Christian School in 1980, which still operates today. Suffice it to say we have been in the same church for more than fifty years.

We are both eternally grateful for the members and attenders over this half century that God has blessed us to work with. They have received truth and paid the price to maintain it. They have also inspired us to continue and are part of the fabric of this book.

Though my hobby is history, my passion is to study the Bible and preach the gospel of the kingdom. By this I mean preaching the Gospel of Jesus Christ as it relates to the government of our lives. Self-control is the mark of the believer, and the strength of the individual will bring blessings to families, businesses, churches, and ultimately the culture surrounding the church. Inevitably, it will be reflected in the quality and institution of civil government in the nation in which you live.

In this book I have endeavored to answer the basic question posed by our subtitle; *is the Declaration still relevant today?* Most people who celebrate July 4 and its annual festivities have never even read the document. Others think that its meaning is archaic, out of date, and thus they ignore it. Some who admire the ideas state that the phrases and meanings owe their origin to the Enlightenment.

In a systematic, way, as a life-long student of both the Bible and the history of the United States, I hope to present ideas as the colonial

Pastor did throughout America's first two hundred years. They would present a Biblical doctrine, give it context in the Scriptures, and then apply it to the current events of the time. Each chapter will follow this general pattern in relation to the Declaration's unique ideas. These ideas, I believe, after years of research, owe their origin to the Bible as they were communicated by the clergy.

The book is written to whoever has an interest in the roots of the ideas contained in the Declaration of Independence. For the American who does not consider themselves religious or is not interested in the Bible, consider my remarks as informative and giving context to a time separated from us by hundreds of years as well as a relatively unknown ideology today.

For the believer who has surrendered to Christ's Lordship by His grace, the connections between Biblical doctrine and their application in the culture ought to inspire you to internalize and live out the type of character necessary for you to be "salt and light" to the community where you live. Character and integrity are more important than power.

For those who are from nations outside of the United States, this book is written to help each of you see that any nation can be discipled in the same truths presented here, regardless of its history and present condition. I include a leading idea at the end of each chapter to demonstrate that the truth illustrated transcends the nation of America. We can all learn examples from history that can inspire us to influence our own nation.

The United States, like all nations, is flawed in its history and even the best of its fruit of liberty. It is flawed because people are flawed. I do not believe the Declaration, or any other American document, is without error, for the Bible is my only perfect standard.

I do not write this book to suggest that the nation of America is a perfect example of these truths. *I do write with a passionate purpose to demonstrate that despite a nation's flaws, the power of God's ideas can grow amid the weeds, especially when that nation confesses (or declares) the truths of God's Word.*

I am *not a Christian nationalist.* My allegiance is not to a political party or politics in general but to truth as I have found it in the Word of God and person of Jesus Christ. History testifies that the nations that have had the greatest liberty have empowered individuals, decentralized their governments, and respected the family, church and smaller spheres of jurisdiction. *Influence is more effective than power.*

The nations are desperate today for solutions and hope for the future. Nations are not formed or reformed from the top, but from the bottom. This is the way of the kingdom of God. They are also formed jurisdictionally (empowered by various spheres of authority), not from a mold of conformity or the centralized control of an all-pervasive civil power.

The book is written in several sections.

Section 1 – Chapters 1-3 – <u>The Core Ideas in the Declaration</u>

After a brief Prologue of biblical doctrine on the jurisdictional role of civil government, we begin with the story of how this thinking culminated on July 4, 1776. The role of the individual, home and church and the fulfillment of their distinct responsibilities made this story possible. We highlight how the jurisdictional separation of church and state is illustrated by the "Creator-Redeemer distinction."

Section 2 – Chapters 4-6 – <u>The historic context of the Declaration of Independence</u>

My goal here is to demonstrate that the Declaration *went further* than Magna Charta in expressing the ancient ideas of liberty drawn from the Bible. The Declaration *extended* the ideas in the Mayflower Compact drawn up by the Pilgrims in 1620 to a national level. Finally, the Declaration is the *foundation* for the United States Constitution, and the tendency to ignore the Declaration creates confusion as to the true foundation of the nation.

Section 3 – Chapters 7-11 – Key Phrases in the Declaration

Here we examine the heart of the Declaration. The key phrases are examined, laying out the Biblical doctrines, and showing how the phrase in the document expresses that truth. I also insert a chapter demonstrating the fact that the Declaration itself convicted people's practice of slavery.

Section 4 – Chapters 12-15 – The Significance of the Declaration

In these chapters, it is my intent to demonstrate how the Declaration is critical to understanding our initial role in the world. Today's "great reset" is contrasted with the Declaration, which was a great reset in its time. We culminate with the full expression of the Biblical doctrine of interposition as to how the Continental Congress lawfully resisted tyranny by avoiding passivity on one hand and vengeance, anger and lawless violence on the other.

Section 5 – Chapters 16-18 – The Price and Influence of the Declaration

We highlight the somber significance of signing the Declaration and the price paid by those who did so. Concluding with the legacy of how the Declaration has inspired nations around the world, it is my hope and prayer that the ideas expressed, rooted in God, will be a catalyst for the discipling of many nations in the years to come.

So, *is the Declaration of Independence relevant today?* If you read with an open mind, and consider the evidence, I think you might agree that the answer to this question is a resounding YES. But don't take my word for it! I invite you to read on and expand your understanding of this document which is the birth certificate of the United States of America.

Dr. Paul Jehle, 2026

PART ONE

The Core Ideas in the Declaration

Chapter 1

INDEPENDENCE DAY:
The Story of July 4

The time is now near at hand which must probably determine, whether Americans are to be, Freemen, or Slaves
– General George Washington, July 2, 1776

Prologue:
The Doctrine of Jurisdictional Responsibility

Tell us, therefore, what do you think? Is it lawful to pay taxes to Caesar, or not? ...And He said to them, Render to Caesar the things that are Caesar's, and to God the things that are God's
Matthew 22:17, 21 (see also Mark 12:17 and Luke 20:25)

The week before His crucifixion, Jesus was challenged in the Temple by the Pharisees. Their intention was to trick him into saying "everything belongs to us (the church) or everything belongs to Rome (the state)." Jesus shocked them as He did regularly, outlining a *third way – the jurisdictional way.*

Jesus stated clearly that though God is sovereign, He has given responsibilities to the legitimate institution of civil government, which He ordained. He has also given responsibilities to the Church. God is not like other 'gods', He has designed authority and responsibilities to be shared.

His main point to Rome was that there are things outside the jurisdiction of civil government. His point to the religious leaders asking the question was that civil government has a legitimate calling, though it was at that time corrupt. Herb Titus has written:

> These words of Jesus Christ, while addressing a question regarding paying one's taxes, answer two of the most significant political and legal questions of the ages. The first question is: What authority may rightfully be exercised by a

> civil government? ...The second question is: Who determines a civil government's lawful authority?[1]

Professor Titus then explains that the Bible clearly limits the authority of the State. Those growing up in colonial America understood that only God and His Word could answer the two questions asserted by Titus above. They heard this from the pulpit and were reasoning in this way long before July 4, 1776.

If humans are the ultimate authority for everything, they will continually make excuses to give more power to whatever sphere of authority they are in. For more than 150 years, those who came and settled colonial America did so for the idea of liberty. Though imperfect people, most were attempting to live out what they had heard from the Bible, known to them as the Word of God.

The jurisdictional responsibilities of the <u>individual</u> (to fear God and obey His commands), <u>family</u> (adhere to the marriage covenant and raise your children in the fear of the Lord), <u>business</u> (to earn a lawful wage for the purpose of serving others), and <u>church</u> (walk in covenant with other believers and hold each other accountable to remain faithful) were taught.

They were also taught that it was God who ordained civil government in Genesis 9. The duties and responsibilities of this institution were rehearsed by colonial pulpits, especially from Romans 13.[2] In Jonathan Mayhew's Preface to his sermon in 1750, he notes the objection some might make.

> A notion that this is preaching politics, instead of CHRIST. However, to remove all prejudices of this sort, I beg it may be remembered, that 'all scripture—is profitable for doctrine, for reproof, for CORRECTION, for instruction in righteousness.' Why, then, should not those parts of scripture which relate to

civil government be examined and explained from the desk, as well as others?

Obedience to the civil magistrate is a Christian duty: and if so, why should not the nature, grounds and extent of it be considered in a Christian assembly? Besides, if it be said, that it is out of character for a Christian minister to meddle with such a subject, this censure will at last fall upon the holy apostles. They write upon it in their epistles to Christian churches: And surely it cannot be deemed either criminal or impertinent, to attempt an explanation of their doctrine. It was the near approach of the Thirtieth of January, that turned my thoughts to this subject: on which solemnity the slavish doctrine of passive obedience and non-resistance.[3]

The truths in Romans 13:1-8 were rehearsed by Mayhew. His major points were as follows:

1. That the end of magistracy is the good of civil society, as such:
2. That civil rulers, as such, are the ordinance and ministers of God; it being by his permission and providence that any bear rule; and agreeable to his will, that there should be some persons vested with authority in society, for the well-being of it;
3. That which is here said concerning civil rulers, extends to all of them in common: it relates indifferently to monarchical, republican and aristocratical government; and to all other forms which truly answer the sole end of government, the happiness of society; and to all the different degrees of authority in any particular state; to inferior officers no less than to the supreme:
4. That disobedience to civil rulers in the due exercise of their authority, is not merely a political sin, but an heinous offence against God and religion:

5. That the true ground and reason of our obligation to be subject to the higher powers, is the usefulness description of magistracy (when properly exercised) to human society, and its subserviency to the general welfare:
6. That obedience to civil rulers is here equally required under all forms of government, which answer the sole end of all government, the good of society; and to every degree of authority in any state, whether supreme or subordinate: From whence it follows:
7. That if unlimited obedience and non-resistance, be here required as a duty under any one form of government, it is also required as a duty under all other forms; and as a duty to subordinate rulers as well as to the supreme:
8. And lastly, that those civil rulers to whom the apostle enjoins subjection, are the persons in possession; description the powers that be; those who are actually vested with authority.

> THERE is one very important and interesting point which remains to be inquired into; namely, the extent of that subjection to the higher powers, which is here enjoined as a duty upon all Christians.[4]

Mayhew then went on to delineate the conditions that might warrant resistance of some kind. The preaching on Romans 13 set it in context of the Roman Empire as well as God's purpose for it to be a ministry of justice and a standard for good civil government, not to justify its conduct.

Events just do not happen. They are effects of causes over time. Consider Rev. Foljambe's election sermon delivered January 5, 1876 in Malden, Massachusetts. He carefully delineates the jurisdiction of the Providential Hand of God, and this was also a doctrine well understood in 1776.

> The events of history are no accidents. There are no accidents in the lives of men or of nations. We may go back to the

underlying cause of every event, and discover in each God's overruling and intervening wisdom. It has been said that history is the biography of communities; in another, and profounder, sense, it is the autobiography of him 'who worketh all things after the counsel of his own will' (Ephesians 1:11) and who is graciously timing all events in the interests of his Christ., and of the kingdom of God on earth.

Tracing the history of men, we find the most trivial and seemingly fortuitous things issuing beyond all human expectations of intention in the sublimest events; we see men planning and working with only their own more immediate and material interests in view, and yet a power behind them is noiselessly and effectually, though possibly for generations unobserved, overruling their actions to the furtherance of higher, more widely extended, and more permanent purposes.

Human freedom and human responsibility in bringing about either good or evil, are not to be pushed aside; providence is not fatalism; but, on the other hand, man's free activities do not prove the despotism of a blind chance, shifting as man's caprice may dictate. Neither social order, moral progress, nor a Christian civilization, can spring out of chance. These demand a prevision and adjustment of causes keener and mightier than man with his wisest forethought and highest intelligence can exercise.

There are influences which man can wield, and should control, aright; there are others which God alone originates and shapes. There are, again, other influences which are under human management, but which become mighty for good only by their timing; and this timing is sometimes visible, but more frequently an invisible, interposition of God's overruling care, only truly seen after many generations have passed away. God's hand is seen in the starting, speeding, retarding, and

> matching such coincident and colliding influences as mark the progress and constitute the varied crises of history.[5]

Let's turn back the clock and see how this understanding of jurisdiction culminated in the story of July 4. Those delegates debating the ideas of independence grew up as children taught by their parents who trained them in business practices, and they also took them to church. Colonial resistance to tyranny was the fruit of the dramatic story of the Declaration of Independence.

Tuesday, July 2, 1776

John and Sam Adams left Philadelphia's State House, later to be called Independence Hall, on Monday afternoon the 1st of July, 1776, knowing that there *must* soon be a miracle. A straw vote had been taken and the colonies voted 9 to 4 to declare independence. This was not enough; it needed to be unanimous to have the moral force necessary to be heard around the world. On Tuesday they reassembled, and the Providence of God brought unanimity. This chapter will tell the story of how that occurred.

On the same day, Tuesday, July 2, George Washington, Commander in Chief of the Continental Army, wrote his orders for the day. As was his custom, he would write a statement expressing his sentiments as to why ordinary farmers should defend their homes, towns, and colonies against the tyrannical practices of England. They had not come to this conclusion lightly, for it had taken 15 years of debate to arrive at this moment. The statement within the order given in New York, if it was possible to have been read by John and Samuel Adams, might have given them passion to expect unanimity in future days.

> The time is now near at hand which must probably determine, whether Americans are to be, Freemen, or Slaves; whether they are to have any property they can call their own; whether their Houses, and Farms, are to be pillaged and destroyed, and

they consigned to a State of Wretchedness from which no human efforts will probably deliver them.

The fate of unborn Millions will now depend, under God, on the Courage and Conduct of this army — Our cruel and unrelenting Enemy leaves us no choice but a brave resistance, or the most abject submission; this is all we can expect — We have therefore to resolve to conquer or die.

Our own Country's Honor, all call upon us for a vigorous and manly exertion, and if we now shamefully fail, we shall become infamous to the whole world — Let us therefore rely upon the goodness of the Cause, and the aid of the supreme Being, in whose hands Victory is, to animate and encourage us to great and noble Actions.

The Eyes of all our Countrymen are now upon us, and we shall have their blessings, and praises, if happily we are the instruments of saving them from the Tyranny meditated against them. Let us therefore animate and encourage each other, and shew the whole world, that a Freeman contending for Liberty on his own ground is superior to any slavish mercenary on earth.

The General recommends to the officers great coolness in time of action, and to the soldiers a strict attention and obedience, with a becoming firmness and spirit.[6]

The Child Independence

Fifteen years before, in 1761, all of Boston was astir, for a showdown was about to take place that in the 18th century was as exciting and popular as the Super Bowl is today. This battle was no financial extravaganza, and nor was it merely an entertaining highlight of rare talent. This debate would have consequences far greater than a football game.

The ideas brought on stage would culminate several centuries of thought on the topic of liberty. It would be condensed into several hours of speeches by key individuals taking the sides of the colonists and the Crown. Only invited guests could see this live, and there was no television to let the others in. They would have to wait for the reports in the papers.

Of the event that was about to take place, John Adams wrote fifty years later that *"here this day, in the old Council Chamber, the child Independence was born."*[7] The conflict that took center stage had been brewing for years and even decades since the early 1600's when the colonies of Virginia and Massachusetts had been founded. In these two colonies, and in all New England, the people grew up learning fundamental principles of government from the pulpits of their churches for 140 or more years prior to 1761.[8]

Though the original charters granted by England to the colonies had given the legality of land and government to these dissenters, the colonies understood the fact that they all had the *"fundamental rights of Englishmen."*[9] The fundamental rights of Englishmen were based upon Biblical common law, for this was the long-standing tradition of England.

England, however, desired to control the colonies. They had not been planted by her care to flourish in the self-government that her charters declared. They were in effect to be dependent children, having government-granted rights and not the kind of God-given rights that Englishmen had understood as their heritage. The monopoly that England desired was expressed most clearly in her policies of trade for the 100-year period between 1660 and 1760. The Colonies saw their own Assemblies as self-governing mini parliaments. They were united with England because they had the same King.

England did not look at it this way, and her assertion of control was expressed in what was known as *"writs of assistance."*[10] The "writs of assistance" were general warrants asserting the Crown's right to search and seize private property from any merchant who violated the monopolistic trade restrictions placed by the mother country.

The show-down was a court case pitting the 63 merchants whose financial survival was on the line against the Crown's "acts" and "laws" restricting trade. Did the local self-governing Court of Massachusetts have the right to bring justice in this case? Did England's laws passed by the Parliament across the ocean have a binding effect upon all the Provincial Assemblies along the Atlantic seaboard?

Even though the merchants had indeed violated the "laws" passed by Parliament, were these laws constitutional? Didn't these laws violate an Englishman's right to privacy except through a local warrant given with "just cause"? Didn't these laws also violate an Englishman's right to be taxed only by their consent (through representatives)?

All these questions rested on an even larger premise that this case brought into question. Was Parliament the final authority, or was there a higher law it had to obey? At stake was whether the law of God written in the Bible and nature was still followed as the final authority in England.

Jeremiah Gridley was to argue the Crown's position. Two of his former law students, James Otis and Oxenbridge Thacher, were to defend the merchants. Otis and Thacher made it clear that they expected no payment from the merchants for their service. This was a cause for the liberty of all, and the cost of losing would be equally shared by all.

Only 12 barristers (lawyers in training) were allowed in the courtroom, and a young 24-year-old John Adams was one of them. He was the only one who took notes and this is how we know the content of this most famous court case.[11]

At 9 A.M. Gridley rose to speak first. He advocated that English laws had been violated by the merchants, which all could see that they had. He also asserted that Parliament had passed them properly. If the mother country needed revenue, why shouldn't she seek it through monopoly? If general search warrants could be issued to catch criminals hiding in private homes, why shouldn't they be issued to catch those who violated the laws of monopoly enforced by the Crown?

Was not the collection of taxes a necessary right of the Crown? Wouldn't the "loss of individual liberty" be rewarded for the protection gained from such a small sacrifice? He was lucid, clear, and articulate. Surely all could see the merchants had no case.

When Thacher completed his half-hour defense by asserting that Massachusetts had been singled out unfairly and the laws were not properly executed in the Colonies, the merchants began to get uncomfortable. This case could not be won by arguing the pragmatics of whether the law as written was followed, but rather whether the law itself was constitutional by the fundamental principles upon which the English constitutional system was built.[12]

James Otis rose at 2 in the afternoon to begin a speech that would change the face of the continent. He would assert through a five-hour oration that the real question was whether the "writs" were void because they violated the laws of nature and nature's God. He rose with fire in his eyes and brought forth with eloquence "the birth of the child independence" with some of these stirring words.

MAY IT PLEASE YOUR HONORS,

I was desired by one of the Court to look into the books, and consider the question now before them concerning writs of assistance. I have accordingly considered it, and now appear, not only in obedience to your order, but likewise in behalf of the inhabitants of this town, who have presented another petition, and out of regard to the liberties of the subject. And I take this opportunity to declare, that whether under a fee or not (for in such a cause as this I despise a fee) I will to my dying day oppose with all the powers and faculties God has given me, all such instruments of slavery on the one hand, and villainy on the other, as this writ of assistance is.

It appears to me the worst instrument of arbitrary power, the most destructive of English liberty and the fundamental principles of law, that ever was found in an English law book... I argue this cause... as it is in favor of British liberty... in opposition to a kind of power, the exercise of which, in former periods of English history, cost one king of England his head, and another his throne.... I will admit that writs of one kind may be legal; that is, special writs... to search certain houses... may be granted by the Court... the writ prayed for in this petition, being general, is illegal... Now one of the most essential branches of English liberty is the freedom of one's house. A man's house is his castle; and while he is quiet, he is as well guarded as a prince in his castle. ...What a scene does this open! Every man, prompted by revenge, ill humor, or wantonness, to inspect the inside of his neighbor's house, may get a writ of assistance.[13]

John Adams wrote about this speech in a letter to William Tudor in 1817:

Otis was a flame of fire! With a promptitude of Classical Allusions, a depth of research, a rapid summary of historical events & dates, a profusion of Legal Authorities, a prophetic

> glance of his eyes into futurity, and a rapid torrent of impetuous Eloquence he hurried away all before him. American Independence was then & there born. The seeds of Patriots & Heroes to defend the Non sine Diis Animosus Infans; to defend the Vigorous Youth were then & there sown. Every Man of an immense crowded Audience appeared to me to go away, as I did, ready to take Arms against Writs of Assistants. Then and there was the first scene of the first Act of opposition to the Arbitrary claims of Great Britain. Then and there the Child Independence was born. In fifteen years i.e. in 1776, he grew up to Manhood, & declared himself free.[14]

Otis refuted the premise that the Crown was basing its argument upon. He upheld in eloquent terms the fact that no government has the right to enact what Heaven has forbidden. Despite his logic and eloquence, however, the merchants ended up losing this case by arbitrary rule of the royal judges. This began the constitutional debate period between the Colonies and the Mother Country that culminated in the writing of the Declaration of Independence. The Stamp Act of 1764 continued to assert the right of the Crown to have a monopoly on every aspect of the Colonies, disregarding their English rights.

It was a continuation of the many Acts that regulated commerce such as the Woolen Act of 1699, the Hat Act of 1732 and the Iron Act of 1750.[15] Virtually every aspect of colonial life had been regulated by an act of Parliament but rarely had any of them been enforced. Thus, life went on in the Colonies as if they did not exist.

But in the 1760's, England desired to enforce these Acts and that is where the conflict began. The Parliament and Crown, in 1773, stated that all taxes except that of tea would be repealed, hoping to get the Colonies to purchase the principle of control at the expense of their desire for tea.

Ben Franklin replied that the Crown;

> Has no idea that any people can act from any other principle but that of interest; and they believe that three pence on a pound of tea, of which one does not drink ten pounds in a year, is sufficient to overcome all the patriotism of an American.[16]

Teenage Independence

In 1774 the First Continental Congress began on its knees, asserting by demonstration and example that the rights debated came from the God of the Universe, and that it was at His bar of Justice that the ultimate appeal was to be brought. The colonists applied the "lower magistrate" principle of John Calvin in lawfully resisting a government which usurped the authority it was given.

The Declaration and Resolves of the First Continental Congress, completed on October 14, 1774, once again expressed to England that the Colonies were entitled to all the same fundamental rights as their brethren in England, including the foundation of common law.[17]

The Second Continental Congress in 1775 had to deal with war. Lexington and Concord had taken place, so was it lawful to take up arms against the Crown? What right does a government have to disarm its citizens in the name of protecting them? Once again, the Colonists appealed to the higher source of law. They stated in the *Declaration of the Causes and Necessity of Taking Up Arms* on July 6, 1775.

> "Our cause is just.... With hearts fortified with these animating reflections, we most solemnly, before God and the world, declare, that, exerting the utmost energy of those powers, which our beneficent Creator hath graciously bestowed upon us, the arms we have been compelled by our enemies to assume, we will, in defiance of every hazard, with unabating firmness and perseverance, employ for the preservation of our liberties; being with one mind resolved to die freeman rather than to live slaves."[18]

As the year 1776 dawned, Boston was occupied by the British, and the war was not going particularly well. The necessity of declaring independence from the Crown was gaining ground among delegates but many were still cautious, hoping for reconciliation through the promised "commissioners of peace" to arrive from England, or for Parliament to simply wake up and see her injustice.

The debate over independence was not over its principle, but over its timing. The Crown declared the Colonies to be in rebellion, revoking its charters in August of 1775. Then in December of 1775, it cut off all trade, treating them as full enemies. It was the knowledge of these acts that set the stage for the third Continental Congress that met in early May of 1776. May 6 brought a proposal for each colony to set up their own government and it was finally passed. On May 15, John Adams wrote the preamble to this resolution which stated:

> Whereas his Britannic Majesty, in conjunction with the lords and commons of Great Britain, has, by a late act of Parliament, excluded the inhabitants of these United Colonies from the protection of his crown; And, whereas, no answer, whatever, to the humble petitions of the colonies for redress of grievances and reconciliation with Great Britain, has been or is likely to be given; but, the whole force of that kingdom, aided by foreign mercenaries, is to be exerted for the destruction of the good people of these colonies; And,

> whereas, it appears absolutely irreconcilable to reason and good Conscience, for the people of these colonies now to take the oaths and affirmations necessary for the support of any government under the crown of Great Britain, and it is necessary that the exercise of every kind of authority under the said crown should be totally suppressed, and all the powers of government exerted, under the authority of the people of the colonies, for the preservation of internal peace, virtue, and good order, as well as for the defence of their lives, liberties, and properties, against the hostile invasions and cruel depredations of their enemies....[19]

On the 17th of May a day of fasting and prayer was called to be observed throughout the Colonies. The higher power and source of all law was to be petitioned, for greater justice of their cause was thought to be enacted from Heaven than from the British Isles. Greater harmony was also thought to exist between the Colonies and the God of Heaven than the King of England. On June 7, Richard Henry Lee proposed a resolution that would begin the great debate on complete separation from England.

Harvesting the Manhood of Independence

> RESOLVED, That these United Colonies are, and of right ought to be, free and independent States; that they are absolved from all allegiance to the British Crown; and that all political connection between them and the State of Great Britain is, and ought to be, totally dissolved.[20]

On June 10, the debate was at such a standstill that it was tabled for three weeks by both sides to give time for reflection. It ought to be apparent that the Colonies were moving in no spirit of rebellion, for even at this late date they were not fully sure that they had the right to separate. The debate with England, however, was now only one-sided, with document after document going un-answered except for a step-up of war.

It might also be noted that at this time individuals called "conservative" were those who desired to preserve the status-quo - they wanted to remain a part of England. A "radical" or even a "liberal" wanted to act fully on the root principle that justified separation and independence. The tension mounted as the days went by until Monday, July 1st, when debate would resume.

Monday morning finally arrived, and John Adams went to his usual seat in Carpenter's Hall about 8:30 in the morning, informing the doorman to immediately give him and Hancock any letters that arrived, and then he put his briefcase of papers and materials on the windowsill. Sam Adams was there shortly after (always known for clock-like punctuality) and sat talking with his cousin about the need to answer any argument against independence.

John wondered whether any new argument existed in favor or against Lee's resolution. He felt the issue had been fully discussed but was willing should the need arise. On the other side of the hall sat Dickinson from Pennsylvania, ready to speak against independence. Even if there was a majority for independence, they discussed, it would not work - for they knew that *unanimity* was required to stand against England.

When Hancock arrived, and the group of delegates were called to order, he read letters from George Washington and other matters that took nearly three hours to complete. A little after noon, Hancock resolved that Congress should be put into a "committee of the whole" so that they could debate and a straw vote be taken that would not officially count.

This being done, Hancock gave the mace very ceremoniously to the Clerk (Benjamin Harrison) and took his place with the other Massachusetts delegates. Immediately, Dickinson was on his feet ready to debate the former resolution for independence.

My conduct, this day I expect will give the finishing blow to my once too great, and my now too diminished popularity. Yet, I had rather forfeit popularity forever, than vote away the blood and happiness of my countrymen... If we declare a separation without waiting for France, we may be overwhelmed with debt... we shall ruin ourselves, and Britain will be ruined with us. France will rise on those ruins... (in the middle of his opening remarks letters were delivered to Hancock and John Adams, who opened them and whispered to each other - Maryland for independence!)

To escape from the protection of Britain by declaring independence, all unprepared as we are, would be like destroying our house in winter and exposing a growing family before we have got another shelter. Before this resolution is put to a vote, maybe we should look into the future, into the Doomsday Book for America... our great Union may become unwieldy and split into separate commonwealths... In that case, Hudson's River would make a very proper boundary for a separate commonwealth to the northward!" (Dickinson had spoken eloquently, from the heart, with no regard for personal gain, and then in great emotion stopped and sank into his chair and a long silence followed his speech)[21]

Delegates sat nervously, and Sam Adams scratched larger holes in his silk stockings, urging John to speak up. John could not let Dickinson have the last word and thus rose to his feet.

I could wish for eloquence, for all the powers of the ancient orators of Greece and Rome. The preceding speaker has been eloquent, for his talent for expression is known throughout the continent. Yet, how simple the argument, and how plain the issue! Every honest person with open mind and senses alert, can hear the moment strike for action, for he knows when the path turns beneath his feet...[22]

Amazingly, no one took notes of Adams' speech. Thomas Jefferson said that it kept all of them on the edge of their seats. Daniel Webster, in his eloquent speech in Boston after the death of Adams and Jefferson on the 50th anniversary of the Declaration, finished it (from what sources we do not know); in this way:

> Sir, before God, I believe the hour is come. My judgment approves this measure, and my whole heart is in it. All that I have, and all that I am, and all that I hope, in this life, I am now ready here to stake upon it; and I leave off as I began, that live or die, survive or perish, I am for the declaration. It is my living sentiment, and by the blessing of God it shall be my dying sentiment, independence, now, and independence forever! [23]

John, however, felt his speech "was a waste of breath".[24] In the middle of one of his sentences, thunder was heard, and the rain came down. Shortly after, while still speaking, the delegation from New Jersey burst through the door, rain still running off their coats! Adams sat down. Judge Stockton, one of the delegates, asked that the argument in favor of independence could be reviewed once again.

Patiently, John recounted his points. Then, Rev. John Witherspoon, a newly appointed delegate with fiery boldness, stared at the New York delegation and said in his nasal tone of voice: "the distinguished gentleman from Massachusetts remarked as we came in that the colonies are ripe for independence, I would like to add that some colonies (looking at New York) are rotten for the want of it!" Sam Adams immediately shouted "hear, hear" but was brought to order by the clerk.[25]

The clerk then called the role. Massachusetts (four stood - unanimous for independence). New Hampshire (unanimous), Rhode Island (unanimous), Connecticut (unanimous). New York (no one stood up). Pennsylvania (4 to 3 in the negative). New Jersey (yes), Delaware (split - thus a no). Maryland (yes by letter). Virginia (yes), Georgia (yes), North Carolina (yes), and South Carolina (no). Thus, by a vote of 9 to 4, the colonies had approved independence in a practice straw vote.

John and Sam Adams, among others, went home that day knowing that a miracle must take place before the official vote was taken the next day. From the afternoon of the 1st, until a little after noon on the 2nd, a providential miracle that brought unanimity for independence took place.

Dickinson and Morris stayed home, which gave Pennsylvania a majority for independence. This was an example of the Christian convictions of Dickinson, knowing he would be a cog in the wheel, so to speak. They were far more united than the partisan politics we often witness in our day due to the common theology from the Bible they shared and ultimately desiring the same goal.

South Carolina, seeing the logic of unity and reason for independence, changed its vote to the affirmative. McKean from Delaware said that George Read, the one who split his vote by a negative, was the type of individual who made up their mind up to vote no on everything! However, just prior to the actual vote taking place, Caesar Rodney from Delaware arrived soaking wet with mud running down his clothes but casting his deciding vote for independence!

New York seemed to be the problem, until instructions were received to vote for independence, and thus its vote was promised and assured. Twelve for, one promise coming - a *unanimous vote!* With relief and a burden lifted, John Adams wrote to Abigail the next day:

> The Second of July, 1776, will be the most memorable Epocha, in the History of America. I am apt to believe that it will be celebrated, by succeeding Generations, as the great anniversary Festival. It ought to be commemorated, as the Day of Deliverance, by Solemn Acts of Devotion to God Almighty... With pomp and parade, with shows, games, sports, guns, bells, bonfires and illuminations from one end of the continent to the other from this time forward forevermore... I can see that the End is more than worth all the Means. And that Posterity will triumph in that Days Transaction, even altho we should rue it, which I trust in God we shall not.... I am well aware of the Toil and Blood and Treasure it will cost Us to maintain this Declaration, and support and defend these States... yet through all the Gloom I can see the Rays of ravishing Light and Glory.[26]

On Thursday, July 4, the actual wording of the Declaration was still being debated. The debate began late the afternoon of the second and throughout the day of the 3rd. Every clause was reviewed, debated, discussed, hashed out, some removed, and some revised. Jefferson preferred the phrase "pursuit of happiness" to the word property for it signified productivity and the freedom one had with property they owned.

The most debated section of the Declaration were the indictments against the King of England. Clause 20 where Jefferson denounced King George for introducing slavery into the colonies was particularly objectionable. When some defended the fact that people freely and voluntarily practiced slavery and were not forced to by the Crown - John Adams sprang to his feet proclaiming;

> Freedom is a mere masquerade in a country that sells humans in chains![27]

John Adams banged his hickory cane on the floor to emphasize his point, but clause 20 was entirely removed.

Jefferson had originally stated that the Colonies were "eternally" separated from England. This was far too harsh, and instead the words "enemies in war, friends in peace" was adopted. Ol' Ben Franklin wanted to shorten Jefferson's words "sacred and undeniable" in describing truth to simply "self-evident" and even Jefferson acknowledged that one word was better than three, even with a hyphen. All in all, most agreed it was a better Declaration after its revision.[28]

The question of an official seal was brought up. Franklin, Jefferson and Adams discussed what it might be.[29] Their suggestion was that on one side a picture of Israel being led by God's Pillar of Fire out of Egypt be rendered, while on the other side the Anglo-Saxon Common Law - Guardian of Freedom be pictured. Instead, however, later, the all-seeing eye of Providence on top of a pyramid and the eagle of liberty were chosen - once again declaring the true and ultimate source of law - God Almighty.[30]

Although the official signing would not take place for more than a month (August 2), the mood changed once the document was completed. One historian remarked that a swarm of mosquitoes and horse-flies from a nearby farm came into the room, biting the legs of the delegates, driving them to complete the document quickly.[31]

Hancock is reported to have declared that he would write his name "so that George the Third might read it without his spectacles." One delegate remarked that "we shall hang together" to which Franklin replied in his usual wit - "or we shall hang separately". Fat Mr.

Harrison of Virginia leaned over to little skinny Elbridge Gerry of Massachusetts and proclaimed, "I shall have the advantage over you; for my neck, probably, will be broken at the first drop, whereas you may have to dangle for half an hour!"[32]

The reader should note that those who debated independence in 1776 only differed on its timing, *not on the fundamental principles of liberty.* We have a much greater challenge today. The fundamentals are no longer taught or understood. If the roots are not understood, the fruit of liberty will not be something as cherished as it was in 1776. The delegates pledged their lives, fortunes, and sacred honor, and no one was more grateful than Sam Adams, who had tirelessly worked for independence for more than 20 years.

He must have pondered every principle of the Declaration - the laws of nature and nature's God - that higher law to which all are accountable; the self-evident truth given by the common grace of God. The truth that all rights come from God and are defined by the Bible - that government in the Bible is by covenant and consent of the governed, and above all, that the Declaration is really one of *dependence on God* before independence from England must have been rehearsed in his mind.

Most of all, the entire Declaration was left in the hands of the Supreme Judge of the world before the court of Heaven.

Leading Idea – ***Great achievements often start with God-fearing ideas in the heart of individuals and are cultivated by families, rehearsed in churches, discussed in towns, and finally acted upon in public.***

Chapter 2

THE GOD OF THE DECLARATION

When in the Course of human events, it becomes necessary for one people to dissolve the political bands which have connected them with another, and to assume among the powers of the earth, the separate and equal station to which the Laws of Nature and of ***Nature's God*** *entitle them...*
Declaration of Independence

Who is the God of the Declaration?

To fully understand the meaning of the Declaration we must consider who the God is that was referred to by our patriotic forebears in the document. The Declaration refers to "Nature's God", the giver of "Self-Evident" truth, Creator, the Supreme Judge, and Providence. All of these were common phrases to describe God at the time. By direct implication this God also gives unalienable rights; those given by this Deity that cannot be revoked by government.

But do all religions refer to their "god" with these same characteristics? Are all Gods the same? Could anyone of them bear all these titles?

It is common today to have God viewed as a creation of the mind of man. Did the framers simply use the titles of God common at the time to get other nations on their side? Did the majority of those who ratified this document attempt to worship this God or was this a mystical one no one could define?

Some may say those who signed the Declaration appealed to a god of inequality since they were practicing such with slaves and native Americans. Those who ratified it were all men and thus they may have appealed to a god of male chauvinism. Some simply say that the Declaration was a propaganda document inspired by the ideas of the Renaissance where the mind of man was viewed as "divine."

Atheists like Richard Dawkins, who wrote *The God Delusion,* agree with Robert Pirsig's statement that;

> When one person suffers from a delusion it is called insanity. When many people suffer from a delusion it is called religion.[33]

Dawkins quickly gets to his main premise when he states;

> Any creative intelligence, of sufficient complexity to design anything, comes into existence only as the end product of an extended process of gradual evolution.[34]

The original definition of the word evolution at the time of our founding was "A series of things unrolled or unfolded; as the *evolution* of ages."[35] It simply meant a process of unfolding the meaning of things or the progression of growth.

Today's definition focuses on "*Biology.* change in the gene pool of a population from generation to generation by such processes as mutation, natural selection, and genetic drift."[36] This process of biological development today is assumed to be godless, from chaos to order – all by chance.

Douglas Wilson, in his book *The Deluded Atheist,* quotes Dawkins in relation to America's founding:

> The paradox has often been noted that the United States, founded in secularism, is now the most religious country in Christendom, while England, with an established church headed by its constitutional monarch, is among the least…

> The genie of religious fanaticism is rampant in present-day America, and the Founding Fathers would have been horrified.[37]

Wilson's response is pertinent:

> Horrified, aye. The preachers at the time of the American Founding… made the average Religious Right evangelical today look like the Rev. Casper Milquetoast. At Yorktown, all George Washington's colonels (with one exception) were elders in Presbyterian churches… Over half the Continental Army were Presbyterians, and the rest were Congregationalists and Baptists, fellow Calvinists all. The black-robed Presbyterian preachers were called "the black regiment" because of their importance to the war effort.[38]

Christopher Hitchens' book *God is Not Great* poses another perspective on the godless nation theory. Douglas Wilson, in his book *God Is,* quotes Hitchens stating:

> Our belief is not a belief. Our principles are not a faith. We do not rely solely upon science and reason, because these are necessary rather than sufficient factors, but we distrust anything that contradicts science or outrages reason. We may differ on many things, but what we respect is free inquiry, open-mindedness, and the pursuit of the ideas for their own sake.[39]

Wilson responds;

> Okay, so he has faith in certain of his principles, but this faith of his is not like our faith in our principles because ours are… wrong.[40]

The Atheist who claims the Declaration is a secular document may do so from a premise that the *faith* of the framers was not religious because Christianity (the one they don't like) is *wrong*. This is circular reasoning at its best. Atheism, in any event, is simply another *belief system.*

Though the vast majority of those who signed the document were believers in Christ,[41] not all were, and thus, as the argument goes, finding inconsistencies in those who signed it will somehow diminish the significance of the document they signed.

Our focus, however, should not be on the frailty of the humans who enacted it, but the nature of the God they appealed to as the source of their rights. After all, this Declaration was no joke, for those who signed it would be labeled as traitors and sought to be arrested, tried and hung for treason.[42]

As we now analyze the Declaration to deduce the nature of the God they appealed to, let's ponder the fact that in today's world, the statement by Paul the Apostle in his sermon on Mars Hill may be pertinent.

> Acts 17:23-25 states, *"the One whom you worship without knowing, Him I proclaim to you. God, who made the world and everything in it, since He is Lord of heaven and earth... He gives to all life, breath, and all things."*

Considering this passage, we now highlight the way God was described and why we believe the God of the Declaration is the God of the Bible.

The Laws of Nature and of Nature's God

The Declaration opens with the idea that the United States has a right to be a separate nation because of ***"the laws of nature and of nature's God."*** Did this phrase come from the Renaissance? No, it was derived from the Biblical premises of William Blackstone's *Commentaries on the Laws of England.* These volumes were very familiar to the delegates writing the Declaration. They remained the main teaching on law in our nation up through the Civil War.

The "laws of nature" was a phrase that meant "creation law." Blackstone wrote;

> When the Supreme Being formed the universe, and created matter out of nothing, he established certain laws... Man, considered as a creature, must necessarily be subject the laws of his creator.... this will of his maker is called the law of nature.[43]

Five times Genesis 1 declares that God created living things "according to their kind." Then, in verse 26 he said, *"Let us make man in our image."* So, Blackstone is correct, there are laws that God has imputed into everything, and we are to follow the rules of the Creator. But how can we know those rules? We can see them in creation, but due to the fall, our understanding is flawed.

The phrase "of nature's God" meant the "law of God." Blackstone wrote;

> The doctrines... we call the revealed or divine law, and they are to be found only in the Holy Scriptures... upon these two

foundations, the law of nature and the law of revelation, depend all human laws.[44]

Only the God of the Bible has revealed Himself in written revelation *and* creation.

Self-Evident Truth

"We hold these truths to be self-evident" is a phrase depicting the biblical doctrine of epistemology or simply how we discern what is true. The Bible reveals that God gives self-evident truth, called in theology "common grace" as declared in Romans 1 and 2.

Romans 1:20 states that "For since the creation of the world His invisible attributes are clearly seen, being understood by the things that are made, even His eternal power and Godhead, so that they are without excuse." In other words, God reveals Himself through His creation in such a way that everyone can discern certain truths, and we are all *"without excuse."*

Romans 2:24-25 states "for when Gentiles, who do not have the law, by nature do the things in the law, these, although not having the law, are a law unto themselves, who show the work of the law written in their hearts, their conscience also bearing witness…"

The idea of self-evident truth is not a Renaissance idea that man is autonomous and can determine what is true all by himself. To the Renaissance man, there is no self-evident truth, only self-created truth.

Self-evident truth is built on the premise that God has revealed truths such as life, liberty and property from Genesis 1:28; *to be fruitful and multiply (life), replenish the earth (liberty to invent), and dominion (own a portion of earth).* Gary Amos writes:

> These beliefs were not some Newtonian Enlightenment concoction of John Wise or Cotton Mather as a first step toward deism. Nor were they invented by early Puritans such as William Ames in the 1600s. These ideas from the Bible had been taught and believed by Augustine, Aquinas, Calvin, and Hooker. To attribute them to deism and the Enlightenment is absurd.[45]

Of course, Newton, Wise and Mather were not "Enlightenment" thinkers, but Amos' point is well taken. The main ideas came from the Bible.

All Men are Created Equal

The Declaration further declares that ***"all men are created equal."*** This is a unique biblical doctrine - all people, male and female, are equal before God. Corrupt nations have made people unequal for the purpose of controlling them based on race, wealth, gender or royalty.

But the only God who has placed all human beings as equal in position before the law is the God of the Bible. It is precisely this premise that became the foundation for the progressive equality of the races, sexes and putting leaders and people under the same rule of law. It gave us *"the consent of the governed"* rather than "ruler's law" (rule by the King).[46]

In America we *progressed toward true equality* in several areas because of the God we enthroned; for we were not practicing full equality at the time of the Declaration. As believers, when we profess Christ as Lord, we are also not practicing total submission to Him in every area of our life, for a declaration of the Lordship of Christ is by nature a declaration beyond where we are presently living.[47]

Unalienable Rights

The Declaration says we are ***"endowed by our Creator with certain unalienable Rights."*** These rights of life, liberty and property (or the pursuit of happiness) were given, as already stated, in Genesis 1. The only God that has ever given unalienable rights, empowering men and women to self-government, is the God of the Bible. Gary Amos writes:

> Outside Christianity, few secular rights theorists have any substance for the language of rights. Except for a handful of these writers, the concept of 'rights' has become obsolete. Within modern Christianity the same problem exists. Theologians and preachers speak only the language of 'duty.' For both Christians and non-Christians the bottom has dropped out of rights theory. This situation signals a crisis in modern political thought and threatens Western freedoms, since the concept of rights is 'theory-dependent.'
>
> ...America was founded on 'unalienable rights' – those that a man may not unconditionally sell, trade, barter, or transfer without denying the image of God in himself. God the Creator endows man with these rights, annexing them to the human person. They are inalienable. For to deny these rights in a man is to deny that he is a human being.[48]

We can be thankful that the God of the Bible empowers His subjects to freely choose to serve Him rather than being mere robots.[49]

Appealing to the Supreme Judge

After listing the violations of English Law that King George III practiced in relation to the Colonies, proving he was indeed a tyrant rather than a public servant,[50] the delegates of the Continental Congress that were in Philadelphia that hot summer of 1776 ***"appealed to the Supreme Judge of the World"*** for the rectitude (righteous or morally upright conduct) of their intentions.

They appealed their cause to the highest court – the court of heaven. They placed their *lives, fortunes and sacred honor* in the Hands of one whose justice is perfect and who never fails. The God of the Bible is a Supreme Judge, and specifically Christ *"has been given authority to execute judgment"* (John 5:27). The idea that one can appeal their cause to God is unique to the Bible.

The Protection of Divine Providence

In closing the Declaration, the delegates wrote ***"with a firm Reliance on the Protection of Divine Providence."*** They had already referenced God's laws and the fact that He holds all men and women accountable for their actions.

God is the Supreme Judge and State constitutions like that of Massachusetts also called Him *"the Great Legislator of the Universe."*[51] These aren't watered down names of a God no one knows. These are attributes of the God of the Bible. The final reference made to God is that of Providence. Providence, from Webster's 1828 Dictionary which defined words as they were used in his time period was;

> The care and superintendence which God exercises over his creatures... by divine providence is often understood God himself.

The God of the Bible is transcendent (separate from us) and immanent (close to us) at the same time.

A Declaration of Prayer and Dependence upon God

Rus Walton of the Plymouth Rock Foundation,[52] emphasized that the Declaration of Independence was also a Declaration of dependence on God. I call it a proclamation of prayer. John Jay, our first Supreme Court justice, wrote;

> No human society has ever been able to maintain both order and freedom, both cohesiveness and liberty apart from the moral precepts of the Christian Religion. Should our Republic ever forget this fundamental precept of governance, we will then be surely doomed.[53]

In perusing the consistent pattern of prayer proclamations in the Bible and American history, we find that they reflect a consistent pattern. Consider 2nd Chronicles 7:13-14 an example.

(1) A Focus on God and His Sovereignty - When I shut up heaven and there is no rain, or command the locusts to devour the land, or send pestilence among My people…
(2) God's Covenant with His people – If my people, who are called by My name will humble themselves, and pray and seek My face…
(3) Our responsibility to repent – and turn from their wicked ways…
(4) Consecration and restoration – then I will hear from heaven, and will forgive their sin, and heal their land.

The Declaration follows this pattern:

(1) A Focus on God as Creator – the laws of nature and nature's God
(2) God's Covenant – all men are created equal… endowed by their Creator… with unalienable rights – life, liberty

and the pursuit of happiness… secured by the consent of the governed

(3) Repentance – for the rectitude (morally correct behavior or thinking – righteousness) of our intentions

(4) Consecration – with a firm reliance on the protection of Divine Providence, pledging our lives, fortunes and sacred honor.

It was John Adams who wrote the following in his diary when he was 20 years old in 1755:

> Suppose a nation in some distant region, should take the Bible for their only law Book, and every member should regulate his conduct by the precepts there exhibited. Every member would be obliged in conscience to temperance and frugality and industry, to justice and kindness and charity towards his fellow men, and to piety and love, and reverence towards almighty God. In this Commonwealth, no man would impair his health by gluttony, drunkenness, or lust - no man would sacrifice his most precious time to cards, or any other trifling and mean amusement - no man would steal or lie or any way defraud his neighbor, but would live in peace and good will with all men - no man would blaspheme his maker or prophane his worship, but a rational and manly, a sincere and unaffected Piety and devotion, would reign in all hearts. What a Utopia, what a paradise would this region be.[54]

You may ask, what difference does all this make? True, America has never been perfect, but since the God referred to in the Declaration is perfect, the nation can return to the premise which brought into existence at any time.

Consider what John Adams wrote to Thomas Jefferson in 1813;

> The general Principles, on which the Fathers achieved independence, were the only principles in which, that

> beautiful assembly of young gentlemen could unite… And what were these general principles? I answer, the general principles of Christianity, in which all those sects were united: and the general principles of English and American liberty, in which all those young men united, and which had united all parties in America, in majorities sufficient to assert and maintain her independence. …I will avow, that I then believed, and now believe, that those general principles of Christianity, are as eternal and immutable, as the existence and attributes of God: and that those principles of liberty, are as unalterable as human nature…[55]

There it is in a nutshell. The Declaration of Independence is the seminal document that united the Colonies and by the Providence of God gave them a most improbable victory over Britain. When the September 3, 1783 Treaty of Paris officially ended the war and brought peace, its first line was this:

> In the Name of the most Holy & undivided Trinity.[56]

Leading Idea – ***For a nation to be changed and remain stable, it needs a God who bears the characteristics of giving self-evident truth, equality, unalienable rights of life, liberty and property, a Judge to whom we can appeal, and providential care through His Sovereignty***

Chapter 3

THE ORIGINS OF THE DECLARATION

...a decent respect to the opinions of mankind requires that they should declare the ***causes*** *which impel them to the separation* – Declaration of Independence

Where did the basic premises of the Declaration come from? We saw in the last chapter that these truths were contained uniquely in the Bible. It was these ideas, more than any other factor, that were the *causes* of the separation from Great Britain.

The United States of America is unique in that it was built primarily on ideas, not conquest. Those ideas were transmitted faithfully to succeeding generations for more than a century. They were transmitted through the medium of colonial homes as well as the preaching from the pulpits of the colonial churches.

Though the God of the Bible may be the God of the Declaration, *how* God is expressed in a civil document is important. To the believer today, as well as the average American, phrases like "the laws of nature and nature's God", "self-evident truth", "created equal", "unalineable rights", "supreme judge" and "divine providence" are strange to the ears, especially as descriptions of God.

The pastors and their parishoners understood God as both *Creator* and *Redeemer*. The way He was described in both of these manners was a matter of jurisdiction. Consider John Calvin's thinking:

> It is one thing to perceive that God our Maker supports us by his power rules us by his providence, fosters us by his goodness, and visits us with all kinds of blessings, and another thing to embrace the grace of reconciliation offered to us in Christ. Since, then, the Lord first appears, as well in the creation of the world as in the general doctrine of Scripture,

> simply as a Creator, after afterwards as a Redeemer in Christ, - a twofold knowledge of him hence arises…[57]

Christians know Jesus Christ as their redeemer, but we must not forget that as Creator He is the author of the liberty every individual enjoys, in America or anywhere in the world, whether they are believers or not. This is common grace and understood as the “Creator-Redeemer Distinction.”

God is revealed as Creator in the jurisdiction of civil government, whereas Christ is revealed as Redeemer in the jurisdiction of the Church. If this understanding is not clear, the tension in language between church and state can be a constant confusion in the responsibilities of each sphere.

The Committees of Correspondense Sowed the Seeds of Liberty

Samuel Adams wrote his ‘Rights of the Colonists” in November of 1772 and sent it as part of the inauguration of the Committees of Correspondence. The purpose of these committees would be a grass roots effort to unite towns to be united in their ideas. Adams wrote;

> May God grant, that the love of liberty, and a zeal to support it, may enkindle in every town. If our enemies should see the flame bursting in different part of the country, and distant from each other, and distant from each other, it might discourage their attempts to damp and quench it. I am well assured they are alarmed at the measure now taking, being greatly apprehensive of the same consequences from it which our good friend at Plymouth hopes and expects. This should animate us in carrying it into exertion. I beg you would exert your utmost influence in your neighboring towns and elsewhere.[58]

As I wrote years ago:

> James Warren was the 'good friend at Plymouth,' which was the first local town to respond. His wife, Mercy Otis Warren, would compile one of the most celebrated histories of the American Revolution, and was quite adept at the 'power of the pen' herself. Sam Adams would write to Elbridge Gerry in 1772 that 'if each town would declare its sense of these matters, I am persuaded our enemies would not have it in thieir power to divide us.'
>
> Could this town by town communication, unorganized from 'above,' and not controled by any central location, actually spread like a blaze and unify the continent? What were the 'rights' that Sam Admas was to declare?[59]

The treatise sent out to the towns by Sam Adams was put in three parts; the 'Rights of the Colonists as Men,' the 'Rights of the Colonists as Christians' and the 'Rights of the Colonists as Subjects.'[60]

Due to Samuel Adams' understanding of the Creator-Redeemer distinction, he wrote to three audiences at the time; non-believers, believers and those who were British citizens. His terminology about God in relation to these areas are a great example for all of us.

> The Rights of the Colonists as Men – Among the natural rights of the Colonists are these: First, a right to life; Secondly, to liberty; Thirdly, to property; together with the support and defend them in the best manner they can.
>
> The Rights of the Colonists as Christians – These may be best understood by reading and carefully studying the institutes of

> the great Law Giver and Head of the Christian Church, which are to be found clearly written and promulgated in the New Testament.
>
> The Rights of the Colonists as Subjects – All persons born in the British American Colonies are, by the laws of God and nature and by the common law of England, exclusive of all charters from the Crown, well entitled, and by acts of the British Parliament are declared to be entitled to all the natural, essential, inherrent, and inseparable rights, liberties, and privileges of subjects born in Great Britain or within the realm…[61]

But long before Adams' treatise in 1772, and before the springs of the Great Awakening bubbled forth in homes and churches, four truths that eventually find their way into the Declaration were known to have been preached several decades before and embedded in the first two paragrahs of the Declaration.

They articulate and reveal four Biblical doctrines arising from God as Creator that were the *causes* of their separation from England, regardless of one's religious affiliation. Though the springs of revival come in the hearts of individuals, it would be the pastors that would implant them further.

The Role of the Clergy in Disseminating the Ideas in our Declaration

President Calvin Coolidge gave a speech in Philadelphia on July 5, 1926 for the one hundred and fiftieth anniversary of the Declaration. He said;

> The American Revolution represented the informed and mature convictions of a great mass of independent, liberty-loving, God-fearing people who knew their rights, and possessed the courage to dare to maintain them.

He went on to attribute the ideas in the Declaration and our Constitution to the clergy who preached for decades prior to the Declaration. He said that a particular Massachusetts clergyman whose books of 1710 and 1717 were reprinted in 1772 and sent out by the town of Boston. His works, he said;

> Have been declared to have been nothing less than a textbook of liberty for our Revolutionary fathers… the apostle of this movement was the Rev. John Wise.[62]

Though Jefferson was the penman of the Declaration, he did not invent the ideas contained in the document. He was one of five committee members commissioned by Congress to write a Declaration. He admitted the ideas were not new when he wrote to Richard Henry Lee;

> This was the object of the Declaration of Independence. not to find out new principles, or new arguments, never before thought of, not merely to say things which had never been said before; but to place before mankind the common sense of the subject; [. . .] terms so plain and firm, as to command their assent, and to justify ourselves in the independent stand we [. . .] compelled to take. neither aiming at originality of principle or sentiment, nor yet copied from any particular and previous writing, it was intended to be an expression of the American mind, and to give to that expression the proper tone and spirit called for by the occasion. all it's authority rests then on the harmonizing sentiments of the day.[63]

So from Jefferson we learn that the Declaration rehearsed the same principles and sentiments already assimilated by the average American. It was an "expression of the American mind."

Alice Baldwin, in her book *The New England Clergy and the American Revolution,* proves that it was the preaching of the clergy that inspired the Revolution and its corresponding documents. She states that;

> Puritan theology and fundamental political thought (at the time of Revolution are inseparably linked)... the New England clergy preserved, extended, and popularized the essential doctrines of political philosophy, tthus making familiar to every church-going New Englander long before 1763 not only the doctrines of natural right, the social contract, and the right of resistance but also the fundamental principle of American constitutional law, that government, likee its citizens, is bounded by law and when it transcends its authority it acts illegally.[64]

Harry Stout, in his book *The New England Soul*, picks up where Baldwin leaves off. He documents the fact that the content of the thousands of sermons preached weekly by the colonial clergy, especially in New England, laid the groundwork for the Revolution and the Declaration.

If there had been no widespread preaching from the colonial pulpit applying key Christian doctrines to political thought, there would have been no American Revolution, and certainly no Declaration of Independence. Stout documents that the average church-goer in New England heard seven thousand sermons in their life, about fifteen thousand concentrated hours of listening![65]

Bishop Charles B. Galloway, famous American Methodist preacher, gave five lectures on Christianity's influence in the building of America in the Chapel of Emory College in Oxford, Georgia in 1898. In his fourth lecture, he made this comment:

> 'The pulpit of the Revolution,' a distinguished author says, 'was the secret of that moral energy which sustained the republic in its material weakness against superior numbers and discipline and all the powers of England.'..... all through the history of the American commonwealth the holy men who have ministred at her altars of religion by their exposition and enforcement of the ethics of the Man of Galilee have 'connected,' says John Quincy Adams, 'with one indissoluble bond the principles of civil government with the principles of Christianity.'"[66]

So if the general inspiration for the American Revolution came from the colonial pulpit, and the ideas in the Declaration came generally from the Bible, is Coolidge correct that *specifically* one could direct their attention to Pastor John Wise, who put the ideas together in such a way that the key phrases in the Declaration can be traced to his works written more than 50 years prior to that document?

John Adams thought so when writing a letter to Timothy Pickering in 1822;

> As you justly observe, there is not an idea in it (the Declaration) but what had been hackneyed in Congress for two years before. The substance of it is contained in the delcaration of rights and the violation of those rights, in the Journals of Congress, in 1774. Indeed, the essence of it is contained in a pamphlet, voted and printed by the town of Boston, before the first Congress met...[67]

The pamphlet referred to by Adams was none other than John Wise's works combined in one reprint by the unanimous vote of the leaders of the town of Boston in 1772!

The pamphlet that contained the "essence" of the Declaration, reprinted two years before the first Continental Congress was formed, was the same one referred to by Coolidge in 1926 as "a textbook of liberty for our Revolutionary fathers."

Pastor John Wise was from Ipswich, Massachusetts. His 1710 and 1717 works were combined and reprinted by the town of Boston in order to spread the key ideas that would unite the Colonies at their most critical period. They were reprinted in the same year that Sam Adams initiated the Committees of Correspondence to unite the colonies as "men, subjects and Christians."[68]

So what was it that united these patriots at the time of our founding as a nation? J. Wingate Thornton, in his work *The Pulpit of the American Revolution*, states;

> There is a natural and just union of religious and civil counsels, - not that external alliance of the crosier and sword called 'Church and State,' – but the philosophical and deeper union which recognizes God as Supreme Ruler…. the church polity of New England begat like principles in the state. The pew and the pulpit had been educated to self-government.[69]

Ideas preached from the pulpit were applied to civil affairs. Keep in mind that most of those we call founders were in those churches listening!

According to the Bible, the jurisdiction of the home is to bring children into the world and disciple them to be fruitful and productive citizens of both church and state. If the home does not do its job, the church and state will have a difficult time doing theirs. After all, the requirement of leaders in the church begin with a fulfillment of "rule well within a household."[70]

The jurisdiction of the church is to cultivate a conscience trained to be sensitive to the conviction of the of God's Word, the Bible. Believers are to evangelize the lost and disciple the saved to be salt and light.[71] The ideas put forth in the birth certificate of America were preached in the church. The influence of ideas is more powerful than force.

Rev. John Wise and the *Birth of American Independence*

John Fiske, in his classic work on *The Beginnings of New England*, said about John Wise of Ipswich that he was "one of the broadest thinkers and most lucid writers of his time."[72] This is because, early on, John Wise was the leader of the resistance to Governor Andros and his autocratic rule in New England.

Andros arrived in New England in 1687, having been sent over by James II in order to punish the growing self-government of the settlements. The Charters of Rhode Island and Connecticut were rescinded, the Church of England and new parishes were forced upon Boston, and the Old South Church was seized for English style services against the will of its Puritans.

In addition, voting rights were removed, arbitrary taxes enacted, private property deeds seized where the "King" assumed ownership, suspension of *habeas corpus*, censor of the press, and abolishment of the General Court put total power in the hands of one individual – Governor Andros.

The man who led the lawful resistance, among others, was John Wise, pastor of the church at Ipswich, who organized the town to interpose. As a result, Wise was imprisoned and fined. At his "trial", it was openly declared that the people of New England had no privileges any longer except to be sold as slaves.

On April 18, 1689, led by John Wise, the citizens and town leaders arrested Andros and his Council and imprisoned them. They then publicly read a "declaration of independence" from the balcony of the Town Hall in Boston.

Written by Cotton Mather, it repeated the reasoning of John Wise, quoting from Magna Charta and claiming that their God-given rights under the law were violated without their consent. Though set in the context of attacks on the church, it was America's *first* declaration of independence.[73] Here are excerpts:

I. WEE have seen more than a decade of years rolled away, since the English World had the Discovery of an horrid Popish Plot; wherein the bloody Devoto's of Rome had in their Design and Prospect no less than the extinction of the Protestant Religion…

II. …our *Charter* was with a most injurious pretense (& scarce *that)* of Law, Condemned before it was possible for us to appear at *Westminster* in the legal defense of it…

III. The Commission was as *Illegal* for the form of it, as the way of obtaining it was *Malicious* and *unreasonable:* yet we made no resistance thereunto as we could easily have done; but chose to give all *Man-kind* a demonstration of our being a people sufficiently dutifull and loyall to our King…

IV. Yet more Absolute and Arbitrary, with which Sr. *Edmond Andros* arrived as our Governor

VI. …Accordingly, we have been treated with multiplied contradictions to *Magna Charta,* the rights of which we laid claim unto....

VIII. …in all our *Titles to our Lands;* and, though *besides* our purchase of them from the Natives, and, *besides* our actual peaceable unquestioned Possession of them… we were every day told,

That no man was owner of a Foot of Land in all the Colony...

IX. ...those of them which were true Lovers *of their Country,* were seldom admitted to, and seldom consulted at the Debates which Produced these unrighteous things...

XI. We did nothing against these Proceedings, but only cry to our God; they *have caused the cry of the Poor to come unto him, and he hears the cry of the Afflicted.* We have been quiet hitherto; and so still we should have been, had not the Great God at this time laid us under a *double engagement* to do something for our security

XII. We do therefore seize upon the persons of those few *Ill men* which have been (next to our sins) the grand authors of our miseries: Resolving to secure them, for what Justice, Orders from his Highness with the *Parliament* shall direct... In the meantime firmly believing: that we have endeavored nothing but what mere Duty to God and our *Country* calls for at our Hands, we commit our *Enterprise* unto the Blessing of Him, *who hears, the cry of the Oppressed;* and advise all our Neighbors for whom we have thus ventured ourselves to join with us in Prayers and all just Actions for the Prosperity of the Land.[74]

A month later, on May 26, 1689, after the official news arrived that the Glorious Revolution had put William and Mary on the throne, formal impeachment papers were drawn up against Andros. He was again seized after trying to escape dressed in women's clothing. He was put in chains and sent back to England![75]

Though the town was founded in 1634, the legacy of her most famous pastor, John Wise, who inspired resistance to Andros, caused the town seal to read *"birthplace of American independence."*[76] Ass seen in the above document, though the declaration was against tyranny, they proclaimed their rights from the doctrines of God as Creator.

It was Wise who helped put a stop to the unlawful Salem Witch Trials. Wise also opposed the hierarchy of the Mather's over individual churches, prompting his work in 1710 entitled *The Churches Quarrel Espoused,* a satire on arbitrary power as the only proper rule for Englishmen.[77]

Then, in 1717, Wise articulated a thoughtful and logical work on key principles of church government based on the Bible but confirmed through right reason and the "light of nature." He again appealed to God as Creator, with its title *A Vindication of the Government of New England Churches.*

This, combined with the 1710 satire, was republished in 1772. Due to its language, it was applicable for the time period and conflict arising at the time of the Revolution.

Copies of the book were purchased by men such as John Scollay (one of the leaders of the Boston Tea Party), Colonel Barrett of Concord (who withstood the British at the Old North Bridge), Rev. Edward Emerson of Concord (who was probably with the militia that day) and William Dawes (who rode with Paul Revere).[78]

On April 18, 1775, 86 years later to the day, John Wise 'rode' with the Minutemen (in book form) on the anniversary of the first "declaration of independence!"

Historian Henry Martyn Dexter, writing in 1880, put it well when he said of Wise;

> He did not himself see, nor did his generation comprehend, either the exact bearing, or the entire force, of the principles which he enunciated. It was in his intent to justify, and bring the churches back to, the Cambridge Platform as their fundamental law; but in so doing he generated a momentum… these two books taken together, and considered in the light of their time, and the influence which it is easy to see that they exerted, were very remarkable.[79]

John Wise articulates four key Ideas that helped inspire the Declaration of Independence

Now let's examine some of the Biblical doctrines John Wise wrote about in his seminal work, *Vindication of the New England Churches.* The doctrines taught by the colonial clergy in general and John Wise in particular are unique in the history of nations. Rarely does the pulpit have the freedom, wisdom and clarity to preach these truths for over 150 years with such unity and application to society.

The first doctrine is ***the law of liberty***. The question is not *whether* religion is the basis of law, but *which* religion is the basis of law. Law is defined as simply "direction and regulation." The question is what the law directs you to obey, and what it attempts to restrain. It is the *law of liberty* when God's law directs us to obey Him and restrains sin and evil.[80]

John Wise said that man has "an original liberty stampt upon his rational nature."[81] According to Wise, God is the author of both the law of nature and revelation (the Bible). The phrase in the Declaration says "the laws of nature and of nature's God."

The second doctrine is that of ***individuality*** or ***equality***. Each individual is unique, the Bible declares in Genesis 1 and 2, though we are all made "in the image of God." After all, God first created an individual in the Garden. Jurisdictions are delineated with responsibilities for the individual, family, church, business, and civil government.

In a natural state, says Wise, we are "equals, no servitude or subjection can be conceived without inequality."[82] In other words, if we claim equality externally, we actually assert the inequality of man. In the Declaration, it says that we are all "created equal."

The third doctrine involves the purpose of civil government to ***protect God-given rights***. The three great rights of mankind – *life, liberty and property,* are given by God in Genesis 1:28. Civil government protects God-given rights, it does not provide them (Romans 13:1-7).

Wise asserted that "the end of all good government is to cultivate humanity, and promote the happiness of all, and the good of every Man in all his rights, his Life, Liberty, Estate, Honor, etc. without injury or abuse done to any."[83] The Declaration uses the phrase "that to secure these rights, governments are instituted among men."

The final doctrine is that of ***authority***. Though God ordained civil government, the question is who gives civil government the practical authority to operate in its sphere of jurisdiction? The individual was created (Genesis 1-2) before church or civil government was instituted (Genesis 8-9). It was God's idea to have it function "at the hand of every man" or by the consent of the governed.

Here John Wise could not be clearer. In his words;

> The first human subject and original of civil power is the people. For as they have a power every man over himself in a natural state, so upon a combination they can and do bequeath this power unto others.[84]

When the Declaration says that governments "derive their just powers from the consent of the governed" the people have the original authority given them by God and they delegate it. That is why all Constitutions, when so constructed, are deemed *express powers* documents. The only power civil government has is what is clearly expressed in its Constitution.

Wise also articulated that the best form of government is one that combines the *one, few* and *many.* The government of ancient Israel, known as the *Hebrew Republic*, with its combination of monarchy (president – Moses), a legislature (with a house and senate), and a democratically electorate, was the model the colonial clergy referenced as the best form of government.[85]

Ancient Israel, following Biblical Law, had an appeals system of justice where individuals were innocent until proven guilty. This lasted for four hundred years (basically during the book of Judges), but the people refused the responsibility of governing themselves, and chose a King to be like the surrounding nations. As a result, as warned by Samuel, she declined as her government grew and centralized power.[86]

John Wise was far ahead of his time because he drew his ideas from the Bible. He sowed many of the seeds that would eventually grow and be established in our Declaration and Constitution.

The Great Awakening:
Link between the Biblical ideas of the Clergy and the Declaration

Why would so many clergy so passionately articulate principles of liberty from the God of Creation, as well as Christ the Redeemer, from about 1740 on with such intensity? It was because of the Great Awakening and primarily from the travelling preacher George Whitefield. Richard Bushman writes:

> The very magnitude of the revivals, which won for the Awakening thie apellation "Great," is one indication of their importance. From Whitefield's 1740 tour until 1743, the period when the revival was at its peak, thousands were converted. People from all ranks of society, of all ages, and from every section underwent the new birth. In New England virtually every congregation was touched. It was not uncommon for ten or twenty percent of a town, having experienced grace, to join the church in a single year.
>
> In the middle colonies, the Presbyterians were most affected, although Whitefield, himself an Anglican, preached to people of all denominations. The Awakening did not penetrate far into the South until after 1744, but then Presbyerians evangelists made rapid inroads into Anglican strongholds in Virginia as well as among their own congregations in the backcountry. It is safe to say that most of the colonists in the 1740's, if not converted themselves, knew someone who was, or at least heard revival preaching.[87]

Whitefield connected all the colonies by his extensive travels. As Tony Cooke writes:

> George Whitefield (1714-1770) has been rightly called 'America's Spiritual Founding Father.' Born, raised, and educated in England, he made thirteen trips acoss the Atlantic and had an unparalleled spiritual impact on the American colonies. Each transatlantic trip would have taken around twelve weeks. In his thirty years of ministry, Whitefield

preached around 1,000 times a year. This inclues an estimated 18,000 wermons and 12,000 talks and exhorations according to one estimate.

It was not unusual for Whitefield to preach to crowds of five or six thousand, and one time there were approximately 20,000 in attendance. Of course, crowds this large necessitated that meetings be outdoors. The population of the American colonies was far less than that of the nation today, and travel was practically always by horseback. Yet, it is estimated that 80% of American colonists heard Whitefield preach at least once.[88]

Harry Stout writes about the fact that due to Whitefield's exposure to play-acting and drama, he combined both in the pulpit:

> Whitefield's American legacy was doubly significant. He not only saved souls and swelled church memberships but rallied as well an entire group of disparate and previously unrelated peoples into a common movement for revival, a group that looked to him as its spokesman. Out of his revivals there emerged a pan-American – indeed, an Algo-American – common cultural identity.[89]

The revivals of the 1730's and 1740's indicated a deep spring *coming to the surface.* They did not originate with Whitefield, but flowed somewhat "underground" or unnoticed by many. It has been my observation that at least two or three decades preceding the outburst "above ground" so to speak, a great preparation is occuring in the hearts of people. As Joel Beeke indicates:

> Major historical movements, whether religious, political, or social, are the product of a period of fermentation. Spokesmen for these movements often seen to appear suddenly on the

> scene, but in most cases lesser-known individuals pave the way for great leaders. Thus Martin Luther and the Reformation cannot be understood apart from the forerunners like John Wycliffe and Jan Hus.
>
> Simarily the Great Awakening, while associated with such great leaders as Jonathan Edwards and George Whitefield, had its precursor. One was Theodorus Jacobus Frelinghuysen, whom Whitefield referred to as 'the beginning of the great work.'[90]

Frelinghuysen arrived in New York in 1720 at 28 years of age. As a Dutch Reformed minister, he gravitated to New York and New Jersey where many from the Netherlands were already located. But he found that many showed no fruit of conversion. He noted that the

> Necessity of a new heart had almost entirely been lost sight of… formalism and self-righteousness almost universally prevailed. Christians were not ashamed to ridicule Christian experience, and many had become very resolute in opposing it.[91]

Revival broke out in his wake, and the colony of New Jersey was transformed. All five of his sons became ministers, and his two daughters married ministers. He was the spark, and Gilbert Tennant continued the work in the middle colonies while Jonathan Edwards led the movement in the north.

Another example of a revival river flowing beneath the surface was the boyhood testimony of Edwards. Between the ages of 11 and 13, he would set up a "booth in which he and his boy companions used to meditate and play." Ola Winslow writes "the bulding of the booth in the swamp was a group response to the same quickening of religious interest."[92]

The children were "playing" church, doing what their parents were doing in earnest. The river of revival often begins privately in home and church before it bursts forth as an awakening in culture.

A third example was the repentance for the Salem Witch Trials of 1692. At the public prayer, fast and humiliation day of 1697, Judge Samuel Sewall stood in church and repented for his role. In 1706 Ann Putnam, who as a 12 year old child falsely accused so many, stood in the Salem Church and asked for forgiveness. Amazingly, she was restored to communion.[93] Soon after, revival springs flowed forth![94]

In concert with the theology of the time, the river of revival that would change the landscape only comes by the sovereign hand of God. There are no gimicks that always work.

In the southern colonies, God used Samuel Davies, among others. Patrick Henry was taken by his mother to hear Davies when he was just a teen. His mother would quiz him on the way home about the major points of his sermon.

There is no question that Patrick was inspired by Davies, and it may have been this influence upon him as a teen when he was converted. He later wrote that Davies "was the greatesr orator" he had ever heard.[95]

But Whitefield connected the dots throughout the colonies. Ira Stoll writes of Whitefield coming to Boston in 1740:

Whitefield preached to seven thousand in Harvard Yard in Cambridge, where, he reported, the president (Samuel Langdon) treated him 'very civilly.' He preaced to a crowd of blacks in Boston about the apostle Philip's conversion of the Ethiopian eunuch. He prayed with the governor (Jonathan Belcher) of the colony and with the poor at the almshouse…

Joseph wrote in his diay, 'It is wonderful to behold a young man (about 26) preaching thus twice a day, with great earnestness, the Gospel of Christ. Many, particularly among the youth, seem to be affected.[96]

One of the youth affected (and likely converted) was 18 year old Samuel Adams. Shortly after the visit to Harvard, where Adams graduated that same year, he joined Brattle Street Church, which you couldn't do without a confession of faith subsequent to conversion.[97] His pastor, Samuel Cooper, would become a close friend and advisor, for he was the leading patriot pastor of Boston. Adams would soon join his cousin John, along with James Bowdoin, John Hancock and Joseph Warren who all sat under his preaching for many years.

The Great Awakening did not just reach back to the time of John Wise. It went forward and prepared the patriot leaders with refining the ideas needed for a unanimous Declaration of Independence. Samuel Adams letter of November 11, 1765 to George Whitefield is a case in point.

We are the descendants of ancestors remarkable for their zeal for true religion & liberty. When they found it was no longer possible for them to bear any part in the support of this glorious cause in their native country England, they transplanted themselves at their own very great expense, into

> the wilds of America... Here they resolved to set up the worship of God, according to their best judgment, upon the plan of the new testament, to maintain it among themselves, and transmit it to their posterity, & to spread the knowledge of Jesus Christ...[98]

Many are ignorant today of how Thomas Jefferson, the member of the Committee to draft the document in 1776, was impacted by the sentiments drawn from the Bible and Christianity regardless of whether he personally ascribed to them. In Mark Beliles and Jerry Newcombe's book "Thomas Jefferson and the God who Gave us Liberty"; they write:

> The attempt to drive out all expressions of religion, especially Christianity, from the public square in Thomas Jefferson's name shows a deep misunderstanding both of Jefferson and of American history. It's time to set the record straight. Separation of the institution of the church from the institution of the state is something Jefferson believed in. Special status of one denomination could not be permitted, but that is far from the separation of God and the state, or the exclusion of general religious principles from expression in the public arena, including in the curriculum of higher education at state schools.
>
> What has made America so great for more than two centuries? One reason is the fact that our nation recognizes that our rights come from God. Regardless of Jefferson's personal doubts, he articulated for all time a very Christian understanding that God is the source of our rights. This gave America a foundational view of government that was non-secular.
>
> It is vital for our nation to recognize and protect God-given rights. Jefferson helped put America on that trajectory, and his true legacy on that point should not be distorted because of

> political correctness or because of personal theological doubts he himself entertained as an older man.[99]

It is one thing to have ideas preached from the pulpits with the same basic theology regardless of whether it was in the clothing of the Episcopal, Presbyterian, Congregational or Bapist denominations, but quite another to have it fueled by the Spirit of God in a revival!

Leading Idea – ***The theology of liberty, drawn from the Bible, is most potent when coupled with the infusing of the Spirit of God in order for it to bring a people to the place where they will stand for truth in the public square.***

PART TWO

The Historic Context of the Declaration

Chapter 4

THE DECLARATION AND THE MAGNA CHARTA

That the Church of England shall be free, and have her whole rights, and her liberties...
Magna Charta, 1215 AD

July 4, 1776, was the culmination of a process of time that brought ancient ideas of liberty to the highest expression in history at the time. The story of liberty in the Western world began centuries earlier, however. The ideas in the Declaration were not new as President Coolidge told us.

Ideas of liberty were declared in 1215 with the document known as Magna Charta. Signed on the 15th of June 1215, it was an attempt to restore the ancient Christian liberties of the British Isles. The 1775 Seal of Massachusetts during the American Revolution illustrates the significance of this document to our own independence.

A colonist stands with a sword in one hand and the Magna Charta in the other. This individual, representing the colonists, is willing to defend his God-given liberties based on the ancient written Charter of English liberty called Magna Charta.

The Roots of Magna Charta

During what is known as the Constitutional Debate period between the colonies and Great Britain (1765-1775), Sam Adams, writing in the Boston Gazette in 1769, said:

> Our writer… tells us that formerly the right of taxation was in the King only. I should have been glad if he had pointed us to that time. We know that kings – even English kings – have lost their crowns and their heads for assuming such a right. 'Tis true this strange claim has occasioned much contention, and it always will as long as the people understand the great charter of nature upon which Magna Charta itself is founded,

- No man can take another's property from him without his consent. This is the law of nature; and a violation of it is the same thing, whether it be done by one man who is called a king, or by five hundred of another denomination.[100]

We learn several things from this quote. First, Magna Charta was an attempt at *restoring* ancient liberty, not just taking rights back from the King. In other words, pre-dating the Magna Charta was a period in English history when Kings had no such "prerogative" as claimed by George III.

Second, it rested on a higher law, the "great charter of nature", which in the words of William Blackstone (in 1755) is "the will of his Maker".[101]

Finally, the idea that "no man can take another's property from him without his consent" arises from this law of nature resting on the Bible. Remember, as Blackstone put it, "upon these two foundations, the law of nature and the law of revelation (the Bible), depend all human laws; that is to say, no human laws should be suffered to contradict these."[102]

What time was Sam Adams referring to when Kings did not claim such life, liberty and property rights in the Crown? It was prior to the Norman (French) invasion of England in 1066. In 890 King Alfred had written his Doom Book (book of the law) which was a compilation of the Ten Commandments and their application to society, along with the Beatitudes of Jesus. This was the apex of English liberty for the individual and the protection of his life and property.

At that time, the King was elected. Alfred copied the government of Israel prior to its choice of a King – the Hebrew Republic. This comprised the "ancient liberties" and was the foundation for what is known as the English Common Law.[103]

According to legend, it was the Galatian believers, to whom the New Testament book of Galatians was written, that took the gospel to the British Isles in the first century. The revival among the Celts is well known, and that pagan populace of what would later be known as Ireland, Scotland and England were largely converted before the end of the 2nd century.

When St. Augustine and St. Patrick were sent a century or so later, they found the Bible and particularly the Ten Commandments at the heart of its culture. Leslie Hardinge writes:

> Wherever Patrick established a church he was believed to have left a copy of "the books of the Law and the Books of the Gospel." The Liber ex Lege Moisi is the only work surviving from Celtic sources which answers to the description, "books of the law."[104]

King Alfred, the only king to be known as England's "Great", translated the *Liber ex Lege Moisi* (liberty from the Law of Moses) and added the Beatitudes from the New Testament. His *Code of Law* became unique, rooted in God's Law, and "common" to both King and people, thus establishing the Common Law of England brought to America. Its ultimate root, of course, was the Bible.

The bottom-up, decentralized structure of government, patterned after Exodus 18 with rulers over ten (neighborhoods), fifty (villages), hundred (counties) and thousands (Burroughs or castles) was brought from England and replicated almost verbatim out of the Bible in the wilderness of colonial America.

So, it is important to look a bit deeper into the content and context of this momentous event which became the cornerstone of English constitutional law and the ancestor of all the colonial State constitutions in America and eventually our Declaration and Constitution.

When the Norman Invasion took place in 1066, and the last Saxon King Harold fought to the death at the battle of Hastings, France forced its top-down, centralized philosophy of government upon the defeated English by force.

It appeared as if the world of King Alfred that featured the liberty of the individual, family and church, with is clear jurisdictions, drawn from the Bible, was gone for good. However, when centuries of freedom loving ideas are forced underground, they only temporarily disappear under the façade of forced submission.

Just as one tiny seed can split a rock, so the seeds of liberty sown from the words of Scripture would sprout again under the Providential Hand of God. For the next 150 years, the Christian culture of England flowed underground. On the surface, it was French, but beneath it were the seeds of liberty waiting for the moment when it would burst into the sunlight!

Stephen Langton and the Magna Charta

The individual who brought these truths into view was Stephen Langton. We find him in the archives of Paris, studying Biblical Old Testament Law and the ancient origins of Britain's constitution. His fame as a teacher of theology caused Pope Innocent III to appoint Stephen as the Archbishop of Canterbury.

While in Paris, Stephen Langton is also credited for first dividing the Books of the Bible into chapters for easier study. He also pioneered a restoration of Canon Law that respected individual liberty.[105] But Langton's appointment by the Pope to be Archbishop was strongly opposed by King John, the monarch of England.

For years John resisted having Stephen even step within his dominion. However, John had other things to worry about, particularly his Barons. These "lower magistrates" had the lawful authority of interposing between the King's tyrannical acts and the people who were most injured by them. Pressured from within and without, King John relented and Langton arrived in July of 1213.

Immediately, Langton began to mediate lawfully between the Barons and the King, teaching the Baron's what he had found in his research of the law, namely, that they must take an oath to the law and not just the King. He was teaching them jurisdictional, lawful resistance.

He also let King John know that the Barons would die in defense of their liberties. As Rev. Leeming writes:

> In this war we see Stephen Langton as a bishop fighting for the independence of his Church as well as an Englishman fighting for the history of his country.[106]

Thus, the Magna Charta was born from the pen of Stephen Langton, who is virtually unknown today!

The signing of the Magna Charta was an epoch in the restoration of the rule of law. But it was only the beginning, for over the next few centuries a constant struggle would ensue regarding how to deal with Kings who refused to follow the written law.

It eventually led to the other two English documents considered as part of the English Constitution – the *Petition of Right* (1628) and *Bill of Rights* (1689). But it was the Magna Charta that was referred to continually by our Founders in the United States as the cornerstone of liberty under law and the fact that all rights are given by God, not government.

Magna Charta represents the "fountain" of English liberty being restored from its underground well preserved in custody of the Saxons by the providential Hand of God. Magna Charta was a giant stop sign to the King.

Unlike the Charter of Henry I in 1100 which attempted to stop the King from his arbitrary acts without diminishing his power, this document limited the King directly and that is why it is considered the "first step" toward a restoration of self-government under God.

King John was forced to sign the document it but never intended to keep it, going into a fit of rage only hours after the signing on the 15th of June, 1215. Even Pope Innocent III, who had asserted his power to get Langton to Canterbury, now repudiated the document!

Magna Charta is not a constitution of due process, it is a listing of grievances and a demand that the King abide by the law – a tradition that Kings were not used to following.[107] Tyrants in church and state don't give up power easily!

Magna Charta was quoted and referenced in Colonial America as well as in the State papers written during our Revolution. From the Charter of 1606 asserting the rights of Englishmen to the various colonial documents that established self-government, Magna Charta was either directly or indirectly referenced.

However, now free from the control of English Kings who ignored the law, those coming to colonial America began to look further back to the root of their liberty asserted by King Alfred – the law of God as written in the Bible.

By the time of the Revolution, the pastors looked to God as the source of their rights. The Framers, instructed by these pastors, went *further* than Magna Charta. They appreciated its step in limiting the

King but had no intention of ever having kings again. Our rights came from God, not government.

We weren't simply *limiting* civil government, we were placing it in the hands of the people who would consent to give express permission for government to act! The degree to which the people followed God would be seen in the nature and structure of their civil government.

Our Bill of Rights ratified in 1791 contains phrases that can be traced to clauses of Magna Charta. They now rest on a surer footing, however. Magna Charta was a first step in overcoming tyranny and returning to Government under God, but it was the end in that process.

Magna Charta does not delineate the source of rights but was a step in restraining tyrants who claim to have all power. American liberty is the child of English liberty. But when American liberty came of age, the English colonists were more English than the mother country! The child went further than the parent!

In America, we no longer viewed Kings as getting their power from God and then distributing it to "subjects". With the Bible in our hand, we understood that the *people* are the "kings" and the source of civil authority just as they are also the source of ecclesiastical authority ("priests" – see Revelation 1:5). We began our resistance to tyranny on our knees in colonial churches, led by the clergy.

Magna Charta and the Declaration are Similar

First, *both are a list of grievances against lawless kings.* King John violated the common law, unwritten but inherited from Saxon England, by exercising arbitrary power, interfering with inheritance laws, rights of widows, debtors, lenders, businessmen and military service. He also violated the due process of law. Chapter 39 of the Magna Charta states "no free man shall be seized or imprisoned, or stripped of his rights or possessions…except by the lawful judgment of his equals or by the law of the land."[108]

The Declaration also lists grievances – nearly two thirds of the document is written against King George III. He was a man with little self-control and many thought him insane (power corrupts). He violated individual rights and the written law, including due process as well. As the Declaration states, King George III has deprived "us in many cases, of the benefits of trial by jury."

Second, both are *documents of interposition*. In other words, they lawfully resist tyranny by asserting the biblical lower magistrate principle of having those in a lower office hold those in a higher office to the rule of law.

In the case of Magna Charta, the Barons, who already held power, resisted the tyranny of King John lawfully. In the case of the Declaration, the Continental Congress was the body that asserted that King George III was acting like a tyrant. This is not lawless revolution, but lawful interposition.

Third, *both are written as lawful justifications for civil war*. The Barons (nobleman in charge of defending the king) had taken up arms against the King. They were armed to ensure obedience to the law.

The Declaration was written after King George III severed the relationship of the Crown to the Colonies.[109] The Colonies had no option left but self-defense. The Continental Congress armed the militias. They did not arm themselves with their own authority.

Fourth, *they both articulate a defense of liberty under God*. The Magna Charta begins "Know ye, that we, in the presence of God… unto the honor of God and the advancement of Holy Church."[110]

The Declaration ends "with a firm reliance on the protection of Divine Providence."

The parallels are amazing in one sense, separated by 550 years, but united in their resistance to the lawless Kings of their times and asserting the rights of the people through the lower magistrate. However, there are key distinctions between the two as well, affirming the fact that the Congress that met in Philadelphia had the advantage of both 550 years as well as the freedom to base America's government more squarely on the original foundation of English Liberty – God's Law.

The Declaration goes Further than Magna Charta

Note that the opening paragraph of the Magna Charta, as quoted at the beginning of this chapter, stated its seminal purpose – to recover the liberties of the Church from the tyranny of the King. As we have previously noted, *true liberty would be a friendly jurisdictional separation of church and state under God's Law.* So let us now identify how the Declaration went a step further.

First, Magna Charta was a stop sign to the King's tyranny. The Declaration went further and was the charter of a new nation built on the ancient foundation of King Alfred's England.

Second, Magna Charta limited the power of the King, but the Declaration sowed the seeds for the eventual elimination of monarchy and the rule of kings.

Third, Magna Charta listed the rights of life, liberty and property as being violated, but the Declaration listed them as self-evident and unalienable, given by God, and thus made them rest on a more solid foundation.

Fourth, Magna Charta gave rise to Parliamentary supremacy where the legislature was supreme over the King. The Declaration gave rise to Constitutional supremacy, where the law ruled over the executive, legislative and judicial branches.

Fifth, Magna Charta was the seed of restoring the rule of law but the Declaration was the fruit of asserting the rule of law (self-government under God).

What can we learn from these similarities and distinctions? God has given us a line of liberty from the days of the Bible to the birth of our nation. It rests on the Ten Commandments which liberated the ancient Israelites from Egypt's tyranny and extends to the grace of God and the Gospel. May we tell this Providential story of liberty and its roots to our children and grandchildren.

Leading Idea – It is a better to restore the ancient roots of liberty drawn from the Bible like the Declaration rather than merely limiting tyrannical power like Magna Charta

Chapter 5

THE MAYFLOWER COMPACT AND THE DECLARATION

In the Name of God Amen. We whose names are underwritten, the loyal subjects of our dread sovereign Lord, King James... - Mayflower Compact, November 11, 1620

The Doctrine of Biblical Covenant

At the mouth of two witnesses, or at the mouth of three witnesses, shall the matter be established – Deuteronomy 19:15

Then take with thee one or two more, that in the mouth of two or three witnesses every word may be established – Matthew 18:16

It is obvious in these two passages that two or three individuals have the responsibility of trying to resolve a conflict, for jurisdictional responsibility begins with the individual.

Neither shall they say, Lo here! Or lo there! For, behold, the kingdom of God is within you. – Luke 17:21

Thy kingdom come, thy will be done, on earth as it is in heaven. – Matthew 6:10

The word kingdom and government are synonymous. The government of God is established first in the heart of believers and the self-government of others. All government starts with God, but He first places it in the heart, at the bottom, so to speak.

Historian Bill Federer has documented that throughout recorded history the most common form of government has been a tyrannical monarchy that does not respect the rights of its citizens. In fact, 95% of all governments throughout history take this form![111]

But the kingdom or government of God is different. The King seeks to reside in His subjects, empowering to rule themselves from within – for this is the fountain of liberty.

This is a most unique Kingdom and is quite unusual and exceptional among all the nations that have existed. Wherever true Christianity has gone, this concept arises, and one example is the history of the United States of America. The way this process begins is to form a covenant.

We might assert that the doctrine of covenant in the Bible, both vertical with God and horizontal with others, has some of the following minimal points.

1. *God deals directly with the individual first, and then with groups.* The individual's responsibility is to learn how to walk with God so that self-control can work (John 3:3).

2. *We are dual citizens, having responsibility toward heaven and earth.* God never intended that we would live isolated lives and remain in hiding from our cultural responsibilities. We are citizens, first of heaven, but then also of earth (1st Peter 2:9).

3. *We have the right of self-government.* As individuals, we are to take the first step in solving problems with others in our families, businesses, the community, as well as the church (Matthew 18:15-18). This is the exhortation in the initial passages above.

4. *The rule of law applies equally to all.* Equality is to be defined internally, not externally. In a covenant, we combine ourselves together to achieve a goal we could not perform on our own. We are equally accountable to both the stipulations of the agreement and its consequences.

The Mayflower Compact and the Declaration

The ideas brought on board the Mayflower in the hearts of most of its passengers from the Church at Leyden, were expressed in the Mayflower Compact. In the Bible, a covenant has two parts – its charter (purpose) and its bylaws (due process).

The Old Testament Law is structured in this way – the ten commandments are the fundamental laws, and the statue laws apply them and guide the due process of justice. As theologian R. J. Rushdoony explains:

> First, certain broad premises or principles are declared. These are declarations of basic law. Second… the major portion of the law is case law, i.e., the illustration of the basic principles in term of specific cases.[112]

The Mayflower Compact of 1620 was the charter of the Pilgrims. Their by-laws were the 1636 constitution formed 16 years later. Though not specific cases, it was the bylaws that were utilized to apply the basic premises. This line of thought continued throughout colonial history here in America.

It culminated 156 years later when the Declaration was written as the charter of America. Its by-laws, first the Articles of Confederation, and then the U.S. Constitution, was the due process outlined as to how the rights defined would be protected, and how one would apply the law to specific cases.

On a broad scale, on July 4, 1837, John Quincy Adams, our sixth President and son of our second, offered part of his two-hour oration in Newburyport to honor the origin of the Declaration's ideas from its root (basic premise) to its fruit (in this case the Declaration).

> In the chain of human events, the birthday of the nation is indissolubly linked with the birthday of the Savior... it forms a leading event in the Progress of the Gospel dispensation... Is it not that the Declaration of Independence first organized the social compact on the foundation of the Redeemer's mission on earth? That it laid the cornerstone of human government upon the first precepts of Christianity and gave to the world the first irrevocable pledge of the fulfillment of the prophecies announced directly from Heaven at the birth of the Savior and predicted by the greatest of the Hebrew prophets 600 years before.[113]

The Mayflower Compact

The Mayflower Compact was signed on board the *Mayflower* while it lay anchored in what is now Provincetown Harbor in 1620. Mutinous talk on board was evidently the catalyst[114], and they were also out of the geographic area designated by their original patent and charter approved by the King. Could they form a government on their own without the King's permission?

The answer to this question had been taught to the members of the Leyden Church by their Pastor John Robinson since they formed their own church by covenant in 1606 in a little town called Scrooby, England without permission from the Bishops.

The Pilgrim Church, while they were meeting secretly at Scrooby Manor in England, ratified their church covenant from the premise that they could form a church from "two or three" as the Bible instructed. William Bradford described it this way;

> They shook off this yoke of antichristian bondage, and as the Lord's free people joined themselves (by a covenant of the Lord) into a church estate, in the fellowship of the gospel, to

> walk in all His ways made known, or to be made known unto them, according to their best endeavors, whatsoever it should cost them.[115]

This church covenant, drawn up by themselves as instructed in the Bible, became the precursor to all covenants that extended beyond the church. Pastor John Robinson had anticipated the need for his church to create a civil government in the new world and had given his advice in his farewell letter upon their departure in July of 1620.

> Whereas you are become a body politic, using amongst yourselves civil government, and are not furnished with any persons of special eminency above the rest, to be chosen by you into office of government; let your wisdom and godliness appear, not only in choosing such persons as do entirely love and will promote the common good... not being like the foolish multitude who more honor the gay coat than either the virtuous mind of the man, or glorious ordinance of the Lord."[116]

When realizing they had been blown off course and were not within the boundaries of their Charter, and amid some who threatened mutiny, they drew up the Mayflower Compact. It was a new government formed without express permission from the King. The cornerstone of American self-government was born in this way.

The Ideological Link between the Compact and Declaration

Professor and constitutional scholar Herb Titus makes this assertion;

> Of the several English colonial charters establishing a civil government in the New World, the 1620 Mayflower Compact stands out. Like the other charters, the signers of the Compact identified themselves as 'loyal subjects' of the English king,

> but unlike the other charters, the Pilgrim fathers did not receive from the King authority to constitute a civil order. Rather, without the king's blessing, they undertook 'one with another (to) covenant and combine (them)selves together into a civil Body Politick.' By claiming the right as a self-governing people to establish a civil government without regard to the king's permission or pleasure, the Pilgrims – as the American Bar Foundation acknowledged n 1978 in celebration of the nation's bicentennial – 'applied to the affairs of civil government the philosophy of the church covenant which was the basis of Puritan theology.'[117]

The ideas contained within the Mayflower Compact are significant and foreshadow the Declaration that was to come 156 years later. Since breaking a covenant has consequences, it is important to demonstrate this with Pilgrim Edward Winslow.

Edward Winslow was only 25 when he came on the Mayflower. He and his brother Gilbert signed the Mayflower Compact. He lost his wife during the first winter, and remarried Susanna White who had lost her husband during the first winter. Their marriage was the first one in the Spring (May) of 1621.

Edward served as Assistant Governor three times and was also an agent in London. He co-authored the diary of their first year in the new world with William Bradford called *Mourt's Relation* which also explained what we know as Thanksgiving. He authored *Good News from New England* and other pamphlets. He became a friend of Chief Massasoit of the Wampanoag, learning his language.[118]

Edward returned to England in 1646 to join with the Puritans in the English Civil War against Charles I. After the Revolution in 1649, he worked for Cromwell and never returned to Plymouth. He died in 1655 after contracting a fever in an expedition against the Spanish.

Winslow was in England when Charles I broke his covenant with England and was tried, convicted and executed. The resistance to Charles I is described in G. Robertson's *The Tyrannical Brief*;

> 'A just power is…derived from and conferred by the people' who consent and voluntarily submit to a form of government… This law – if the King becomes a tyrant he shall die for it – is the law of nature and the law of God, written in fleshly tables of men's hearts.[119]

In 1689, when William and Mary came to the throne in 1689, accepting the English Bill of Rights, the popular sovereignty principle arose again, forcing King James II who;

> Having endeavored to subvert the constitution of the kingdom by breaking the original contract between king and people, and having…violated fundamental laws and withdrawn himself out of the kingdom, has abdicated the government and the throne is hereby vacant.[120]

This concept of Biblical covenant, patterned from the Old Testament among the Israelites, was preached as the model for setting up a righteous government by the clergy of the colonies for 100 years. Eric Nelson's book *The Hebrew Republic*, highlights the concepts birthed in the reformation and preached by the clergy in America.

> …the idea that the Declaration was birthed from non-religious premises (is false for he) …asserts that it was rooted… in the full fervor of the Reformation…. (Christians) began to regard the Hebrew Bible as a political constitution (with) the right of choosing, yea of changing their own Government by the grant

> of God Himself in the People. (Nelson also affirms that Christians) began to regard the Hebrew Bible as a political constitution… (with) the right of choosing, yea of changing their own Government by the grant of God Himself in the People.[121]

The Compact and the Declaration Compared

The Mayflower Compact was inspired by Pastor John Robinson from Leyden, Holland. The Declaration of Independence was inspired by Pastor John Wise of Ipswich, Massachusetts.

The Compact clearly set forth the flow of power from God to the people, and then to government when it began, "In the Name of God, Amen. We whose names are underwritten, the loyal subjects of our dread Sovereign Lord King James."

The Declaration did the same, stating that everyone was "Endowed by our Creator with certain unalienable rights, that among these are Life, Liberty and the pursuit of happiness."

The Compact indicated that we are dual citizens of heaven first and then with responsibilities on earth when it stated, "Having undertaken, for the Glory of God and advancement of the Christian faith and honor of our King and Country."

The Declaration did the same, stating that we owe allegiance to the earth, "laws of nature", and heaven, "nature's God."

The Compact indicated that government, like covenant, is enacted by consent, "solemnly and mutually in the presence of God and one of another, Covenant and Combine ourselves together into a Civil Body Politic."

The Declaration stated similarly, "That to secure these rights, Governments are instituted among Men, deriving their just powers from the consent of the governed."

Finally, the Compact declared the equality of individuals before the law, stating that they were "to enact, constitute and frame such just and equal Laws."

The Declaration simply stated that "all men are created equal."

Though the Pierce Patent of 1621 made the Pilgrims legal in the eyes of England, the Pilgrim laws that were subsequently published copied the Mayflower Compact as its preamble, indicating that they functioned under *that* Covenant.

Col. John Eidsmoe succinctly summarized, from an historic perspective, the importance of this document as the foundation for America when he said the Compact is

> Described by John Quincy Adams in 1802 as 'the only instance in human history of that positive social compact.'"[122]

Leading Idea – ***The Mayflower Compact of 1620 lays the foundation for the idea of covenant, drawn from the Bible, that is eventually extended ideologically to the Declaration of Independence***

Chapter 6

THE DECLARATION AND THE CONSTITUTION

Done in Convention by the Unanimous Consent of the States present the Seventeenth Day of September in the Year of our Lord one thousand seven hundred and Eighty seven and of the Independence of the United States of America the Twelfth... - Constitution of the United States, Article VII

Colossians 2:6 declares quite simply, "as you therefore have received Christ Jesus the Lord, so walk in Him." All of us who profess to be Christians, or followers of Christ, should seek to practice what we profess. It is like the role of the Charter and By-Laws discussed in the last two chapters.

It is this concept of profession and practice that describes the Declaration and its relationship to the United States Constitution.

Charters and By-Laws Designed to be Inseparable

When the Declaration of Independence was proclaimed on July 4, 1776, the Continental Congress had already received a draft of a new constitution from Ben Franklin a year before. It was the first draft of the Articles of Confederation.[123] In essence, they had begun to consider the by-laws before the charter was finalized.

The motion by Richard Henry Lee on June 7, 1776, stated the colonies "are, and of right ought to be, free and independent States" and also included the statement, "a plan of confederation be prepared and transmitted to the respective colonies for their consideration and approbation."[124]

In essence, the Declaration was the charter of our nation, it's birth certificate, and the Articles its first Bylaws. The Declaration was not a reaction to recent conflicts, and neither was it done in rebellion to authority. It was the culmination of a long process of intermediate steps, always seeking reconciliation.

The *Resolves of the First Continental Congress* in 1774 stated that rights were from the law of nature and were life, liberty and property.[125] The colony had the right to resist encroachments from the Crown that violated the written charter given to each colony by appeal. It capped what has been known as the "constitutional debate period" which attempted peaceful negotiation and preceded any conflict of arms.

The *Second Continental Congress* in 1775 sought reconciliation, but authorized force as a last resort to resist the unlawful encroachments of England. By August of that year, George III declared the Colonies to be in rebellion, and the Prohibitory Act of December 22nd severed the relationship of the Colonies with the Crown and Great Britain. On May 10 of 1776 the Continental Congress asked each colony to form their own government. It is important to note the following conclusions of this Congress.

1. A colony can sever its relation to another if done lawfully
2. If a colony or group of colonies do so, they are separate from, but equal to, all nations

Note that by natural (creation) law, people must be able to flee tyranny.[126] To be blessed of God, however, they must do so lawfully through interposition (submitting to the lower magistrate.)[127]

One of the most intriguing confederacies that brought unity with diversity and predated both the Articles and Constitution was the Iroquois Confederacy. As John Eidsmoe has written,

> Unlike the Incas, the Iroquois left no lasting pyramids or temples. Unlike the Maya, they left no written records of their history and accomplishments. Unlike the Aztecs, they did not conquer or terrorize their neighbors.
>
> But the Iroquois accomplished what the Incas, the Maya, and the Aztecs did not – a confederate republic which established order, security and justice, and yet preserved individual freedom and the autonomy of each tribe or republic. As Bruce Johansen says, few people today know that 'a republic existed on our soil before anyone here had ever heard of John Locke, or Cato, the *Magna Charta*, Rousseau, Franklin, or Jefferson.'[128]

Not only did it last for hundreds of years, but it adopted decentralized jurisdictions of power with a Great Law of Peace. The role of a Creator, together with a clear religious focus, brought about a strong emphasis on family life, roles of men and women that brought about greater equality, the military in subordination to civil power, and impeachment of officers, to name a few.[129]

Eidsmoe writes:

> Benjamin Franklin with the Great Law of Peace. In 1754, a congress convened in Albany, New York, to consider a plan for uniting the northern colonies and to formulate an alliance with the Iroquois against the French. Franklin commented favorably on the proposed union and pointed to 'the strength of the League which has bound our Friends the Iroquois together in a common tie which no crisis, however grave, since its foundation has managed to disrupt.'[130]

Though not the same as would be brought forth in either the Articles or federal Constitution, there is no question that it was similar in many aspects, inspired by natural law. For as Romans 2:14 declares, "the Gentiles, which have not the law, do by nature the things contained in the law."

The Articles of Confederation

The Articles were the by-laws and naturally united with the Declaration. On June 12, three weeks before the Declaration, a committee was formed, consisting of one member from each of the thirteen colonies to draft a plan of confederation.[131]

Though the committee worked secretly, John Dickenson produced what was essentially the first draft in June of 1776.[132] It was not fully ratified until Maryland, the thirteenth state, did so on March 1, 1781.

Author and historian Archie Jones writes:

> The Articles of Confederation embodies many of the same Christian political and legal principles that were woven into the state constitutions, declarations of rights, and bills of rights, and that later would be fashioned into the fabric of the Constitution of the United States. However, these principles were applied with different emphases in the Articles

Interestingly, Jones goes on to state:

> There were no disputes over religion in the debates over the Articles of Confederation. Virtually all the framers of the first draft, the great majority of the Continental Congress and the committee which put the Articles into its final form were Christians. The Articles contain three unmistakable references to God which form the framework of the political provisions contained in the paragraphs of its numbered articles.[133]

The Articles reference the "Year of our Lord" twice and the "Great Governor of the World." Though appearing to some as merely the rhetoric of the time, it is consistent with what we have noted previously.

There is an unmistakable ideological link between the concepts in the Declaration and our first Constitution, the Articles of Confederation. A.D., or Anno Domini, is a clear indication of dating the world in relation to the Dominion (or reign) of Jesus Christ from the time of his birth, death and resurrection.[134]

References to God in a civil constitution have clear implications, and the following clear principles embody the Articles:

1. God is Sovereign, and thus the State is not
2. Man is sinful, and thus power in any person's hands must be checked
3. Government should be representative (by "the consent of the governed")
4. The "rule of law" should be maintained for people and rulers
5. Decentralized power – or the one and many – should characterize the power structure
6. Other concepts, based in the Bible, such as the protection of innocent life, protecting private ownership of property, and due process of justice to protect liberty are enjoined.[135]

When the Articles were deemed insufficient to maintain unity among the States, especially during the American Revolution, a stronger federal union was proposed, and debates began in May of 1787 for a "constitutional convention."

The delegates from the various colonies were sent to "revise" the Articles of Confederation. The five-month long meeting, held in secret to avoid unnecessary public scrutiny, concluded that a new Constitution, and not just a revision, was in order.
The draft of this new Constitution was sent to the States, and individual conventions were held where delegates at the local level debated every line.[136]

The Constitution became the New Bylaw of the Declaration

At no time during the Constitutional Convention was there any repudiation of the Declaration or any discussion about replacing it. In fact, up through the time of the Civil War, when the relationship of the States and Federal government was tested, it was the foundation of the Declaration that was appealed to for the purpose of bringing harmony.

Note the date of the Constitution;

> Done in convention by the unanimous consent of the states present, the seventeenth day of September, in the year of our Lord one thousand seven hundred eighty-seven, and of the independence of the United States of America, the twelfth.[137]

The Constitution is dated from the Declaration, indicating it as the foundation for the document. Note also the fact that the "year of our Lord" remains as a reference to the dating of the world.

The relationship between the two documents was tested in 1811 when trade embargoes and threats of secession came from the northern states. It was tested again by 1860 when the threats of secession came from the southern states over the issue of slavery.

In both cases, however, the key question was a constitutional one - was the nature of the union between the States *confederated* (a loose alliance) or *consolidated* (a tight alliance)?

In the former, one could nullify a law of Congress by vote of an individual state, or presumably, secede from the Union if necessary. In the latter one, a state could not secede without violating the very covenant of the Constitution.

Robert Hayne of South Carolina wrote to James Madison, sharing his arguments for the confederated viewpoint. He was debating Daniel Webster of Massachusetts whose view was that the union was a consolidation. Madison's answer was that both extremes were wrong. Though he agreed a state had a right to secede, it could only do so by following the same process by which it entered the union. Madison wrote to Hayne in 1830, stating the following,

> It appears to me that in deciding on the character of the Constitution of the U. S. it is not sufficiently kept in view, that being an unprecedented modification of the Powers of Govt. it must not be looked at thro' the refracting medium either of a consolidated Government, or of a Confederated Govt: that being essentially different from both…

Madison states that the Constitution is neither confederated (like the Articles) nor consolidated (like a union), but a combination of both. It is thus a vertical (national) and horizontal (state) covenant. If after attempting to appeal through constitutional due process, the Supreme Court, or an amendment, it does not resolve the conflict, then the last resort is to return to "original rights."

> In the event of a failure of all these Constitutional resorts against usurpations and abuses of power and of an accumulation thereof rendering passive obedience & non resistance a greater evil, than resistance & revolution, there can remain but one resort, the last of all, the appeal from the

> cancelled obligations of the Constitutional compact, to original rights and the law of self-preservation.[138]

Note that Madison is reversing the steps the colonies took to form the union of states in the first place. The final resort of the States, if passive obedience and non-resistance is a greater evil, is resistance and revolution, cancelling the Constitution itself, but returning to self-preservation; which are the ideas put forth in the Declaration of Independence.[139]

The Declaration was a proclamation of the right of secession from the empire of Great Britain after following all the lawful steps to reconcile, without which it could not have been blessed by God nor could it have been protected by Divine Providence.

The Preamble and the Declaration

The Preamble was a summary of the main ideas embedded in the Constitution. Remember that the Constitution is the due process of how to carry out the premises or goals of the Declaration. Cleon Skousen writes about the drafting of the Preamble;

> The Committee on Detail had made up a very most preamble but it was unacceptable to the Committee on Style, especially the chairman, Gouverneur Morris. Morris was a 36-year-old bachelor who was not only a talented lawyer with a gifted pen, but was also prominent in the field of finance. He had lost a leg in an accident and was not the least embarrassed about this wooden leg, which he would use to thump the floor when he approved of a speech or performance.
>
> Gouverneur Morris was quite certain that very few people would bother to read the text of the Constitution, and so he

> wanted to set forth… the …magnificent objectives which the Founders intended this form of government would attain.[140]

Let us now compare the Preamble with ideas in the Declaration.

The Preamble begins *we the people... do ordain and establish* and the Declaration asserts *by the consent of the governed.*

The constitution is an express powers document, where the only power government has is written in the document. All others, by their omission, cannot be assumed.

The Preamble's purpose *in order to form a more perfect union* corresponds to the Declaration's assertion of *instituting a new government.*

The constitution, as previously noted, is neither consolidated nor confederated, but a combination of both. The federal (national) government rules in every place specifically ceded to it by the states (see Art. I Sections 9 and 10).

The vertical and horizontal aspects of this covenant are delineated further in Article IV and the 9th and 10th Amendments. It is thus "a more perfect union" in a better balance than merely confederated.

The Preamble *establishes justice* and the Declaration states *all men are created equal.*

The concept of justice, drawn from the Bible, where one is innocent until proven guilty, tried by a jury of his peers, and is equal before the law, is declared as a key principle of our government.

The Preamble *insures domestic tranquility* and the Declaration *derives their just powers from consent.*

1st Timothy 2:2-3 tells us that a government that is "good and acceptable in the sight of God our Savior" is that which "may lead to quiet and peaceable life in all godliness and reverence."

The Constitution created a government that is sovereign in its well-defined jurisdictions, such as the legislative, executive and judicial, and the states.

Two-thirds of the Declaration articulates that the King of Great Britain exceeded his jurisdiction, claiming powers that violated the written charters and assemblies of the colonies. Thus, the Declaration states that "A Prince, whose character is thus marked by every act which may define a Tyrant, is unfit to be the ruler of a free people."

The Preamble *provides for the common defense* and the Declaration declares the right to have *enemies in war, in peace, friends.*

The defense of the people's life, liberty and property is the primary function of government, according to Romans 13:3-4. Extended to the nation, its purpose is national defense.

The Preamble *promotes the general welfare* and the Declaration declares government is to *effect their safety and happiness.*

Promoting the general welfare means to do what is best for all, allowing people the freedom to "try, buy, sell and fail."[141] In contrast, special welfare is attempting to bring external equality through the redistribution of wealth. Madison's speech to the first U.S. Congress is applicable here.

> If Congress can apply money indefinitely to the general welfare, and are the sole and supreme judges of the general welfare, they may take the care of religion in to their own hands; they may take into their own hands the education of children, establishing in like manner schools throughout the

> Union; they may undertake the regulation of all roads, other than post roads. In short, everything from the highest object of State legislation, down to the most minute object of policy, would be thrown under the power of Congress, for every object I have mentioned would admit the application of money, and might be called, if Congress pleased, provisions for the general welfare.[142]

In short, this would be an equivocation of the meaning of general welfare, turning it into special welfare, taking money without consent from some, and giving it to others, thus destroying the individual's need to take responsibility for their own private welfare.

Finally, the Preamble *secures the blessings of liberty to ourselves and our posterity* and the Declaration *secures those rights.*

Those who signed the Declaration and drafted the Constitution were thinking of the generations that would follow them. That is why they asserted that government was to "secure" rights and not provide them. They may have been thinking ahead when they wrote;

> "And for the support of this Declaration, with a firm reliance on the protection of Divine Providence, we mutually pledge to each other our Lives, our Fortunes, and our sacred Honor."

That which some have deemed to be left out in this Preamble is a reference to the fact that their premise was to be upon "the laws of nature and nature's God," the "Creator" and the protection of "Divine Providence." How come the Preamble makes no mention of the *source* of their ideas?

After all, a nation that does not acknowledge God, particularly the God of the Bible, can justify anarchy, and do whatever it wants to do, including lying, stealing and terrorizing others. But this is a critical point, for the Constitution *must be interpreted* by ultimately relying on the Declaration and its fundamental premises.

The Divorce of the Declaration from the Constitution

A divorce of the Declaration from the Constitution has caused…

(1) A misreading of the Preamble "we the people…"

Though the anti-federalists, as they came to be called, would have rather had the Preamble begin *we the states* instead of *we the people,*[143] it might have been best for it to have declared that the source of its union was the Declaration.

As generations of Americans have not been taught the source of the ideas in the Declaration, it can be easily misread that the people are the ultimate source (or the states for that matter), rather than the document that delineates the Biblical premises upon which we stand.

James Wilson of Pennsylvania, when lecturing in 1790 on the Law of Nations, attempted to clarify the misunderstanding that the people are the ultimate source of power. He stated:

> Let us again beware of being misled by an ambiguity, sometimes, such is the structure of language, unavoidable. When I say that, in free states, the law of nations is the law of the people; I mean not that it is a law made by the people, or by virtue of their delegated authority; as, in free states, all municipal laws are. I mean that… as the law of nature, in other words, as the will of nature's God, it is indispensably binding upon the people, in whom the sovereign power resides.[144]

The Declaration declares… "to which the Laws of Nature and Nature's God entitle them"

(2) An Ignorance of the fact that one's rights are God-given Without the Declaration as a reference point, it is easy to misread that our rights are government granted rather than God-given. With no accountability to a higher law other than the Constitution itself the document can be interpreted as if civil government is the ultimate source.

The Declaration declares... "they are endowed by their Creator with certain unalienable rights"

(3) The idea that Government or the State is Sovereign and the people have no right of Appeal

We are increasingly given little confidence of any appeal to the centralized encroachment of government as if we have no right to question anything. But the Declaration declares the right to appeal and the Constitution delineates the process by which we can do so.

> "...that whenever any form of government becomes destructive of these ends, it is the fright of the people to alter or to abolish it, and to institute a new government, laying its foundation on such principles, and organizing its powers in such form, as to them shall seem most likely to effect their safety and happiness."

In short, removing the Declaration conveniently removes most references to God as the ultimate accountability, and leaves all questions as procedural, technical and residing within government itself. Governments that stretch their power will rarely, if ever, restrict them on their own.

In summary, then...

The Declaration is the foundation for the Constitution

Just as the Constitution needs the Declaration, so the Declaration needs the Constitution. If the Declaration stood alone, there would be no due process of protection. A charter demands a set of bylaws.

"That to secure these rights, governments are instituted among men, driving their just powers from the consent of the governed..."

The Declaration validates the Constitution

Representative government is rooted in the equality and integrity of the people. The Constitution rests on the assumption that rights are God-given. The people can charter a new government (after following a lengthy process of appeal) as a last resort if the present one continues to violate its covenant.

The structure of the Constitution assumes the premises of the universal principles found in the Declaration. Ultimately, it validates the fact that there is a higher power than the Constitution itself to which we can appeal.

"...appealing to the Supreme Judge of the World for the Rectitude of our Intentions"

The Declaration requires the Constitution for Due Process

Parliament was attempting to rule the Colonies outside of their jurisdiction. The Declaration declared the right of these colonies to resist, and the Constitution brought a solution for the separation of powers. There was also no supreme law in England, it was one of parliamentary supremacy. The Constitution instituted the supremacy clause in Article VI.

> This Constitution and the laws of the United States which shall be made in pursuance thereof, and all treaties made, or which shall be made, under the authority of the United States, shall be the supreme law of the land; and the judges in every state shall be bound thereby, anything in the constitution or laws of any state to the contrary notwithstanding. (Article VI)

There was no lawful way to interpose or appeal in the British Constitution. The Constitution instituted interposition in Article IV, Section 4.

> The United States shall guarantee to every state in this Union a republican form of government, and shall protect each of them against invasion; and, on application of the legislature, or of the executive (when the legislature cannot be convened), against domestic violence.

There was no way to amend the English Constitution. But Article V introduced this process in the Constitution.

> The Congress, whenever two thirds of both Houses shall deem it necessary, shall propose Amendments to this Constitution, or, on the Application of the Legislatures of two thirds of the several States, shall call a Convention for proposing Amendments, which, in either Case, shall be valid to all Intents and Purposes, as Part of this Constitution, when ratified by the Legislatures of three fourths of the several States, or by Conventions in three fourths thereof, as the one or the other Mode of Ratification may be proposed by the Congress…

As Dr. William Allen has written, "virtually every clause condemning the action of King George III was remedied by the Constitution and its provisions."[145]

Leading Idea – ***A nation's constitutional covenant must rest on the foundation of its declared premises of law to consistently apply due process and achieve justice***

PART THREE

Key Phrases in the Declaration

Chapter 7

ALL MEN ARE CREATED EQUAL

*We hold these truths to be self-evident, that **all men are created equal**...*

The Declaration of Promise

All men are created equal

The phrase "all men are created equal" is under attack in our culture. On one hand, for decades now, Christians were not to revere this phrase for the ideas came from the Enlightenment and the Renaissance and were secular in nature.

Today, the opposite extreme appears before us. The Declaration's ideas are not valid, for the phrase "all men are created equal" does not mean what it says and those who signed the document knew it.

Those who signed it were hypocrites, wanting rights for only white males, deliberately ignoring women, and were racist since nearly two thirds of them owned slaves. So, how do we understand this phrase in the Declaration?

In short, there will always be a gap between promise and fulfillment. The Declaration of Independence is a document whose ideas were derived from the Bible with its terminology rooted in the Reformation. The ideas did not originate with either Thomas Jefferson or those who signed it.

It was a ***declaration of promise***, not a declaration of achievement. Without this distinction in mind, those who signed the document will be looked at as incredibly hypocritical on one hand or terribly ignorant on the other. Neither is the case.

We should make no excuse for the inconsistencies of those who signed the Declaration. However, we must set it in context with the

Biblical doctrine of promise and fulfillment, for both are part of the gospel.

Creation is a Promise

Why did God create us? A discussion of rights and responsibilities should begin here.

Then God said, Let us make man in Our likeness... so God created man in His own image; in the image of God He created him; male and female He created them. – Genesis 1:26-27

The Hebrew word for man in these verses is *adam* and means *"a human being, an individual or the species mankind."*[146] It is thus a generic word that includes both male and female. The immediate context of the two verses indicates the same, for both the singular "man" as well as "male and female", him and them are used. Some translations use the phrase "human being" as well.[147]

Theologians have concluded that the creation of mankind indicates a unique position of being in the likeness and image of God. God made human beings with at least these traits:

1. Mankind (male and female) are rational with the ability to think logically.
2. Men and women are sub-creators, able to be productive, inventing things.
3. Men and women are stewards, vice-regents with God in managing this world.
4. Men and women have a choice to love what God loves and hate what God hates.[148]

These are wonderful promises. Men and women were given unalienable rights of life, liberty and property that was part of the Creation mandate to steward the earth and bless the developing civilizations. But rights are always accompanied by responsibilities. God's declaration of promise was interrupted by the sin of Adam and Eve.

Sin is the Origin of Sexism and Racism

As a result, God said;

"I will put enmity between you (the serpent) and the woman...
between your seed and her seed...
Your desire shall be for your husband, and he shall rule over you"
– Genesis 3:15-16

The consequences of sin were devastating. When God confronted the man, he blamed "the woman whom you gave to me" (Genesis 3:12.) When God confronted the woman, she blamed "the serpent" (v. 13.) God declared that in relation to the devil, there would now be a war between the believer's seed (the woman) and evil enhanced by the devil.

It was sin that laid the groundwork for a battle between the sexes and races. God's plan was equality with different roles, but sin desired *superiority* out of pride. Note that this pride knew no limits due to race, culture or ethnicity. Sin knows no boundary and is a pervasively deep heart problem.

Genesis 3:16 indicates a tendency for a woman to be in an unholy subjection to her husband and men in general. This would quickly spread to polygamy and racism.

In the ancient world, only the nation of Israel, due to her reception of the Ten Commandments, made chattel slavery (where humans are owned by others) illegal.

"He who kidnaps a man, whether he sells him or he is
found in his possession,

shall surely be put to death" – Exodus 21:16

In the Bible, the word "slavery" is used in several contexts other than chattel or owning an individual's person and labor.

Indentured servitude (Ex. 21:12 - a voluntary, limited service to acquire a life skill), voluntary servitude (Ex. 21:5 - a life-long dependency voluntarily chosen)

Criminal restitution (Ex. 22:3 – a limited, forced restitution of goods due to a crime being committed), and

Captives from war (Lev. 24:44-46 – where one nation acquires slaves because of conquering in war).

The last category, theologians agree, has been repealed by the New Testament year of jubilee so there are no legitimate "*holy wars*." (most favored or hated nations)[149]

The Hope of Redemption to Fulfill God's Promise

In the garden of Eden, before the man and woman were kicked out due to their sin, another promise was given to restore their irresponsibility and give them hope of fulfillment. Amidst the consequences of sin - strife between the sexes and people in general, God cursed the serpent, the devil, but said:

> *I will put enmity between you (the serpent) and the woman, and between your seed and her Seed, He shall bruise your head, and you shall bruise His heel.* – Genesis 3:15

Theologians have noted the hope of fulfilling God's creation mandate in this verse set in the midst of judgment for sin. The seed of the woman, Christ the Redeemer, would fatally bruise the head of the serpent, but it would cost the bruising of his heel (death on the cross.) As Charles Spurgeon put it:

> The old serpent's head is bruised with a fatal bruising, while the wounded heel of our Saviour is the joy and delight of our hearts.[150]

The gospel of Christ, wherever it has gone, has begun to bring fulfillment of the promise in Creation by a change of heart and a restoration of lives, families and the improvement of culture.

The Gospel is a Promise of Fulfillment

Shifting from God as Creator to Christ as Redeemer, Rome was a dark place to live unless you were part of the nobility. Slaves comprised 40% of the population. Women were considered less than a man with no legal equality. As Jeremiah Johnston puts it

> People were divided by race, by free or slave status, and by gender.[151]

Male slaves were worth 10 to 12 times more than female ones, and baby girls were more likely to be abandoned.[152] What is worse;

> The Roman Law of Twelve Tables (Leges Duodecim Tabularum), which may date in its earliest form to the fifth century BC, required fathers to put to death any child who was deformed. One of these laws reads: 'A notably deformed child shall be killed immediately.'[153]

The Scripture declares that God the Father sent Jesus into the world in the *fullness of time.*[154] In the midst of the darkest of times and one of the worst cultures the world had ever known, God sent Jesus who

> ...delivered us from the power of darkness and conveyed us into the kingdom of the Son of His love, in whom we have redemption through His blood, the forgiveness of sin." (Colossians 1:13-14)

His life and sacrifice set a standard that was in great contrast to the time in which He lived. If we receive Jesus as Lord, we are "sealed with the Holy Spirit of promise, who is the guarantee of our inheritance until the redemption of the purchased possession." (Ephesians 1:13-14)

Christ and the theology of Christianity is built on both a *promise* and an *inheritance.* We are positionally in heavenly places the moment we are converted. However, our feet are on earth and we must "work out our salvation with fear and trembling." (Philippians 2:12)

<u>The Doctrine of Sanctification – overcoming Sexism and Racism</u>

Though we are presented perfect before heaven at our conversion; *sealed with the Holy Spirit of promise,* we will not fully inherit the blessings in our experience until the *redemption of the purchased possession.*

It is our confession that confirms the Holy Spirit's regeneration, "for with the heart one believes unto righteousness, and with the mouth confession is made unto salvation." (Romans 10:10) If our conversion was one of achievement, we would live perfectly the moment we were converted.

Our conversion, however, will lead to sanctification and growth (living more like our confession) if it is true and righteous.[155]

In addition to the world of inequality between slave and free, wealth and poverty, male and female, the Roman Empire and the Jewish exiles were filled with racial discrimination and hatred. Johnston writes;

> The world of the first century was littered with racism and oppression. In the mind of a first-century Jew, Gentiles (Africans, Romans, Greeks, Syrians, Asians, etc.) were created to fuel the fires of hell. When a Jew called a Gentile 'uncircumcised,' he spit it. It was the name of profound contempt. If a Jewish person married a Gentile, the Jewish parents held a funeral service for their child. In their eyes, their child was dead. On the flip side, Gentiles regarded Jews to be sub-human. Historically, the Jews have been an oppressed people, living under the thumb of one Gentile nation after another (e.g., Egypt, Assyria, Babylon, Greece, Rome).[156]

The Declaration of Promise that Paul the Apostle stated was astounding when one considers life in the first century. "From Roman and Jewish perspectives, every part of this astonishing declaration is problematic."[157] What was that declaration?

There is neither Jew nor Greek, there is neither slave nor free, there is neither male nor female; for you are all one in Christ Jesus. – Galatians 3:28

The unity in Christ transcends, at the deepest level of the heart, the natural and pervasive attitudes of division and derision known everywhere and in every culture. Imagine beginning to demonstrate a loving attitude toward others, even though your tradition and culture, for generations, taught you to hate.

What kind of statement did Jesus make when he had more female disciples than males who administrated his trips, prepared the meals, and scouted out lodging throughout his ministry?

His declarations of kindness toward the Romans, Greeks, and others, astounded the disciples. He also demonstrated that the law alone could not redeem. This is why in the book of Philemon the emphasis is on first treating the slave as a brother. It begins in the heart, but it must also be codified into law.

This is what a *declaration of promise* does. It sets forth the power of hope in the heart to proclaim something far ahead of where you are living. It may take generations to fulfill the promise.

For a nation to declare the standard of God's justice is imperative, but it will only bring equitable achievement as people, and those who know God, allow Him to do a work in their hearts and attitudes. Psalm 33:12 declares this truth.

Blessed is the nation whose God is the Lord; the people He hath chosen for His own inheritance.

God blesses a nation through the condition of His people. He also curses a nation through the condition of His people. What is our condition? What is your condition?

Do not be too quick to place blame for poor attitudes toward people in our ancestors alone. We are not as pure as we think we are, nor are we as loving and kind as we might profess.

Our mannerisms, terminology and attitudes demonstrate the fact that we often see things through our eyes without much perspective, and thus we are often "respecter of persons." We can be thankful that God is no respecter of persons but instead enjoins us to "not hold the faith of our Lord Jesus Christ, the Lord of glory, with partiality." (James 2:1)

***All* Men are Created Equal**

But does the word “all” in the Declaration mean all races, or just all whites? Again, the phrase may have been derived from the Scriptures and as Acts 17:26 declares

> And He has made from one blood every nation of men to dwell on all the face of the earth, and has determined their reappointed times and the boundaries of their dwellings.

In the Bible the creation account indicates that all races were created in His image. Of the 56 who signed the document, at least 29 (52%) were trained in schools primarily to produce ministers.[158] Consider also that at least 34 of the 56 (61%) were slave owners.[159]

How can this be? We might think that either their education was shallow and their Christian confession weak, or the facts of their slave owning has been greatly exaggerated. Neither is the case.

In the context of history, slavery was universal, existing in virtually every nation on earth, blinding the eyes of those who practiced it. In America, anti-slavery societies began springing up immediately after the Declaration.[160]

There were founders who made it clear where they stood regarding the abolition of slavery. Samuel Adams had declared that “no slave will live in my house.”[161]

John Adams, during the debates on the wording of the Declaration about the slave clauses and some defending them, sprang to his feet proclaiming, “freedom is a mere masquerade in a country that sells humans in chains!”[162]

Abigail Adams wrote to her husband John during the first Continental Congress of 1774,

> I wish most sincerely there was not a slave in the province. It always seemed a most iniquitous scheme to me – (to) fight ourselves for what we are daily robbing and plundering from those who have as good a right to freedom as we have.[163]

She also wrote to John, wondering if Virginians would be committed to independence when they practiced slavery.

> I have, sometimes been ready to think that the passion for liberty cannot be equally strong in the breasts of those who have been accustomed to deprive their fellow creature of theirs.[164]

Col. George Mason, delegate from Virginia at the Constitutional Convention in 1787, declared these famous words during the discussion on slavery in August.

> This infernal traffic originated in the avarice of British merchants… Every master of slaves is born a petty tyrant. They bring the judgment of heaven on a country. As nations can not be rewarded or punished in the next world they must be in this. By an investable chain of causes and effects providence punishes national sins, by national calamities.[165]

It is important to note that when considering slavery's pervasiveness globally that all races have been owned as slaves. What was *exceptional* was a Declaration, possibly the first civil document in history, to publicly take a stand against it and begin the progression to end it!

Those who signed the document in Philadelphia that hot summer of 1776 declared a truth that transcended their culture, world history and many of their own practices.

Abraham Lincoln, in his famous speech in Springfield, Illinois, rebutting the Supreme Court case *Dred Scott vs. Sanford* on June 26, 1857, agreed with the basic assessment above, that it was a claim of promise for the equality of all races even though many did not immediately act on it.

He knew the Declaration was not one of achievement, but of promise, for he declared the following:

> Chief Justice Taney, in his opinion in the Dred Scott case, admits that the language of the Declaration is broad enough to include the whole human family, but he and Judge Douglas argue that the authors of that instrument did not intend to include negroes, by the fact that they did not at once, actually place them on an equality with the whites.
>
> ...this (an) obvious violence to the plain unmistakable language of the Declaration.... I think the authors of that notable instrument intended to include all men... They defined with tolerable distinctness, in what respects they did consider all men created equal - equal in "certain inalienable rights, among which are life, liberty, and the pursuit of happiness." This they said, and this they meant.
>
> They did not mean to assert the obvious untruth, that all were then actually enjoying that equality... They meant simply to declare the right, so that the enforcement of it might follow... They meant to set up a standard maxim for free society, which should be familiar to all, and revered by all; constantly looked to, constantly labored for, and even though never perfectly attained, constantly approximated, and thereby constantly spreading and deepening its influence, and

> augmenting the happiness and value of life to all people of all colors everywhere.[166]

Lincoln indicated that the freeing of slaves in the generations following the Declaration "ameliorated" (declined) once again due to the economic advantages of the practice.

All Men are Created Equal

Was the Declaration merely for males? Some have suggested that the Declaration's statement was self-consciously for males, and that the signers had no intention of applying equality to women. After all, in the world of 1776 women were not treated individually as equal before the law since the primary focus of development had treated them with rights within marriage and the family.

Again, it was Abigail Adams' private correspondence with her husband John, a few weeks before Independence was declared, that would eventually be published and inspire a movement toward equality in the way of women's suffrage.

It took decades for this to occur, but the point is worth repeating, the use of the term "men" in this context is derived from Christianity and particularly the creation account and thus it never meant "males," but mankind as noted previously.

On March 31, 1776, Abigail Adams wrote her coy remark with her husband:

> I long to hear that you have declared an independency. And, by the way, in the new code of laws which I suppose it will be necessary for you to make, I desire you would remember the ladies and be more generous and favorable to them than your ancestors. Do not put such unlimited power into the hands of the husbands. Remember, all men would be tyrants if they could. If

> particular care and attention is not paid to the ladies, we are determined to foment a rebellion, and will not hold ourselves bound by any laws in which we have no voice or representation.[167]

John's response on April 14 indicated that he understood both her serious point as well as the fact that her ideas of a "rebellion" was not a threat as much as a reiteration of a personal discussion between them for he said, "in practice you know we are the subjects."[168]

Suffice it to say that Abigail's sentiments, built on the Declaration itself, inspired the women's suffrage movement that would eventually culminate with the passage of the 19th Amendment in 1920.

All Men are Created Equal

The concept of equality based on the doctrines of Christianity is quite distinct from the definition put forth from the Renaissance or Enlightenment. Christian equality derived from Scripture is one of position before God and the Law. No one is born better or worse than others for all are made in the image of God yet marred by sin.

Equality of position allows for a base of unity. Equality in external talents, character development, work ethic, and one's station in life is quite diverse. A Biblical view of equality rests on unity with diversity, while the Enlightenment was societal, where government would "equalize" external things such as wages, income and wealth.

John Adams, in a letter to John Taylor on April 19, 1814 stated this truth on the meaning of equality as given in the Declaration of Independence.

> Inequalities are a part of the natural history of man... That all men are born to equal rights is true. Every being has a right to his own, as clear, as moral, as sacred, as any other being has. This is as indubitable as a moral government in the universe. But to teach that all men are born with equal powers and faculties, to equal influence in society, to equal property and advantages through life, is as gross a fraud, as glaring an imposition on the credulity of the people, as ever was practiced . . . by the self-styled philosophers of the French Revolution.[169]

Unalienable Rights – the <u>Promise</u> of the Declaration

The unalienable rights of life, liberty and property, derived from the Creation account in the Bible, is the standard God has put forth for all societies at all time periods and in all cultures. Webster defines right as a *just claim.* He states; "all men have a right to the secure enjoyment of life, personal safety, liberty and property."[170] Thus, his definition a right is a *just claim on a promise given.*

Two of the most prominent weeds of sin in American culture, from which we must repent and pursue reconciliation, are the mistreatment of the American Indian and the slavery of the African American. Their rights were secured by God long before the nation was formed, but it was confirmed by the Declaration of 1776.

Unfortunately, they were a promise to be claimed to be realized more consistently over decades. From the native American to the African American and women's suffrage, the Declaration has been the document that has been appealed to and claimed for the progress toward true equality.

Martin Luther King, Jr., in 1963, understood the truth that the Declaration was one of promise. In his famous "I have a Dream" speech, he gave these powerful remarks:

> ...when the architects of our Great Republic wrote the magnificent words of the Constitution and the Declaration of Independence, they were signing a promissory note to which every American was to fall heir... It is obvious that America has defaulted on this promissory note... we refuse to believe that the bank of justice is bankrupt... we refuse to believe that there are insufficient funds in the great vaults of opportunity in this nation.... I still have a dream. It is deeply rooted in the American dream. I have a dream that one day this nation will rise up, live out the true meaning of its creed: We hold these truths to be self-evident, that all men are created equal.[171]

There are many ills that remain in our society today but let us remember that in 1776 when the Declaration was ratified, it was a *declaration of promise.* As such, it was the death knell to slavery around the world, beginning a progressive movement to end its practice.

It was a claim to true equality of position before God and the law. As Brown University's professor emeritus of history, Gordon Wood recently wrote:

> What is important is that slavery began to be attacked and eliminated from that moment (1776) on... the first anti-slave convention in history was held in Philadelphia in 1775. The American Revolution made slavery a problem for the world when it had not been a problem before, having existed for thousands of years without substantial criticism. All this is lost in today's climate.[172]

Let us rehearse some thoughts from Alexis de Tocqueville, the French journalist who penned the book *Democracy in America* as a result of his tour in the 1830's. His observations were as follows;

> Upon my arrival in the United States the religious aspect of the country was the first thing that struck my attention; and the longer I stayed there, the more I perceived the great political consequences resulting from this new state of things. In France I had almost always seen the spirit of religion and the spirit of freedom marching in opposite directions. But in America I found they were intimately united and that they reigned in common over the same country.
>
> Religion in America... must be regarded as the foremost of the political institutions of that country; for if it does not impart a taste for freedom, it facilitates the use of it. Indeed, it is in this same point of view that the inhabitants of the United States themselves look upon religious belief. I do not know whether all Americans have a sincere faith in their religion -- for who can search the human heart? But I am certain that they hold it to be indispensable to the maintenance of republican institutions. This opinion is not peculiar to a class of citizens or a party, but it belongs to the whole nation and to every rank of society.
>
> In the United States, the sovereign authority is religious...there is no country in the world where the Christian religion retains a greater influence over the souls of men than in America, and there can be no greater proof of its utility and of its conformity to human nature than that its influence is powerfully felt over the most enlightened and free nation of the earth.... Christianity, therefore, reigns without obstacle, by universal consent... .... Christianity is the companion of liberty in all its conflicts -- the cradle of its infancy, and the divine source of its claims.[173]

Let us avoid the extreme that we were founded on evil ideas. Let's also avoid the extreme that all we need to do is make America great again. Our prayer ought to be; *Lord, make our nation a godlier nation than at any other time in our history by humbling us before you and asking for your mercy, that we might live up to our Declaration of promise!* Amen.

Leading Idea – *The Declaration is a promise of Biblical equality, so let's continue to overcome the sins of our culture as God empowers each of us to do so to achieve it more fully*

Chapter 8

THE DECLARATION AND ROBERT CARTER III

It was no coincidence that Carter's first religions conversion took place in the wake of the Declaration of Independence, and that his second (political one) took place in the wake of the ratification of the Constitution: the timing of his great changes always coincided with great changes in the life of the new nation. – Andrew Levy in,
The First Emancipator; Slavery, Religion, and the Quiet Revolution of Robert Carter

The Parable of the Leaven

Another parable He (Jesus) spoke to them; 'The kingdom of heaven is like leaven, which a woman took and hid in three measures of meal till it was all leavened.' – Matthew 13:33

In preparation for doing a tour in costume at Colonial Williamsburg, Virginia, I remember standing in front of the home of Robert Carter III waiting for my tour group. It was not open to the public, but I desired to know more about this individual.

I spent several hours in the archives and providentially found a book newly published about Robert Carter III labeled "The First Emancipator."[174] I was not only intrigued, but fascinated. I read it, realizing that the story of this individual illustrated the parable of Jesus noted above.[175]

The kingdom of heaven (rule of God that begins in the heart of individuals[176]) is like leaven. Leaven (like yeast, baking soda, baking powder) produces carbon dioxide that ferments it, causing bubbles to rise and the dough to expand.

Like a tiny seed that eventually splits a boulder over time, so conviction of sin takes place in the hearts of individuals and eventually a tipping point occurs that makes changes politically.

I believe the Declaration of Independence was such a tipping point and the life of Robert Carter III is an illustration of this point.

Lesson One – *Changes in a nation begin with changes in the heart of individuals. Sins like slavery must produce conviction in the heart of common people before politically corrected*

Of the eighty-eight structures at the recreated historic Colonial Williamsburg, most are homes.[177] In colonial America, the home extended a form of trade and business to the community as a part of its mission. Children were taught trades at a young age.

The home was the first church where worship and prayer took place. It was also the first system of economics where children would learn the values of stewarding goods and money. Furthermore, it was the first "civil government" where justice would be applied and the first foreign policy where strangers would be entertained.

The initial lessons from the generations of the Carter family were not exemplary. John Carter, the *great grandfather* of Robert III came to Virginia at 22 years old in 1635. He served in the House of Burgesses and helped build Christ Church. Despite his professed religious values, he became a leader in acquiring slaves or "tithables." He owned more slaves than anyone in Virginia by the time he died in 1669.[178]

Lesson Two - *Though slavery was universal all over the world and among every nation, individuals and nations that profess the Christian faith are especially responsible to correct its evil.*

John's son Robert, grandfather of Robert III, also served in the House of Burgesses in 1691, as Speaker of the House in 1696, and on the Governor's Council in 1700. In addition to his public service, he was the second wealthiest individual in Virginia by 1726, owning 300,000 acres, 47 plantations, 18 buildings, and a brick mansion with 15 children from three different wives (at different times). Though he taught his children to dream big, unfortunately this meant owning more than 700 slaves and selling thousands more![179]

Lesson Three – *It is one thing to practice a sin such as chattel slavery, but it is another to pass it down to your children and grandchildren. Multi-generational sin is called iniquity in the Bible.*

By the time Robert, junior grew up, the name "Carter" was not popular. A family that owned and sold more slaves than anyone else was reviled. Robert II died at 29 in 1732. His father Robert I, known as "King" Carter, also died the same year, thus 4-year-old Robert III lost his father and grandfather in the same year; but had been given his first slave at age 3! Levy writes:

> By his fourth birthday, an age when the typical gentry boy was still wearing a petticoat, a frock, and a rope around the waist tied to something or someone sturdy, Robert Carter III had suddenly inherited one of the largest fortunes in America. As well, he had inherited sole possession of the most respected, and the most reviled, name in Virginia... Robert Carter III joined this stage as Robert Carter I and Robert Carter II left it, as the mansion that represented their family burned and fell to ruin, as if his destiny, to dismantle the empire his grandfather and father built, were foreordained.[180]

Robert attended the Grammar school at William and Mary at age 9 and by 11 he inherited more than 100 slaves and 65,000 acres of land.[181] The amazing thing about God is that sin's power is limited by God's overruling Providence according to His purposes. Robert Carter III was the fourth generation of slave owners, and by God's design, this cycle would end with him!

> **Lesson Four** – *For I, the Lord your God, am a jealous God, visiting the iniquity of the fathers upon the children to the third and fourth generation (Exodus 20:6). Robert III, at a young age, would carry a burden of guilt and shame, but God would bring forth an amazing redemption!*

In 1749, at the age of 21, Robert III sailed to England. On board was Lawrence, half-brother of George Washington.[182] This would eventually bring him into a relationship with some of the most ardent patriots. A greater Providence was that it brought him into contact with their faith as well.

In 1754, after his return, Robert III married Frances Ann Tasker, daughter of the former Governor of Maryland. Within 18 years they had 17 children though only 12 would live to adulthood. Robert was part of the Governor's Council and by 1761 moved his growing family to Williamsburg where he purchased a home adjacent to the Governor's Palace and next to George Wythe.[183]

At the same time, new influences were arriving in Virginia, bringing a surge of faith that would influence his life:

> The Presbyterians, Methodists, and Baptists who now seeped into Virginia, however, were not merely religious dissidents;

> they were cultural and political rebels, the 'negative image,' as Rhys Isaac has written, of the gentry. They didn't drink or gamble. They dressed plain. They didn't dance. And when wealthy Virginians mocked and persecuted them, they wore their martyrdom as a badge of honor: William Fristoe, a Presbyterian minister, called it 'clearer proof of the genuine quality of religion among us.'[184]

In the next decade Robert would be influenced by his father-in-law Governor Faquier, particularly because of his faith and his Will. His funeral was not to be "pompous" and in his Will he questioned the practice of slavery, all because it "was contrary to the spirit of Christ's religion."[185]

Robert refused to participate in a slave auction when settling one of his relatives' estates.[186] He grew apart from his family legacy, and even named his children after his wife's family, not his.[187] God was moving in his heart.

These influences, and other Virginians like John Blair, George Washington, George Wythe and Thomas Jefferson, would make Robert a patriot by the time of the Revolution. Over time he renounced his allegiance to George III, resisted Governor Dunmore, sent supplies to the Virginia militia and refused to have his children taught at William and Mary.

He moved his family to Nomoni (on the Potomac) in 1772 and hired Philip Fithian to tutor his children.[188] Fithian was recommended by

Dr. Witherspoon, who was one of his instructors at the College of New Jersey.

Converted at a revival in 1766, Fithian's faith had a profound impact upon Robert and Anne as well as the children he tutored in 1773-1774. Philip would have discussions with the Carters, and quite often slavery and its abolition would be the topic. Slowly Robert began to see that the true and sincere faith of Christianity was incompatible with the institution of slavery, for all were created equal.[189]

Fithian read the poetry of Phillis Wheatley to Bob, one of Robert's children. Wheatley's poetry had helped to dispel the myth that African Americans did not have the same intelligence as whites.[190]

Though Robert's great grandfather had freed his slaves in his Will upon his death, the practice of manumission was illegal in Virginia from 1728 to 1783. The turning point for Robert III was none other than the drafting and ratification of the Declaration of Independence.

By the *"laws of nature and of nature's God"* all men were created equal. They were given these rights by their Creator and not by the government.

Furthermore, all governments ought to operate based on self-rule, securing and protecting rights. Since Christianity and the Bible taught these truths, he became convinced he must be converted.

No sect was more adamant for the abolition of slavery at the time than the Baptists. Levy writes about Carter in the early days of 1776:

> …he devoured Tom Paine's *Common Sense* in the early weeks of 1776… he meditated upon the links between his new

> country and the Jews of the Bible… 'Kings they had none,' Carter observed, 'it was held sinful to acknowledge any Being under the title but the Lord of Hosts.'[191]

Shortly after the Declaration was written, Carter

> Experienced what he called a 'most gracious Illumination' where he felt 'the truth contained in the following scripture, where Paul declares 'that he, Paul, was alive without the Law once: but when the Commandment came, sin revived, and he died.'[192]

Robert now understood, by a revelation of the Lord, that the Word of God became alive, his sin was exposed, and he was converted. While many would discount such experiences, Robert Carter III was now a new man!

Lesson Five – *Though God often works through the influence of others already walking with Him to draw us, conversion is a sovereign act of God's grace.*

It was later observed that Carter's "religious conversion" followed the Declaration, and his "political conversion" would follow the ratification of the United States Constitution.[193] He experienced several of his own slaves being converted at this time also.

At the one-year anniversary of Independence, July 4, 1777, Levy writes that;

> At Nomony, Robert Carter gathered together his family, around seven in the evening. In the past, he acknowledged to them, they had not gathered to read parts of the Bible and talk about 'fundamental Christian doctrine.' But now they would

> do it daily, 'so that Hearers, each and every one, may examine whether they had experienced similar Exercises…til,' he added, already thinking of the laws against certain forms of religious practices,' it should be forbidden.[194]

Carter joined the Morattico Baptist Church, declaring his faith openly in their meetings. He became an avid financial supporter as well.[195] His declarations, though often in private, helped ignite a fire already beginning to blaze in his heart and among others in Virginia.

Following the Bill that legalized manumission in Virginia, Levy notes that some began privately manumitting their slaves.

> Before Robert Carter freed his slaves, small slaveholders across Virginia had liberated almost ten thousand of their black servants, and entire states with significant slave populations, such as New Jersey, were learning how to finance emancipations on a public scale.[196]

Carter resisted the discrimination laws against blacks, but also against the Baptists, Quakers and other religious sects that did not align with the State established religion in Virginia. He refused to separate slave families, and though the number of his slaves increased to over 400 by 1785, they were treated so well they continually pledged a willingness to remain.

He also continued to avoid slave auctions. He gave his slaves more autonomy and watched over their health and sanctioned only 'moderate correction in every case' where punishment was due.

By 1788, as the Constitution was being debated in every colony before it was ratified, he wrote that "tolerating slavery indicates great depravity.[197]

Lesson Six – *Carter's* ***Deed of Gift in 1791*** *was an act of manumission that occurred in the wake of his conversion where God used the Declaration and Constitution at our nation's birth*

During great turmoil due to his own children being willing to be slave owners, and losing his wife Frances in October of 1787, he became frustrated that all the petitions and resolutions published by key leaders against slavery seemed to go nowhere politically.

> - George Washington (1786) – "There is not a man living who wishes more sincerely than I do, to see a plan adopted for the abolition of it (slavery)."
> - James Madison (1787) – "We have seen the mere distinction of color made in the most enlightened period of time, a ground of the most oppressive dominion ever exercised by man over man."
> - Benjamin Franklin (1789) – "Savery is... an atrocious debasement of human nature."[198]

In light of the point made at the beginning of this chapter, that a seed of truth takes time to germinate in the hearts of people, consider John Jay's (Governor of New York and first Supreme Court Justice) description of the fact that at the time of the Revolution (and Declaration) people's hearts were being convicted and changed in their attitude toward slavery.

> Prior to the great Revolution... our people had been so long accustomed to the practice and convenience of having slaves that very few among them even doubted the propriety and

> rectitude of it. Some liberal and conscientious men had indeed, by their conduct and writings, drawn the lawfulness of slavery into question… their doctrines prevailed by almost insensible degrees, and was like the little lump of leaven which was put into three measures of meal.[199]

Jay also said it quite succinctly this way:

> That men should pray and fight for their own freedom and yet keep others in slavery is certainly acting a very inconsistent as well as unjust and perhaps impious part.[200]

There were some political victories such as the Northwest Ordinance outlawing slavery in 1787 for the new territory that would become Ohio, Indiana, Michigan, Illinois, and Wisconsin which declared in Article 6, "There shall be neither slavery nor involuntary servitude in the said territory, otherwise than in the punishment of crimes whereof the party shall have been duly convicted…"[201]

For Robert, this was not enough, and his time had come.

Robert Carter III, at 63 years of age, went public and freed more slaves than any other individual prior to 1860. He was "determined to end slavery" and began with what he called his Deed of Gift on September 5, 1791.[202]

To illustrate his religious conversion and break the generational cycle of slavery in his family, it was reported by others that he erected a large pulpit in front of his home in Nomoni and announced the freedom of his 452 slaves in 1791:

> I have for some time past been convinced that to retain them in slavery is contrary to the true Principles of Religion and Justice, and that therefore it was my Duty to manumit them.... I have with great Care and Attention endeavored to discover that Mode of Manumission from Slavery which can be effected consonant to Law and with the Least possible Disadvantage to my fellow Citizens.[203]

Carter implemented an <u>immediate yet gradual emancipation.</u> It could have become a model plan if not for the selfish economic incentives to retain slavery that would occur years later. His method was immediate, yet gradual, because the oldest were freed first, and women when they turned 18 and men when they turned 21 would be set free. This was true love for their independence and productivity to be sustained.

Every January 1st more would be freed. As late as 1852, Julia Carter, Robert III's daughter, was still freeing descendants of Carter's slaves under the same Deed of Gift.

Truly Robert Carter is a fascinating Founding Father that has been forgotten, for it was better to be a slave in 1790, closer to the Declaration when its truths were fresh on people's minds than in 1810, when the love of money would cause owners to cling to slavery as the Declaration's truths of equality faded into the background.[204]

As Andrew Levy describes:

> It was no coincidence that Carter's first religions conversion took place in the wake of the Declaration of Independence, and that his second took place in the wake of the ratification

> of the Constitution: the timing of his great changes always coincided with great changes in the life of the new nation.[205]

Historian Thomas West confirms the fact that Carter freed his slaves at a pivotal point in our history:

> In 1776 the number of free blacks in America was very small. The first census, taken in 1790, counted 27,000 free blacks in the North and 32,000 in the South. Because of the much larger slave populations in the South, by 1810 more Southern blacks had won their freedom through individual manumissions than northern blacks had through manumissions and abolition combined. In that year the census reported 78,000 free blacks (and 27,500 slaves) in the North, but 108,000 free blacks (and 1.2 million slaves) in the South. Delaware owners freed their slaves in such large numbers that it amounted to a near abolition. By 1810, 76 percent of Delaware blacks were free; in Maryland, free blacks numbered a substantial 23 percent.[206]

Dr. Robert Carter III, who is an African American himself, and shares the name of this hero, writes:

> After his conversion, Carter – who often referred to his slaves as his brethren – became convinced that being a humane slaver owner was not enough… Carter was not motivated by the desire for personal gains or fame. Instead, he acted solely for one cause: to abolish slavery. Leading by example, Carter started a trickle that became a flood of manumissions. Within a decade, nearly 10,000 enslaved people were freed throughout Virginia.[207]

Carter's heart change was planted like a seed and would grow into a hopeful promise of abolition. He was not alone, but his sacrifice stood out as a beacon of hope and an inspiration for many to do the same. No nation is free from vices, but those nations that embrace Biblical promises that can be claimed are in a blessed position.

As Martin Luther King Jr. would declare years later, the Declaration *was a promissory note* that served as an ideal for the equality of future generations!

Leading Idea – The seed of godly ideas will gradually leaven culture in a positive way, beginning with individuals who stand for truth out of a love for people

Chapter 9

LIFE

We hold these truths to be self-evident, that all men are created equal, and are endowed by their Creator with certain unalienable rights, that among these are ***Life****, Liberty, and the Pursuit of Happiness*

Life comes from God

The first verse of the Bible declares that all of creation comes from God. Genesis 1:1 – "In the beginning God created the heavens and the earth." But to be more specific, all *human life* comes from God as well. Genesis 2:7 – "And the Lord God formed man of the dust of the ground, and breathed into his nostrils the breath of life; and man became a living being."

It is His breath in our lungs. We have a spirit designed to communicate with God, a soul (mind, will and emotion) that makes us unique among all creation, and a physical body; all crafted by God.

God gave men and women three great *responsibilities* on earth – life, liberty and property. They are given to us in Genesis 1:28. The first was to "be fruitful and multiply." The first right given by God to humanity was the right to life.

We will discuss what the Bible says about life, and then what the Declaration meant in its historic context. All rights, however, come with responsibility.

It is the responsibility of mankind to have children and multiply – we are to trust God that He made the earth capable of sustaining life. The *myth of over-population* should be discarded.[208] Overcrowding is a challenge, but God provided plenty of space for the population of the earth.

Reasoning from the book of Genesis, John Locke (1632-1704), noted by many of the founders as the "philosopher of the American Revolution," noted that;

> No one ought to harm another in his Life, Liberty, or Possessions. For Men being all the Workmanship of one Omnipotent, and infinitely wise Maker: All are Servants of one Sovereign Master, sent into the World by his Order, and about his Business, they are his Property, whose Workmanship they are, made to last during his not one anothers Pleasure.[209]

When starting from a viewpoint that human beings are created by God, Locke asserts that all human life is God's property. It matters not what religion they may espouse, of what race or ethnicity they might share, for each one has a purpose. Locke is correct when saying that an individual's life should not last during another's pleasure, but left for God to decide.

The Sanctity of Life

Writing about the fact that every individual is made in God's image, Gary Amos states;

> Being made in God's image makes man a being of enormous value and inherent worth. This notion was foreign to all ancient systems of thought and accounts for the lack of any strong concepts of subjective rights outside ancient Israel or in non-Christian cultures.[210]

If human life is sacred, it must be protected. Locke reasoned that just as a State of Nature indicates that every human life is to be honored, the entry of sin into the human race made it possible that we could live in a State of War when our life was individually threatened.

> The State of War is a state of Enmity and Destruction: And therefore declaring by Word or Action, not a passionate and hasty, but a sedate settled Design, upon another Man's Life, puts him in a State of War with him… For by the fundamental Law of Nature, Man being to be preferred, as much as possible, when all cannot be preserved, the safety of the Innocent is to be preferred… To be free from such force is the only security of my Preservation; and reason bids me look on him, as an Enemy to my Preservation, who would take away my Freedom.[211]

Self-defense of one's life and the punishment of those who take it without cause is taught throughout the Bible. This is true for the child as well as the adult.

Noah Webster defines justice;

> **1.** The virtue which consists in giving to everyone what is his due; practical conformity to the laws and to principles of rectitude in the dealings of men with each other; honesty; integrity in commerce or mutual intercourse…
> **2.** Impartiality; equal distribution of right in expressing opinions; fair representation of facts respecting merit or demerit. In criticisms, narrations, history or discourse, it is a duty to do *justice* to every man, whether friend or foe.
> **3.** Equity; agreeableness to right; as, he proved the *justice* of his claim.

For centuries true justice has meant a system that attempts to give to each individual "the punishment that fits the crime." This is true equity. True justice is blind, like the statue that is blindfolded so that it is impartial.

Scott Allen, in his book, *Why Social Justice is not Biblical Justice,* writes that social justice is;

> The tearing down of traditional structure and systems deemed to be oppressive, and the redistribution of power and resources from oppressors to victims in pursuit of equality of outcomes.[212]

Not only have societies agandoned true justice, but many no longer see life as valuable and worth protecting in the first place. Such cultures are dying ones and certain to face the cause and effect adjustments from the Creator.

For the Declaration to list *life* as the first unalienable right to be protected by civil government rests solely on the fact that God is the Creator, for He endows such a right.

The opposite philosophy is the Enlightenment, particularly the philosophy espoused by Jean-Jaques Rousseau (1712-1778). Carl Trueman, in his book *Strange New World,* writes of Rousseau's philosophy,

> First, he locates identity in the inner psychological life of the individual. Feelings for Rousseau are central to who we are. And second, he sees society (or perhaps better, *culture*) as exerting a corrupting influence on the self. To the extent that society prevents us from acting consistently with our feelings, to that extent it prevents us from being who we really are.[213]

The world of the delegates in Congress in 1776 was a world shaped by St. Augustine, John Calvin and the Reformation. We were personally created by God, yet fallen in our human nature.

Rousseau's world was that we are not made in God's image, but our own. The nature of self and its feelings identify who we are.

Trueman goes on to say "What Rousseau proposed as something novel and exciting is now the norm."[214] It has given rise to the notion that one must define their own identity and this had led to identity politics which leaves few rights protected since our feelings change so frequently.

That is why it is imperative that we understand the origin of the ideas written in the Declaration. If life is not sacred at its beginning, it will not be treated as sacred at its end, either. When there is no consciousness of a Creator, life is cheap and expendible. Thus, as Dan Wiser wrote in 2024:

> In a disturbing development, assisted suicide and euthanasia have become more prevalent across the West in recent decades. Government and health authorities are encouraging voluntary death, even for patients who do not suffer from a terminal illness but are afflicted by disabilities, poverty, or loneliness.[215]

In contrast to today's culture, this right to life, embraced by the delegates, extended as people say, from "the womb to the tomb."

The Bible teaches that Life Begins at Conception

Psalm 51:5 states "in sin my mother conceived me." The sin nature of every human being is given at conception. Our soul and body begin at conception. It is interesting that God's Word is always ahead of the confirmation of science. Though the biological science of conception was not understood by David, the author of this Psalm, he was given revelation ahead of his time.

Jeremiah 1:5 states, "Before I formed you in the womb, I knew you." The very prophet who lamented at the valley of Hinnom was called by God *even before he was conceived in the womb of his mother.* Our calling predates our conception! And remember, the very Jeremiah who could declare such truth with the backdrop of such evil, was known as the *weeping prophet*, filled with grace.

Psalm 100:3 says, *"It is He that has made us, and not we ourselves."* We are not the owners of our lives, God is. He has called us, created us, and has a purpose for us. Rus Walton, former Executive Director of the Plymouth Rock Foundation, wrote;

> Pro-abortionists claim that terminating a pregnancy is not murder because the fetus is not a human life… Thus, the question: When does life begin? The Bible has always given the answer, and the more science learns through study and research, the more science affirms the Scriptures. Life begins at conception. When a zygote ("genesis" cell) is formed by the fusion of the sperm and the egg, life commences.[216]

Every life is the work of God's Hand in the womb as described in Psalm 139:13-16;

> For you formed my inward parts; you covered me in my mother's womb. I will praise you, for I am fearfully and wonderfully made; marvelous are your works, and that my soul knows very well. My frame was not hidden from You when I was made in secret, and skillfully wrought in the lowest parts of the earth. Your eyes saw my substance, being yet unformed, and in your book they all were written, the days fashioned for me, when as yet there were none of them.

Exodus 21:22-23 declares;

> If men fight, and hurt a woman with child, so that she gives birth prematurely, yet no harm follows, he shall surely be punished accordingly as the woman's husband imposes on

him; and he shall pay as the judges determine. But if any harm follows, then you shall give life for life.

Note that the child, if it does not die, is still worth the penalty as the husband (and wife) determine. However, if it does die, it is "life for life" or in other words equal to the life of an adult! God's Law considers the child in the womb to be a person.

Roe v. Wade in America, 1973

The now famous *Roe v. Wade* decision[217] was rendered on January 22, 1973 by a 7 to 2 margin. Since then, there have been over 65 million (as of this writing) recorded abortions in the U.S.[218] The highest number of abortions (93%) occur in the 1st Trimester.

We are grateful over the years since that there has been a steady decline in the number of abortions per year since the peak of 1.5 million in 1991.

Also, the number of abortion providers has decreased steadily since its peak of 2,908 in 1982 to less than half that number today.[219] But upon what premise was this Supreme Court decision made in the first place? Why would they overturn the pro-life practice of our nation's first three hundred and fifty years?

Herb Titus, legal scholar and constitutional expert, summarized the findings in *Roe v. Wade* by citing the decision; "A child in the womb of a mother was not human life, only 'potential human life.'"[220] With the stroke of a pen, a court decision held that a child in the womb was no longer a human being with the right to life.

Interestingly, in *Dred Scott v. Sandford* (1857) the Court concluded that slaves were "beings of an inferior order… so far inferior that they had no rights which the white man was bound to respect."[221] In essence, we have relegated the child in the womb to a slave status. Though modern culture talks of equality, inclusion and diversity, its hypocrisy is visible for all to see. Today there is no equality with those in the womb, nor inclusivity, and certainly no respect for diversity since some abortions are recommended due to projected handicaps.

One of Abraham Lincoln's reasons for his rebuttal of *Dred Scott*, beyond the fact that it was demeaning to the rights of Scott, was that the Supreme Court has limited jurisdiction to individual cases.[222] He lamented that Scott was a commodity to be returned to his owner, but rejoiced that the decision only applied to that one case, and could not be binding on other States.

The Supreme Court's role is clearly defined in Article III, Section 2 where it reads "The judicial power shall extend to all cases." It extends only to the case before it as the text of the Constitution declares.

As Titus has written;

> A case is a dispute between two parties… None of the other 50 states nor any of their residents were parties. Under Article III… no court has the power to issue a general rule binding on people not before the Court.[223]

In other words, the Court cannot write law (or expect all the States to follow any decision it makes) as it tried to do in both *Dred Scott* and *Roe.*

Dissenting Judge Justice White in *Roe* stated;

> The Court simply fashions and announces a new constitutional right for pregnant mothers, with scarcely any reason or authority for its action.

In *Roe* the Court determined that the mother's liberty of choice was a greater right than the child's life.[224]

The ancient nations of Egypt, Assyria, Babylon and Persia, to name a few, practiced the killing of infants in the womb or newly born if the child was not a benefit to society as determined by the State or Empire. But the early Church at the dawn of Christianity disagreed because Christ brought value to each individual, including children in the womb.

Christian literature (1st Century) of the Didache stated; "thou shalt not murder a child by abortion.." Why? The clause just prior to this states; "Thou Shalt love thy neighbor more than thy own life."[225] In other words, the child in the womb is your neighbor, it is not merely a part of the woman's body.

The early church acted on this, picking up babies set on doorstops intended to be abandoned by Romans who were taught that their life was only as avaluable as the Empire that ruled the society had determined. Tertullian, a 3rd century theologian, wrote;

> ...we are not permitted, since murder has been prohibited to us once and for all, even to destroy the foetus in the womb... It makes no difference whether one destroys a life that has already been born or one that is in the process of birth.[226]

The right to life became the standard definition codified in Common Law after Christianity permeated the British Isles by the 9th century in King Alfred's England.

What did "Life" mean in the Declaration in 1776?

Jurist William Blackstone, whose books on the law were fundamental to those we call founders wrote;

> Life is the immediate gift of God – a right inherent by nature in every individual; and it begins in contemplation of law as soon as an infant is able to stir in the mother's womb. For if a woman is quick with child, and by a potion or otherwise kills it in her womb; or if any one beat her whereby the child dies in her body and she is delivered of a dead child, this… was by the ancient law homicide or manslaughter.[227]

Now it is true, that today, this concept is hotly debated and contested. In fact, several scholars write that since the "quickening" of the child was the point at which a baby's life was protected by law (due to the science of the time), the baby was not protected prior to this and thus not considered a human being.[228]

Modern reasoning imposes this presupposition in spite of the fact that Blackstone (and others) were simply saying you can't prove "beyond a reasonable doubt" that the fetus is alive until the mother feels it move within her. The idea of "quickening" does not indicate a belief that the fetus was not a child prior to the 4th month (possibly the time such a quickening might be sensed by the mother).

Jameson Taylor, in his essay on "The Founding Fathers and the Right to Life" gives us further insight about how the framers understood the right to life:

> James Wilson's "Lectures on Law," given at what eventually was to become the University of Pennsylvania, clearly affirm that the right to life encompasses the unborn. Wilson was one

of only six men to sign both the Declaration and the Constitution and was a Supreme Court justice from 1789 to 1798. Recognized as "the most learned and profound legal scholar of his generation," Wilson's lectures were attended by President George Washington, Vice President John Adams, Secretary of State Thomas Jefferson and a "galaxy of other republican worthies." For this reason, as constitutional scholar Walter Berns states, "Wilson, when speaking on the law, might be said to be speaking for the Founders generally." So what do the Founders say about the right to life?[229]

Wilson clearly answers this question: "With consistency, beautiful and undeviating, human life from its commencement to its close, is protected by the common law. In the contemplation of law, life begins when the infant is first able to stir in the womb. By the law, life is protected not only from immediate destruction, but from every degree of actual violence, and in some cases, from every degree of danger."[230]

John Quincy Adams' speech in 1831 commemorating the Declaration articulated the follwing;

> Ask the Declaration of Independence and that will tell you that its authors held for self-evident truth that the right to life is the first of the unalienable rights of man (and) to secure and not destroy (that right) governments are instituted among men.[231]

The recent *Dobbs* decision in June of 2021 returned the practice of abortions back to the State legislatures where it constitutionally belongs. Justice Samuel Alito in his majority opinion wrote;

> For the first 185 years after the adoption of the Constitution, each State was permitted to address this issue in accordance

> with the views of its citizens. Then, in 1973, this Court decided Roe v. Wade… Even though the Constitution makes no mention of abortion, the Court held that it confers a broad right to obtain one. It did not claim that American law or the common law had ever recognized such a right… the opinion concluded with a numbered set of rules much like those that might be found in a statute enacted by a legislature.[232]

And this is the point, the Court attempted to *enact a law.* The reversal of Dobbs did not outlaw abortion but returned it to individual state legislatures, where decisions could be made closer to the people. This is a step closer to the Constitution, for Amendment 10 states;

> The powers not delegated to the United States by the Constitution, nor prohibited by it to the States, are reserved to the States respectively, or to the people.

Dobbs will not stop federal funding of abortions. It has, however, exposed how divided we are – as of this writing twenty states now restrict abortions, at least 19 do not; and the others may fall somewhere in between. Six states (AK, VT, OR, NJ, NM, CO) and Washington DC have no limits on abortion at all.[233]

But consider the Bill of Rights as it might be applied to the right to life. Amendment V declares that no person can be "deprived of life, liberty, or property, without due process of law." Since the child in the womb is a person, they should be defended as innocent until proven guilty.

How can we deprive them of life without due process of law? What crime have they committed that would allow the death penalty?

The ultimate solution, however, is not in law, but in a revival among the people, for as John Adams wrote in 1798;

> Our Constitution was made only for a moral and religious People. It is wholly inadequate to the government of any other.[234]

Inherent in the right to life in the Declaration is also the right of self-defense. As Locke observed, if someone attempts to take away our life, we are in a state of war with that individual, and we have the right to defend it.

An area we face that deserves mention is the rise of mental health which has become a crisis. Jeremiah Johnston has accurately defined it,

> Mental illness is defined as a physical dysfunction of the brain that causes the inability to think or feel or act in a person's normal manner.[235]

This is a right to life issue. Many treat those suffering from mental illness as if they are deliberately trying to cause harm. However, as Johnston explains,

> There are treatment procedures physical problems of the body (i.e. cholesterol levels) and there are treatments for the unseen illness of the brain. Mental and physical health should be treated as equal.[236]

This is not to say people aren't responsible for their actions, but we must take into account that the brain needs to be fed properly just as the body does. Lack of nutrition and continued exposure to a toxic environment has contributed to these issues and proven treatments must be included if we value life as sacred.

Those who believe in a Creator, as the delegates did in 1776, face a challenge today that they did not face then. The culture of 1776, including much of Europe, all believed in a Creator. As our culture descends into a philosophy substituting self and feeling in place of a personal Creator, it is easy for some to react in anger.

However, we must understand that it is wrong to react in such a way, *for it has been our own detachment from cultural responsibility that is to blame*. Those who believe in a personal Creator should demonstrate such through good works in serving others.

In this way we are being "salt and light" as Jesus declares in Matthew 5:13-16. It is better to demonstrate the solution rather than blame others who might share your viewpoint. This understanding that change begins with the one who sees the injustice allows us to truly be repentant, rather than blaming others.

God is always ready to pardon at the first notion of conviction and repentance. I remember studying in the archives of the Moody Center in Northampon many years ago reading some of Dwight Moody's sermons. I came across this quote; "I cannot preach on hell unless I preach with tears.[237]

I also remember the many quotes of Corrie Ten Boom who experienced the depths of evil under the Nazi Regime's Concentration camp where she stayed and her sister was killed. I was moved by her simple statement; "there is no pit so deep where God's love is not deeper still."[238]

If you are tempted to rise in unbridled anger toward those who tend to quick to justify abortion, assisted suicide and forms of euthanasia of the elderly, take heed. Jesus said that the command to refrain from murder goes to the heart of unbridled anger or vengeance.[239]

Truth must always be shared in love and with mercy and grace. 1st Corinthians 10:12 warns us to "let him who thinks he stands take heed lest he fall."

The way God changes a culture is to first bring that change through those who claim to know Him.

> For the time has come for judgment to begin at the house of God, and if it begins with us first, what will be the end of those who do not obey the gospel of God? – 1st Peter 4:17

Why does God first judge His people for the sins of a culture? The first reason is that *as the church goes, so goes the nation.* The other reason is that *His people are to demonstrate both truth and grace.*[240]

Believers ought to know that none of us are innocent since it was our sin and God's Law that required Christ to be put on the cross!

> Jesus of Nazareth, a Man attested by God to you by miracles, wonders, and signs which God did through Him in your midst, as you yourselves also know – Him, being delivered by the determined purpose and foreknowledge of God, you have taken by lawless hands, have crucified, and put to death; whom God raised up, having loosed the pains of death, because it was not possible that He should be held by it. – Acts 2:22-24

May God bring the correction necessary for us to restore our nations that we might have a culture that respects the sanctity of life. May God also soften our hearts that we might show compassion and love toward others. May we agree with Moses as recorded in Deuteronomy 30:19;

I call heaven and earth as witnesses today against you, that I have set before you life and death, blessing and cursing; therefore choose life, that both you and your descendants may live; that you may love the Lord your God, that you may obey His voice, and that you may cling to Him, for He is your life.

Leading Idea – The protection of life is the first purpose of civil government, from the womb to the natural end of life.

Chapter 10

LIBERTY

We hold these truths to be self-evident, that all men are created equal, and are endowed by their Creator with certain unalienable rights, that among these are Life, ***Liberty****, and the Pursuit of Happiness*

The Origin of Liberty

"Be fruitful and multiply; fill (replenish) the earth and subdue it..." – Genesis 1:28

In Genesis 1:28 God gives three basic rights to mankind – life, liberty, and property. Each of these rights carries proportional responsibilities. We now examine the right to liberty, or the responsibility to *replenish* the earth.

The word translated "replenish" is a Hebrew word meaning to "make full".[241] There are a variety of interpretations, but the interpretation I have studied is creative productivity, using the resources God has given.

Psalm 115:16 states *"the heaven, even the heavens, are the Lord's, but the earth He has given to the children of men."* God empowers us to be productive by harnessing the laws embedded in creation for the glory of God and service of others.[242]

We are made in God's image, and part of that is creativity. We don't create out of nothing like God does, but we create out of what He has given us. The standard for creativity is God's creation. Not all art, music or technology fits God's standard or gives Him glory. Also, the use of technology is to help us be a more efficient steward, not to make us dependent on it.[243]

Thus, technology such as "artificial intelligence," or AI, if not done to enhance our stewardship of God's creation but instead put us into slavery to machines or those seeking our control, is a violation of His commands.

We fill the earth with acts of creative expressions such as tools to aid our stewardship of the earth. This is a filling of the earth in a different form than how we found it. Today, from airplanes to high-rise buildings, we have expressions of man's creativity around us.

Societies and nations that have looked upon liberty as a God-given right have flourished in technology, tools, productivity, and advancement of civilization.

On the other hand, those nations that have looked upon liberty as a government-granted privilege regress, giving only limited freedom to their populations. The *right to liberty* is thus the right to be uniquely creative, but it also requires the responsibility of self-control (with the right attitude), which is why the Bible calls it the *law of liberty* (see James 1:25).

The Law of Liberty

"Of every tree of the garden you may freely eat; but of the tree of the knowledge of good and evil you shall not eat, for in the day that you eat of it you shall surely die." – Genesis 2:16-17

Made in God's image, our thirst for liberty, freedom of choice, and the ability to learn from our own mistakes, is a part of who we are in His likeness. Right after God created Adam and Eve, he placed them in a garden, a piece of private property, where they were to exercise their right to liberty, but under His law.

All the trees could be freely chosen, except one. In other words, initially freedom of choice was greater than any restriction. This command of God was a clarification of the law of liberty.

The evil personified by the serpent was to trick them into embracing *lawless liberty,* to have good and evil determined by their choices rather than God's law. They were supposedly to be "gods" determining right and wrong. Not much has changed, has it?

The result of their sin cost them their freedom. Diminished self-control by rejecting God's law resulted in greater external control, being banished from the garden. The enemy's tricks are the same, but he is wise to disguise them by deception dressed in modern culture.

After the fall the Law was given as an act of mercy so that we might know what is righteous. Each one of the ten commandments is foundational, and the rest of the laws in the Old Testament are applications of these. As an example, Exodus 20:13 (6th commandment,) states *Thou Shalt not Kill.* To murder is to unjustly kill another, taking away their life and liberty.[244]

A case law application of this, however, or what we call statute law, is given in Exodus 21:24 that justice should be *eye for eye, tooth for tooth, hand for hand, foot for foot.* The punishment ought to fit the crime, but there is more. In Matthew 5:38-39 Jesus says to refrain from retaliating with anger. All the laws of God involve both the heart *and* the behavior.

Take another law, Exodus 22:2-3, that states; *"If the thief is caught while breaking in and is struck so that he dies, there will be no blood-guiltiness on his account. But if the sun has risen on him, there will be blood-guiltiness on his account.* If in the act a thief is killed by the self-defense of the owner, he or she shall not be guilty of murder since they have a right to self-defense.

However, if he gets away, and you track him down the next day, to avoid vengeance, you can't take justice into your own hands, and guilt must be determined by a trial of "two or three witnesses." (see

Deuteronomy 19:15; Matthew 18:16) The Law of God thus protects us from both *our evil attitudes* and *others' lawless actions.*

Liberty must be Defended

Consider the historic roots of the citizen militia (soldiers) in defense of liberty. Bill Federer writes;

> In the Denver University Law Review, David Kopel writes, 'New Englanders intensely self-identified with ancient Israel… Thus, ancient Hebrew militia law is part of the intellectual background of the American militia system, and of the Second Amendment… Every male 'from the age of twenty years up, all those in Israel who are able to bear arms'… were obliged to fight, to go forth 'armed to battle.'[245]

As Rev. E. C. Wines in his colossal work on ancient Israel written in the 19th century, wrote;

> Moses' constitution made no provision for a standing army ... The whole body of citizens ... formed a national guard of defense… Thus the landholders (and every Israelite was a landholder) formed the only soldiery, known to the Mosaic constitution."[246]

Author Darrel Cole summarizes key leaders in church history on this issue;

> (Calvin) along with Ambrose, Augustine Aquinas and Luther – that Jesus' goal is to restrain personal retaliation, not to restrain political force, which is, after all, an agent of His Father's wrath and love.[247]

When the church fathers present force as an act of love, it causes us to ponder how this could be. But our true motivation of using force is to defend the innocent, it is not one of vengeance.

> *"Stand fast therefore in the liberty wherewith Christ hath made us free and be not entangled again with the yoke of bondage."* – Galatians 5:1

This verse was quoted by clergymen and political statesmen at our founding when defining and defending civil liberty. Today many think they misinterpreted this verse since its initial context is spiritual liberty. But let's not forget that *all truths begin as spiritual ones.* The real question is whether spiritual principles spoken in the Scriptures can be applied in such areas as civil government.

This verse exhorts us to remain in the liberty that has come through the work of Jesus Christ on the cross. In other words, spiritual liberty begins *within.* It means to stand fast in the freedom of *overcoming sinful attitudes and actions* through the power of Christ and His grace. If we walk in the liberty of internal restraint, we will not have to be entangled by sin (Galatians 5:16).

The word liberty in Greek means "…freedom from the dominion of corrupt desires so that we do by the free impulse of the soul what the will of God requires."[248] We have the liberty to ***do*** the will of God, and also the liberty to ***omit*** or ***restrain*** corrupt desires of the flesh (what the Bible calls sin; or disobedience to God's law.)[249]

The word liberty is both freeing and restraining. It does not mean that we are free to do whatever we want.[250] Liberty has limits. We are free to express righteousness, morality, self-control, and decency; all which express the will of God.

We are not liberated to sin, hurt other people through attitudes or actions, or practice acts of lawlessness. This only leads to tyranny.[251] *The less restraint we have in our hearts is reflected in a greater need for external control.*

Without Christ's redemption, we are slaves to sin, and unable to obey God's laws. Liberty, according to the Bible, is always under law. It is neither ***license*** (doing what you want - a law unto yourself; called ***anarchy)***, or ***oppression*** (doing only what others force you to do; called ***tyranny***). Liberty rests on the character of the individual to exercise self-government, or internal restraint.

This concept has a huge implication for society. The founders of our nation used the Bible as their "political textbook," quoting it more than any other source. It is not liberty without law *(anarchy)*, or law without liberty *(tyranny)*, but liberty in accordance with righteous law. Noah Webster (1828 Dictionary) defined liberty as it was used in our founding period:

> **Liberty -** "the liberty of men in a state of society, or natural liberty, so far only abridged and restrained, as is necessary and expedient for the safety and interest of the society, state, or nation. A restraint of natural liberty, not necessary or expedient for the public, is tyranny or oppression. Civil liberty is an exemption from the arbitrary will of others, which exemption is secured by established laws, which restrain every man from injuring or controlling another. Hence, the restraints of law are essential to civil liberty."[252]

Liberty cannot exist without law. But it is also true that the *source* of liberty will determine its *quality*. Since all laws are religious in nature, the true question is *which religion* will produce the kind of laws that best protect the individual's right to liberty? Noah Webster answered this question when he wrote;

> "Almost all the civil liberty now enjoyed in the world owes its origin to the principles of the Christian religion... and civil liberty has been gradually advancing and improving as genuine Christianity has prevailed... the religion which has introduced civil liberty, is the religion of Christ and His apostles... this is genuine Christianity, and to this we owe our free constitutions of government...."[253] In his Advice to the Young, Webster stated: "the moral principles and precepts contained in the Scriptures ought to form the basis of all of our constitutions and laws."[254]

Religious and Civil Liberty

Romans 13:5 tells us that submission to a righteous civil government should be "not only for wrath but also for conscience sake." In other words, wrath because we are to be punished for our actions, and conscience, because of our religious obligations.

The truth that the State and the Church have distinct responsibilities before God is unique. It is the jurisdictional separation of church (developing the conscience and religious liberty) and state (civil liberty).

Today, more than 26 million martyrs have died for their religious faith in the last 100 years, and that is more than all the previous 1900 years combined!

The dictatorships and subsequent murders by Pol Pot (Cambodia); Adolf Hitler (Germany); Joseph Stalin (Soviet Union); and Mao Tse-Tung (China), pale in comparison to the fact that in the past year alone 340 million Christians were persecuted, 4,761 were killed for their faith, 4,488 churches and Christian buildings attacked, 4,277 detailed without trial.[255]

The Virginia Statue for Religious Liberty

Conscience is internal, and actions are external. The Common Law restricted civil government from punishing the conscience (heart), limiting punishment to actions. One's free expression of ideas in general, and religious ideas in particular, is a derivative of our general property rights. Consider the history of "Religious Freedom Day" in our nation.

Thomas Jefferson gave instructions that on his gravemarker three achievements would be noted: writer of the *Declaration of Independence,* "father" of the University of Virginia, and author of the *Statute of Virginia for Religious Freedom*.

In 1992, the United States Congress established January 16 as Religious Freedom Day since "Bill No. 82" was passed by the Virginia State Legislature on the 16th of January, 1786.

Though written by Jefferson in 1777, its ideas were also championed by James Madison in Congress to pass the First Amendment to the Bill of Rights in 1791. The first paragaph of the Virginia Statue for Religious Freedom states:

> Well aware that Almighty God hath created the mind free; that all attempts to influence it by temporal punishments or burthens, or by civil incapacitations, tend only to beget habits of hypocrisy or meanness, and are a departure from the plan of the Holy Author of our religion, who, being Lord both of body and mind, yet chose not to propagate it by coercions on either…"[256]

Eleven of the original thirteen colonies required one to profess to be a Christian in order to hold office.[257] At the State level Christianity was the foundation of law but initially also "established" by the State. This would change in time by the time of the Civil War when all states would honor religious liberty.

State establishment (often with financial support) of a specific Christian denomination was problematic for it used the force of law to favor one form of Christianity over another. Religious toleration, not freedom, was the result. As historian Philip Schaff has noted:

> The American system differs from the system of toleration... Toleration exists where the government supports one or more churches, and permits other religious communities... under certain conditions... There is a very great difference between toleration and liberty. Toleration is a concession, which may be withdrawn; it implies a preference for the ruling form of faith and worship... It may be coupled with restrictions and disabilities... In our country we ask no toleration for religion and its free exercise, but we claim it as an unalienable right. (emphasis added)[258]

Since all humans are sinful, those with power are tempted to exercise control over others. The second section of the Virginia Statute addressed this problem:

> No man shall be compelled to frequent or support any religious worship, place or ministry... or otherwise suffer on account of his religious opinion or belief.[259]

Some say that when the framers wrote Article VI, forbidding a religious test in order to hold office, that they were intending a "secular" state. But the evidence suggests otherwise, for as Joseh Story wrote;

> The same policy, which introduced into the Constitution the prohibition of any religious test led the more extended prohibition of the interference of Congress in religious concerns.[260]

This idea was, in essence, a protection of religious liberty at the State level that led to the same protection at the federal level when the Constitution was ratified.[261]

Those of our founders who were committed Christians believed that if Christianity did not remain as the the *basis* of our laws at both the state and national level, we would eventually move into chaos. Alexis deTocqueville observed, as a journalist visting in the 1830's that;

> Religion in America takes no direct part in the government of society, but it must be regarded as the first of their political institutions.... I do not know whether all Americans have a sincere faith in their religion – for who can search the human heart? - but I am certain that they hold it to be indispensable to the maintenance of republican institutions. This opinion is not peculiar to a class of citizens or to a party, but it belongs to the whole nation and to every rank of society.[262]

In other words, Christianity held influence as a voluntary religion. And as Jefferson observed, it cannot be sustained by force of law or it violates its very nature!

Jesus taught in Matthew 13:32 that the Kingdom of God is like a mustard seed; *"but when it is grown, it is the greatest among herbs, and becometh a tree, so that the birds of the air come and lodge in the branches thereof."* The Kingdom's influence would shelter all kinds of "birds of the air." Birds are symbols of ideas, both godly and ungodly.

Christianity, by its very nature, when influencing a culture, protects even those who do not espouse its beliefs from the force of those who disagree. No other religion does so. It is thus through *prayer* (1st Timothy 2:1-7) and *voluntary generational influence* of the heart, that Christianity blesses the earth.[263]

As Herb Titus observed:

> If God, Himself, who has all power and authority, has chosen not to use force to impose the true religion upon mankind, Jefferson observed, how dare men 'assume dominion over the faith of others, setting up their own opinions and modes of thinking as the only true and infallible"[264]

The final paragraph of the *Statute* states;

> And though we well know that this Assembly, elected by the people for the ordinary purposes of legislation only, have no power to restrain the acts of succeeding Assemblies, constituted with powers equal to our own, and that therefore to declare this act [to be] irrevocable would be of no effect in law; yet we are free to declare, and do declare, that the rights hereby asserted are of the natural rights of mankind, and that if any act shall be hereafter passed to repeal the present or to narrow its operation, such act will be an infringement of natural right."[265]

Here Jefferson and the Assembly declare that their religious liberty is a "natural right" or one given by God to them directly which is *unalienable.*

Many today suppose that the Declaration and Constitution are secular because they do not *enforce* Christianity by law from the top. Others say they are not Christian because they allow those who do not believe in God or profess Christ to have freedom. But, as historian Verna Hall once wrote;

> The determining fact, we submit, is not whether Christians formed the Constitution, but whether the form is Christian according to the Word of God."[266]

It is in fact true that every religion, if influential in their nation, will produce a corresponding form of government that reflects its tenets. A civil government resting on self-government and leaving it up to the individual and family to voluntarily pass down their faith to future generations is the methodology of only one religion, Christianity. Others must rely on the force of law.

Today we need to heed the warning of Robert C. Winthrop, descendant of Puritan John Winthrop, and Speaker of the House of Representatives from 1847-1849:

> All societies of men must be governed in some way or other. The less they have of stringent State Government, the more they must have of individual self-government. The less they rely on public law or physical force, the more they must rely on private, moral restraint. Men, in a word, must necessarily be controlled, either by a power within them, or by a power without them; either by the Word of God, or by the strong arm of man; either by the Bible, or by the bayonet.[267]

Historian Philip Schaff's comments about the unique nature of church and state relations adopted in America are worth pondering.

Writing in 1888 and comparing the distinction between Europe and America, he states:

> What is the distinctive character of American Christianity in its organized social aspect and its relation to the national life, as compared with the Christianity of Europe? It is a free church in a free state, or a self-supporting and self-governing Christianity in independent but friendly relation to the civil government... Civil liberty requires for its support religious liberty and cannot prosper without it. Religious liberty is not an empty sound, but an orderly exercise of religious duties and enjoyment of all its privileges. It is freedom IN religion, not freedom FROM religion; as true civil liberty is freedom IN law, and not freedom FROM law.[268]

In America, by 1888, Christianity was not supported by taxpayer funds, so it was not a political institution, but voluntarily, in the hearts of her citizens, it was their first allegiance that informed the right of conscience, and secondarily, the right of speech and liberty of action.

Alexis de Tocqueville also wrote;

> On my arrival in the United States the religious aspect of the country was the first thing that struck my attention; and the longer I stayed there, the more I perceived the great political consequences resulting from this new state of things... The Americans the notions of Christianity and of liberty so intimately in their minds that it is impossible to make them conceive the one without the other; and with them the conviction does not spring from that barren, traditionary faith which seems to vegetate rather than to live in the soul.[269]

Now it must be noted that Religious Liberty is distinct from religious toleration. In the former, the right of conscience is an unalienable right, only regulated when the actions of the individual violate the rights of others. In the latter, religious toleration leaves the sovereign authority in the State to grant privileges and thus remain in ultimate control. Philip Schaff puts it this way:

> The American system differs from the system of toleration… Toleration exists where the government supports one or more churches, and permits other religious communities under the name of sects… under certain conditions… There is a very great difference between toleration and liberty. Toleration is a concession, which may be withdrawn; it implies a preference for the ruling form of faith and worship, and a practical disapproval of all other forms. It may be coupled with restrictions and disabilities… In our country we ask no toleration for religion and its free exercise, but we claim it as an unalienable right. (emphasis added)[270]

To maintain true unalienable religious liberty, the ultimate source of freedom must be identified. In America, that was Christianity. It had the largest sway among our population but also was unique in granting more freedom for other religions. It is imperative to note that when defending religious liberty, it must be distinguished from religious exemptions which imply toleration.

The Colonial Church Developed Religious Liberty

The colonial clergy had a unique role in influencing the establishment of laws as well as State governments. What could have caused 13 colonies to unite in the same Biblical philosophy of resistance to tyranny by the time of the American Revolution?

As an example, there were 720 churches preaching the gospel in New England. The ratio of preachers to congregants was the "lowest in the Protestant world." Over five million sermons were preached in a period of 150 years to only half a million inhabitants.[271] As Harry Stout summarized in his research:

> Covenant theology as it evolved over five generations of New England preaching comprised a view of history and corporate identity that could best be labeled 'providential.' In this view God entered into covenant with nations... (and thus) resistance became necessary the minute England declared the colonies' duty of 'unlimited submission' in 'all cases whatsoever' and, in so doing, set itself alongside God's Word as a competing sovereign. Such demands were 'tyrannical' and left New Englanders no choice but to resist unto death or forfeit their identity as a covenant people. As explained from the pulpit, New Englanders' revolution was first and foremost a battle to preserve their historic identity and unique messianic destiny.[272]

Thus, the fabric of New England is inseparably woven by the well spring of Jewish and Christian thought and thus our foundations are indeed Judeo-Christian. The philosophy of government, respecting both religious and civil liberty, stretched from the covenants of the Old Testament to their fulfillment in the New Testament. Religious liberty can be viewed as the *source* of civil liberty, for the protection of conscience will determine the protection of other liberties.

American Liberty: built on Religious and Civil Liberty

Did the founders of our nation apply the Biblical doctrine of liberty to their external, civil affairs? Could liberty spoken of in terms of spiritual freedom also apply to the civil sphere? And most importantly, did our founders sanction the use of force to defend liberty in a lawful manner? These and other questions focus our attention on properly applying spiritual liberty to civil affairs.

Harry Stout, professor at Yale, in his book *The New England Soul*, notes the origin of American liberty and the American Revolution. He states that the colonists believed that "if God's Word was sovereign, then all human powers and authorities would have to be limited."[273] The limitation of civil government's powers meant a protection of liberty for the individual.

This idea of sovereignty or the fact that ultimate governmental authority could only be claimed by God was applied to the *form* of civil government embraced by our nation. Stout states:

> The only solution to the problem of 'tyranny' was a scheme of church government and social order whereby power would be distributed throughout the body of believers in such a way that no single individual or group of individuals could seize control and exert a God-like authority over the rest.[274]

In other words, the Bible's idea of liberty requires a civil government that is decentralized and limited. The colonists did not even want their churches controlled by other churches! The form of government in colonial churches set up a model of liberty for their local and state governments to follow.

Furthermore, the interpretation of Romans 13 and civil magistrates being *ministers of justice* was set in the context of Biblical jurisdiction and the ability to resist unrighteousness magistrates through the doctrine of the lower magistrate.[275]

Throughout colonial history, the clergy preached a doctrine from Scripture and then applied it to the culture in which they lived. The sermon was the main instrument of education – it was the media of the day.[276] What they preached in their churches, highly influenced those who were delegates that approved the Declaration of Independence and also our Constitution.

The Meaning of Liberty in the Declaration of Independence

We have seen that the meaning of liberty is freedom from external restraint in proportion to the individual's exercise of self-control under law. This involves a protection of both *religious* as well as *civil* liberty.

No culture can long endure freedom that abandons the necessity of defining the limits of liberty. For when anarchy comes because of conflicting standards, tyranny will arise on its heels to bring order out of the chaos. This is the lesson of history, and the founders studied this swinging pendulum in history and saw it illustrated in the events that led up to and followed the French Revolution.

Thus, the surest foundation that could be found for maintaining liberty in a culture with as small a civil government as possible was Christianity in the hearts of the people. The reason for this is that Christianity requires a high quality of internal restraint and thus allows for less external controls.

The text of the Declaration states that *"we hold these truths to be self-evident, that all men are created equal; that they are endowed by their Creator, with certain unalienable rights; that among these are life, liberty and the pursuit of happiness."* Liberty, according to the Declaration, is a God-given right. It is not government-granted. Government granted liberty is nothing more than a privilege.

This is what England promised her Colonies - the privilege of the Crown - called the *prerogative*. It simply meant that the Crown, or civil government, had all power, and granted some of it to the people as a privilege.

The Declaration of independence states that it is self-evident (needing no explanation or proof) that the right to liberty is unalienable (can never be revoked or taken away), and comes from an authority above the civil government, namely the Creator.

The origin of your liberty is your god. The *source* of liberty will determine her *quality*. Either God is our Creator and the author of our liberty, or government is our creator and grants us liberty. I submit that the history of America clarifies the fact that the former brings liberty, and the latter brings slavery.

The Declaration states that *"to secure these rights, governments are instituted among men."* The purpose of civil government is to protect the rights given by God. One of these rights is liberty. Civil Government, according to the Declaration of Independence, is not to *grant* liberty, but *protect* it.

The Declaration reminds us that civil government is to make sure that everyone plays by the same rules. Civil government should not play for either side, but fulfill the role of a referee, only interfering when someone breaks the rules. This ensures and protects the liberty and equality of everyone.

We are to be free to succeed, produce and gain respect by our own character and integrity. We are also free to fail, so we learn from our own mistakes and take responsibility for our own actions. Liberty comes with responsibility.

Slavery is the Opposite of Liberty

Rev. Levi Hart, the pastor of a Congregational church in Preston, Connecticut for 46 years, had many his sermons printed for greater distribution. Since most colonial sermons lasted up to two hours in length, the sermons printed were often 40 to 50 pages in length.

In 1775, Levi Hart, a well-known orator and preacher, stated what many had begun to realize - that liberty was a God-given right, and its opposite, slavery, must be totally abolished if we were to be consistent with our own Declaration.

Hart's point was that slavery was the opposite of liberty. Slavery, by its very nature, is the practice of government-granted privilege. It is the acceptance of the inequality of human beings, for it makes one the legal tyrant over another. In his sermon, he stated:

> "If civil liberty consisteth in acting freely, and without constraint, or fear of punishment, for the public good, and tyranny and slavery are the reverse of this - it followeth, that every one who acts for the general good of society, is entitled to the approbation and assistance of the body. None can justly fall under the frowns of society, but those who prefer some private benefit to the public welfare. And every society which suffers, or even connives at the practice, in any of its members, of taking away the liberty or property of those who have done nothing against the public interest, connives at injustice, and is so far guilty of tyranny and oppression.
>
> "Of all the enjoyments of the present life, that of liberty is the most precious and valuable, and a state of slavery the most gloomy to the generous mind - to enslave men, therefore, who have not forfeited their liberty, is a most attrocious violation of one of the first laws of nature, it is utterly inconsistent with the fundamental principle and chief bond of union by which society originally was, and all free societies every ought to be formed. I mean that of a general union for the common good, by which every individual is secure of public approbation so long as he acts for the public welfare."[277]

Levi Hart's clarification on the meaning of liberty understood at the time of our founding is critical. Any restraint upon an individual's liberty is a form of punishment, for it is to enact lawful justice. This is why the slave trade as well as the practice of slavery was so inconsistent with the Declaration of Independence. It punished individuals under the disguise of protecting them in their best interest.

And while all of us would agree that the abolishing of slavery was a good thing, do we re-create it when we punish people with restraints before they have done anything wrong? We need to hear the Levi Hart's of our past as they sound forth the trumpet call of consistency in relation to the origin of American liberty.

Favoritism, whether it be positive (such as special privileges) or negative (such as punishing people through regulation before they have done anything wrong), is the practice of *slavery*.

Just prior to the Civil War, John Stuart Mill, from England, wrote his famous essay on *Liberty*. He reminded all of Europe, as well as the United States, that the meaning of liberty was the freedom to practice self-restraint.

Liberty was not being practiced when you get punished before you do something wrong just in case you might think of doing it. That was why America's great sin of slavery (punishing a race of people when they had done nothing wrong) had to be dealt with at the bar of God's justice during the Civil War. Mill wrote:

> The object of this Essay is to assert one very simple principle... that principle is, that the sole end for which mankind are warranted, individually or collectively, in interfering with the liberty of action of any of their number, is self-protection. That the only purpose for which power can be rightfully exercised over any member of a civilized community, against his will, is to prevent harm to others. His own good, either physical or moral, is not a sufficient warrant. He cannot rightfully be compelled to do or forbear because it will be better for him to do so, because it will make him happier, because, in the opinions of others, to do so would be wise, or even right. These are good reasons for remonstrating with him, or reasoning with him, or persuading him, or entreating him, but not for compelling him, or visiting him with any evil in case he do otherwise.
>
> To justify that, the conduct from which it is desired to deter him, must be calculated to produce evil to some one else. The

only part of the conduct of any one, for which he is amenable to society, is that which concerns others. In the part which merely concerns himself, his independence is, of right, absolute. Over himself, over his own body and mind, the individual is sovereign."[278]

Mill reminds us again of the meaning of liberty. It is freedom to choose. It is the freedom to produce. It is the freedom to think and come to your own conclusions. It is freedom to disagree and debate. It is also freedom to be responsible for your own actions, and have to face the consequences of improper decisions. It is the freedom to fail when what you produce no one else wants to buy.

We cannot force others to pay for our mistakes because it is not fair that we failed. That is asking to be a slave. Justice is when the rules stay the same for everyone. Liberty is the freedom to choose to help your neighbor who is hurting or simply needs a friend. Either we are free to do these things, or we need the government to do them for us or require us to do them.

Patriot's Day was based on true American Liberty

Patriot's Day commemorates the battle of Lexington that took place early on the morning of April 19, 1775. The day was first dubbed "Patriot's Day" in 1894. The town of Lexington was established by the Parish of Cambridge Farms in 1713.

However, the ideological and historic origin of this holiday has its roots in the practice of calling public days of fasting and prayer and the role of the militia from the Pilgrims.[279]

The Bible instructs God's people to inspire ecclesiastical and civil leaders to call public days of fasting and prayer when facing tyranny or a rising tide of iniquity.[280] Why? These are open declarations before God and one another that whenever we face such challenges, we must first radically surrender more deeply to God in our hearts to successfully resist evil.[281] God has designed His church, the *Ecclesia,* to exercise the heart of kingdom government by taking responsibility for preserving liberty.[282]

As students of the Bible, the Pilgrims, when facing major challenges, called days of fasting and prayer. Derek Prince, after visiting with John Talcott in Plymouth at the 350th anniversary of the arrival of the Pilgrims in 1970, studying their writings, wrote,

> One distinctive practice employed by the pilgrims to achieve their spiritual goals was that of united, public prayer and fasting.[283]

Built on the theology of the Pilgrims and Puritans, New England called special days of prayer and fasting to preserve a sensitive conscience. They were regional, beyond a single congregation.

By their very nature, they demanded a depth of unity among believers since though they were called by ecclesiastical and civil leaders, and often there were holidays where work was suspended, but prayer and fasting were voluntary.

Initially, the Pilgrim's harvest festival of 1621, their fast and Thanksgiving-day in 1623, and subsequent special days of prayer and fasting were sporadic and not annual. Historian Thomas Lechford noted as much in 1867 when he wrote, "There are days of fasting, thanksgiving and prayers upon occasions but no holy days, except the Sunday."[284] The only initial "holiday" was the weekly sabbath on Sunday.

It was on April 19, 1694, (note the day), that the Massachusetts State Legislature (General Court) called the first *annual* prayer and fast day. It was called to repent for the travesty of the Salem Witch Trials of 1692. These "trials" violated Biblical due process of being innocent until proven guilty and unlawfully took the life, liberty, and property of many innocent church members and citizens.[285]

Annual public days of fasting, humiliation, and prayer continued for two hundred years until 1894. There would be over 300 such days called in New England alone by either civil or church leaders by 1820![286] David Barton writes:

> Proclamations for days of prayer and thanksgiving like that of Massachusetts, with corresponding sermons, were not unusual. Civil governments on the state and local level had proclaimed over 1,000 days of prayer and thanksgiving or prayer and fasting during the 150 years of colonization. Americans would continue these regular public proclamations throughout the Revolutionary War, the establishment of the constitutional republic, and for well over 100 years.[287]

From the initial conflict with King George III and with the British Parliament in 1760, public days of fasting and prayer intensified. Christianity and Biblical ideas so permeated the clergy and their congregations that the response was immediate and heart-felt. It appeared that God was allowing the focal point of conflict to come to Lexington, and as historian George Bancroft wrote;

> Their names are had in grateful remembrance, and the expanding millions of their countrymen renew and multiply

> their praise from generation to generation. They fulfilled their duty not from the accidental impulse of the moment; their action was the slowly ripened fruit of Providence and of time.[288]

For many years, and specifically from 1765-1775, the Clergy in the Colonies preached that the Scriptures taught the doctrine of the lower magistrate, and that direct rebellion was a sin. Thus, colonial public officials sought to *first go to prayer and fasting, avoid conflict, appeal to England for a redress of grievances, constitutionally boycott* (the Boston Tea Party), and only as a last resort, *stand and take up arms in their own self-defense.*[289]

In every case, they sought reconciliation with Britain. The Pastors were clear that the only justification to use force against British soldiers was if they were commanded to fire first. Only a defensive war was just in the eyes of God, otherwise, He would be their adversary.

In 1775 Lexington had about 700 inhabitants, most of whom were members of the one church on the green. They all knew each other, were in covenant together, understanding the connection between the gospel of the kingdom preached by their pastor Jonas Clark for 20 years, and the fruit of religious and civil liberty in their village.[290]

It was Clark's home that hid John Hancock and Samuel Adams from the British who were sent to arrest them that morning of April 19. When asked whether his men would fight, Clark responded, "I have trained them for this very hour!"[291]

What did he mean? How could you possibly train a congregation for a conflict like this? First, he had trained them that God was Sovereign, and no human government can thus make such a claim. Second, he had trained them to understand that liberty was governed by law. The only form of resistance that is Biblical is through the lower magistrate.

Their pastor had helped inspire the creation of the Continental Congress in 1774 so that their resistance to Britain would be approved by God and "under the law."

Remember, it was the Continental Congress, in June of 1775 (a result of Lexington and Concord,) that said it was time to consider taking up arms in self-defense. Also, in 1776, it was the Continental Congress that wrote the Declaration, not the people.

But most importantly, Clark had trained his congregation in *radical submission to the Sovereign purposes of God so that their hearts would be surrendered and their conscience tender when their lives may be demanded of them.* From reformers such as Calvin, personal self-defense as well as a nation defending itself had been articulated as an act of love.

So, this was no lawless band that stood on the green early that morning of April 19. Captain Parker, a deacon in Clark's church, told the militia that morning; "Stand your ground. Don't fire unless fired upon, but if they want to have a war, let it begin here."[292]

The deacon boards were responsible for storing extra ammunition in the basement of the church. John Parker was 46 years old that morning and had been with Pastor Clark since 1755. He was deathly ill with tuberculosis and would die that fall.

There were about 45 family units represented on the Green that Wednesday morning. At 5 AM on April 19, about 77 of the Lexington "training band" responded to the drumming of 16-year-old William Diamond and 18-year-old fifer Jonathan Harrington. The 144 enlisted men in the Lexington militia had taken this oath:

> We trust in God, that should the state of our affairs require it, we shall be ready to sacrifice our estates and everything dear in life, yea, and life itself, in support of the common cause.[293]

I want each of you to ponder this moment if you can. You are summoned to the green and surrounded by the men and boys of the families you worship with every Sunday.

John Buckman, 31, who owns and runs Buckman Tavern, where many of you have been waiting since 2 AM, stands with his relatives Amos and Isaac Muzzey (also 31). Isaac would be shot in the back leaving the Green.

The Munroe descendants' number 25, or 32% of the militia on the green. William, great grandson of one of the founders of Lexington in 1713, is the Orderly Sergeant under Captain Parker. Robert, age 63, is the flag bearer and a veteran of the French and Indian war. He stands in the front row on the green facing the British. The Munroe tavern, the family business, would be used by the British as a field hospital and nearly burned to the ground in revenge.

Jonas Parker, who had married into the Munroe clan, was 53 years old. He was affectionately known as the "wrestler" of Lexington. On Sunday afternoons when the church would gather on the lawn for lunch, he would carry as many children as possible on his back, shoulders and in his arms.

Known as the strongest man in town, he stood in the front facing the British, having told those in the church that if this day ever came, he would never turn from facing a British bayonet. He kept his word, returned fire after being fired upon, but was bayonetted while reloading, never leaving the Green.

And Prince Estabrook, African American slave, 34 years old, adopted into the Munroe family by reason of his owner. He enlisted in the militia, fighting for freedom he did not yet have, and would be wounded that morning. As a result of the Declaration, he was emancipated and would die at 90.

The Harrington clan had intermarried with the Munroe's, and there were nine Harrington's on the Green that morning. Caleb, 24, was killed, shot in the back, as he ran out of the church, for the British knew that ammunition was stored there. Jonathan Jr., at 30 years of age, was also shot in the back as he left the Green, crawling to the door of his home, and dying in the arms of his wife Ruth of nine years. His young son was probably watching from the upper window.

Then there is Pastor Jonas Clark, standing on the road with his Bible in his hand, encouraging you with his presence. You have a huge respect for him, for though he is the pastor of your church, he has been the shepherd of your town.

He was described by Theodore Gilman in 1911 in this way; "he nerved the arms of the fighters, he informed the minds of legislators, and he unfolded the principles of equity and righteousness on which the contest for independence was based."[294]

He drafted instructions adopted by his town meeting to resist the Stamp Act of 1765. He addressed the Ancient and Honorable Artillery in 1768 about the need to defend liberty. He authored the state papers of Lexington, and due to his long tenure as pastor in Lexington, he addressed the new State Legislature of Massachusetts in 1781 with an election sermon for the new State Constitution.[295]

Most importantly, he taught the individuals and families for twenty years to be restrained from within and through the personal practice of prayer and fasting to ask God for the grace to be governed within at a time when you are tempted to act lawlessly. You are on the green, deliberately leaving the road to Concord free and clear, and your stance is at ease.

You are not to initiate a war. But the British stop, load and prime their guns, and come off the road toward the militia on the Green. Pastor Clark and Captain Parker would spend hours proving to the world that the British fired first.[296] In fact, individuals who witnessed the events early on that Wednesday morning would be deposed, proving their case.

Facing 700 or more British soldiers, the nerves of the militia must have been on edge, being only a tenth as large in numbers. The Regulars run toward you, with loaded guns, and are swearing in your face. It takes amazing restraint to follow Captain Parker's orders and the oath you've taken. You nervously wait, and then Captain Parker gives the order to disperse "but to take care of yourself."

The British demand you lay down your arms, but this would be laying down your rights. You join those who turn to go, some running off the Green chased by the British, and then you hear a gun go off – a British commander screams, "fire, by God, fire!" and many are shot in the back.

Providentially, there were two prayer and fast days called in mid-April 1775 – of course, few would know this at the time;

> **On April 15, 1775...** the Massachusetts Provincial Congress, led by John Hancock, declared: "In circumstances dark as these, it becomes us, as men and Christians, to reflect that, whilst every prudent measure should be taken to ward off the impending judgments...the 11th of May next be set apart as a Day of Public Humiliation, Fasting and Prayer...to confess the sins...to implore the Forgiveness of all our Transgression."

> **On April 19, 1775**, in another Proclamation of a Day of Fasting and Prayer, Connecticut Governor Jonathan Trumbull beseeched that: "God would graciously pour out His Holy Spirit on us to bring us to a thorough repentance and effectual reformation that our iniquities may not be our ruin; that He would restore, preserve and secure the liberties of this and all the other British American colonies, and make the land a mountain of Holiness, and habitation of righteousness forever."[297]

The colonial clergy, including Pastor Clark, had as their first response to tyranny a call to submit to God, remembering that He allows difficulty to mature His church. He rehearsed these sentiments in his anniversary sermon on April 19, 1776;

> However unjust, or cruel the oppressor, and those that thirst for blood may be, in contriving and carrying into execution their wicked, oppressive, or bloody designs, they are no other than instruments in providence and the rod in the hand of the great Governor of the world, for the reproof and correction of His people.[298]
>
> Clark goes on to make his most critical point saying; "However unjust our sufferings may be from man; yet, when we realize the hand of God, the great wise Governor of the world, as concerned herein, silence and submission is our indispensable duty, and no murmur, or complaint ought every to be heard, but we reverence and in humility it becomes us to bow before the Lord…
>
> (He will) bring good out of evil… by the over-ruling hand of Providence… There is no just ground to suppose, that it would have ever entered the heart of Americans, to have desired a dissolution of so happy a connection with the Mother-

> Country, or to have sought independence of Britain, had they not been urged, and even forced upon such an expedient, by measures of oppression and violence, and the shedding of innocent blood...[299]

Today's church may recoil at such a theology, but as the church goes, so goes the nation. The prayer and fast day called by the Continental Congress after Lexington and Concord prayed for King George III:

> "...to forgive our iniquities, to remove our present calamities, to avert those desolating judgments, with which we are threatened, and to bless our rightful sovereign, King George the third... That virtue and true religion may revive and flourish throughout our land; And that all America may soon behold a gracious interposition of Heaven."[300]

But when the churches in New England no longer passionately adhered to the gospel of the kingdom, it was natural that in 1855 some began to discuss doing away with the public fast days. On May 31, 1892, various religious leaders petitioned the Legislature officially to abolish them.

Why? The rising notion was that the civil government was "secular" and the church "religious." Separation of church and state had become isolation of God from government.

Public officials will eventually be a reflection of the church. On March 16, 1894, Governor Greenhalge signed a bill into law "to abolish Fast Day and to make the Nineteenth Day of April a Legal Holiday." Patriots Day was thus the replacement for the Fast Day.

But Greenhalge declared on April 11;

> It may well be called Patriot's Day... Let the day be dedicated, then, to solemn, religious, and patriotic services... especially our gratitude to Almighty God, who crowned the heroic struggles of the founders and preservers of our country with victory and peace.[301]

Though Patriot's day may appear to replace the public fast day, it is merely the external result of such prayers and repentance. The degree to which the church demonstrates humility and self-restraint (often through prayer and often fasting) is the degree to which we will have liberty. In essence, *prayer and fasting is internal, and true patriotism is external.*

Without prayer, patriotism is simply reduced to nationalism (and idolatry). So let us recover the root principle of submitting our hearts to God, especially when He allows evil to appear to triumph. Today, we are in a war of words. Information and misinformation abound, but discerning the truth is critical.

It is important for believers to recognize that the deeper the cross goes within our heart, the more we recognize that He is Sovereignt and we are not. Our pride must die deeper depths, and our humility must the mark of our preparation. As Americans, we must recognize our reverence for God as our Creator goes a long way toward gaining His protection.

We may not stand on a green in the shadow of our church with a musket in hand. But who knows, God may, in His Providence, put us in the place of having to make the momentous decision to *stand our ground* in the battle of information and truth in our day; being unwilling to yield to deception. We may not know the outcome or whether He will cause some of us to pay the dearest price, our own lives, for the sake of future generations.

One thing is certain, the more we deal with the darkness and depravity of our own hearts by consciously submitting to God and the cross of Christ, the more prepared we might be for such a spotlight in the face of evil. It is only in this way that we will see a greater measure of His Kingdom coming and His will being done "on earth as it is in heaven."[302] May the Church of today learn lessons from the Church in Lexington in 1775, and restore the true meaning of liberty under law!

Leading Idea – Liberty described as unalienable in the Declaration reflects the law of liberty whose foundation is self-restraint, even in the midst of evil and tyranny.

Chapter 11

THE PURSUIT OF HAPPINESS

*We hold these truths to be self-evident, that all men are created equal, and are endowed by their Creator with certain unalienable rights, that among these are Life, Liberty, and **the Pursuit of Happiness***

Be fruitful and multiply; fill the earth and subdue it. – Genesis 1:28

Before we look at the phrase "pursuit of happiness" in our Declaration, we must deal with what the Bible says about private property, for after all, the Bible was the book consulted most by all those considered founders of our nation.[303]

The Right to Pursue Happiness
is based on the Stewardship of Private Property

The three great God-given rights given to individuals, with their accompanying responsibilities, are life (be fruitful and multiply), liberty (to fill the earth creatively), and property (to subdue the earth). God tells us to take dominion of the earth. The Hebrew words *rahdah* means to reign or to rule. Author Gary Amos writes:

> It shares the stem of the Latin noun dominium, meaning property or lordship over possessions and lands… Translators used the word dominion in part because it accurately reflects the Biblical idea that property, an attribute of lordship, was given to man before the Fall into sin and is part of the original law of nature.[304]

God owns all, yet empowers mankind (male and female), as stewards over his creation.[305] Inherent in this understanding is the concept of private property. To steward means there are boundaries that define responsibility.

The first piece of real estate given to men and women to steward in the history of the world was the Garden of Eden. Since Adam and Eve failed in their stewardship, eating of the forbidden tree, sin entered creation, and they lost the garden.

We learn from the garden of Eden that the problem of sin is not first in society, but in the heart of men and women. Any nation that does not focus on how to tame the internal will have little success in bringing order out of chaos. As we have already discussed, stewardship of property is both internal and external.

We have the responsibility of stewarding our hearts and conscience (internal knowledge of right and wrong). God holds us accountable for both spheres of stewardship. Adam and Eve did not guard their conscience, and as a result, lost their external property as well.

The sixth commandment, *"thou shalt not steal"* is meaningless without the premise of private ownership. The tenth commandment *"thou shalt not covet"* is meaningless if the internal property of the conscience – that is – religious liberty, does not exist.[306] It becomes clear that the God of the Bible (Judeo-Christian) *empowers individual wealth,* whereas the religion of Statism empowers government wealth.

So, what does the phrase *pursuit of happiness* in the Declaration have to do with the right and responsibility of internal and external property? Thomas Jefferson was the penman of the Declaration,[307] and scholars agree that he took the poetic phrase "pursuit of happiness" from George Mason's *Virginia Declaration of Rights* ratified June 12, 1776. That document stated that,

> The enjoyment of life and liberty, with the means of acquiring and possessing property, and pursuing and obtaining happiness and safety.[308]

Four years later John Adams, penman of the Massachusetts State Constitution, ratified in 1780, stated similarly;

> All men (have)… unalienable rights; among which (are)… the right of enjoying and defending their lives and liberties; that of acquiring, possessing, and protecting property; in fine, that of seeking and obtaining their safety and happiness.[309]

In the classical sense, "happiness" as it was used in 1776, means to be "blessed" like the Beatitudes of Jesus. It is determined by, "whether man pleases God and is blessed in this life."[310] We can conclude that the phrase "pursuit of happiness" meant the responsibility of individuals to possess and protect private property in a conscientious way.

Furthermore, we can conclude that individuals, according to the Declaration, have the right to *pursue* happiness in acquiring and stewarding property. No where in the Bible or the Declaration are we told that we have a *right* to happiness itself.

The Bible and Property Rights

I believe that the Bible is the premiere source of wisdom on any topic. We might say it is the *theology of everything.* A Biblical theology of property rights could include the fact that God created the earth, and as Psalm 24:1 states, "The earth is the Lord's, and all its fullness, the world and those who dwell therein."

Psalm 115:16 states, "The heaven, even the heavens, are the Lord's, but the earth He has given to the children of men." If God owns the earth, as well as what it produces, He determines how it should be stewarded, and He has given men and women that responsibility.

The Tithe and the Tax

God's Law designated voluntary tithes to finance the church's role for the sanctuary, (Levites or ministers, including Christian education), the festive conferences (a second 10%), and the poor (10% every three years); a total of 23 and a third%![311]

The Bible indicates that for liberty in any area to thrive, the State cannot be the ultimate sovereign, it must be limited. How people privately manage their voluntary tithes (and charitable work) will determine proportionately the size of the State under which they live.

The tithe is voluntary, the tax is not. *The more we give privately on our own, including tithes, the less the State will need to forcefully tax its citizens.* This is premised on how the church and others in a community voluntarily reach out to those in need.[312] Historically it can be proven that charitable institutions doing volunteer work help the poor and needy at a far higher percentage than governments can ever do.

The only civil tax approved of by God in the Bible was the poll or head tax. It was the same amount for all regardless of income; small enough so the poor could pay and did not punish the wealthy just for being prosperous.[313] The benefits of a poll (head) tax are many and include:

- Being non-discriminatory – it did demean those who were poor, they had to pay something. It also did not penalize those that were wealthy. It did incentivize neighbors who had wealth to help those who were in need to pay their tax.

- It was paid in precious metals (gold/silver). This means the economic base was in a commodity and thus it naturally curbed inflation. In today's money, the average Israelite 20 years old and up paid about $550 a year.

- It restrained the size of government. One of the greatest catalysts for expanding a government is going to war without just cause just as Samuel warned Israel when they wanted a King (see 1st Samuel 8). *A poll tax can help avoid a "warfare state."*
- It restrained the scope of government. One of the largest areas of a bloated civil government are life-time pensions for those in power as well as a corrupted source of money laundering regardless of true need. *A poll tax can help avoid a "welfare state."*

In the Bible there was no property tax, no income tax, no inheritance tax, and the year of Jubilee restored land to its original owner every 50 years![314] Furthermore, when Jesus fulfilled the year of Jubilee, He abolished all forms of ancient chattel slavery!

Now, through the influence of the gospel and the liberating of the individual from the bondage of sin within, religious and civil liberty are available to any nation! Ancient Israel was the only nation chosen by God, but all nations can now choose Him through the confession of her laws.

True property rights as well as the responsibility of stewardship begins internally in the heart. This is the unique nature of Christianity. Proverbs 4:23 states "Keep thy heart with all diligence, for out of it are the issues of life."

The heart is a form of internal property to be stewarded to insure good behavior. Jesus spoke of the heart (conscience) as property as well, "A good man out of the good treasure of his heart brings forth good things, and an evil man out of the evil treasure brings forth evil things.[315]

Allodial and Feudal Property

Noah Webster, in his famous 1828 Dictionary, identified with clarity the private ownership of land as drawn from the Bible, contrasting *allodial* and *feudal.*

- ***ALLO'DIAL***, *adjective. Pertaining to allodium; freehold; free of rent or service; held independence of a lord paramount; opposed to feudal.* (Note: the derivation from the Latin root allodium – the total property of a person)

- ***FEU'DAL***, *adjective. 1. Pertaining to feuds, fiefs or fees; as feudal rights or services; feudal tenures.*[316]

There are thus two types of ownership, allodial and feudal. William Blackstone, the English Jurist, wrote that private property is "every man's own land, which he possesseth merely in his own right, without owing any rent or service to any superior."[317] Black's Law Dictionary affirms the distinction between the two as well.[318]

If all this was inherently in the Law of God for ancient Israel, why would any nation give up such freedom? Israel chose a King "to be like the other nations"[319], and by doing so, she chose a different form of government, and land was now taxed. When a nation centralizes its civil government, it often embraces a feudal concept of land where the state is the ultimate sovereign.

The Declaration and Private Property

There are some who deny that this Biblical concept of private property laid the foundation for the Declaration, for it is assumed that the Greeks and Romans, or philosophers of the Renaissance, laid the ideological foundations for America. But neither Greeks nor Romans embraced the idea of a Creator, thus all rights were granted by the State.

As such, they were, in essence, alienable privileges.[320] Furthermore, the "social contract" theory of the Renaissance held that land is held in common, under the dictates of the State for the good of the community.

One of the first nations that did embrace the Biblical notion of private property as an unalienable right was Great Britain. King Alfred set up a government modeled after ancient Israel in 890 AD.[321]

This included a *republic (representative government), justice with restitution and the rule of law, trial by jury, private charity for the poor, and generational transfer of land, all while respecting the private property of the individual and family!*[322]

Where did the Saxons of King Alfred's day get these ingredients? As we discussed in chapter 4, they got it from Christianity after their conversion! St. Patrick's book *Liber Ex Lege Moisi* in the 5th century paved the way for the transformation of British Isles![323] The Magna Charta of 1215 sought to restore King Alfred's England since the Norman Conquest of 1066 had imposed feudal land ownership. The Saxons went underground to preserve their liberties.

By the time of the writing of our Declaration, England was functioning according to the Crown "Prerogative" rather than their ancient liberties.[324] But from 1660 to 1760, the clergy of the Colonies preached the Biblical ideas of liberty and unalienable rights given by their Creator, including private property. The writers of our Declaration, influenced by the clergy, articulated the Biblical roots of self-government by consent and land ownership.

John Locke, reasoning from the Bible, wrote that one of the major reasons civil governments are formed is to protect their "Lives, Liberties and Estates...."[325] James Madison, "father of the Constitution," summarized the Scriptural and historic understanding of internal and external Property:

> Property... In the former sense, a man's land, or merchandise, or money, is called his property. In the latter sense, a man has a property in his opinions and the free exercise of them. He has a property of peculiar value in his religious opinions, and in the profession and practice dictated by them... In a word, as a man is said to have a right to his property, he may be equally said to have a property in his rights.... Conscience is the most sacred of all property.[326]

Madison argues that conscience is <u>the most sacred property</u>, especially our *<u>religious opinions</u>*.

The Significant Role of the Gospel

The gospel, which alerts the individual of the need for regeneration, is the root for all "allodial" property. When one learns they have sinned against God and must repent; surrendering to Christ, they are liberated within, and the process of a Biblically informed conscience begins. At the time of our founding as a nation, it was understood that the King and Parliament were wrong to attempt to force a person to do things against their conscience.

As we have already read, George Mason articulated this, limiting the State's jurisdiction to behavior in The Virginia Declaration of Rights, just prior to the Declaration,

> That religion, or the duty which we owe to our Creator, and the manner of discharging it, can be directed only by reason and conviction, not by force or violence... all men are equally entitled to the free exercise of religion, according to the dictates of conscience.[327]

It follows then, if churches no longer preach the gospel, and people lose sight of the hope they have to be governed by Christ from within, society will no longer defend the conscience as property. We will thus lose, proportionately, our external right to property as well.

The allodial property rights understood at our founding have gradually become known as feudal property owned ultimately by the State. As God recedes in a society, the State takes its place as a "god."

Was land ownership in at the time of the Declaration Allodial?

Noah Webster, in his 1828 Dictionary, (definitions as used at our founding), defined <u>Allodium:</u>

> Freehold estate; land which is the absolute property of the owner; real estate held in absolute independence, without being subject to any rent, service, or acknowledgement of a superior. It is thus opposed to feud. In England, there is no allodial land, all land being held of the king; but in the United States, most lands are allodial.[328]

George Bancroft in his classic 1860 _History of the United States,_ articulated the following:

> Every incident of feudal tenure that would have been a restraint on the possession and transmission of real estate was utterly forbidden... in Massachusetts, all the land was allodial.[329]

Thomas Jefferson, giving instructions to the Continental Congress in 1774, wrote;

> ...an error in the nature of our land holdings... Our Saxon ancestors held their lands, as they did their personal property, in absolute dominion, disencumbered with any superior, answering nearly to the nature of those possessions which the Feudalist term Allodial. William the Norman, first introduced that system generally...
>
> America was not conquered by William the Norman, nor its lands surrendered to him or any of his successors. Possessions there are, undoubtedly, of the Allodial nature... The fictitious principle, that all lands belong originally to the King, they were early persuaded to believe real, and accordingly took grants of their own lands from the Crown... It is time, therefore, for us to lay this matter before his Majesty, and to declare, that he has no right to grant lands of himself.... [330]

No wonder when the British needed large trees for their masts, they sent the King's surveyors into the woods of New Hampshire, marking which ones they wanted. How could they do that on private property? They claimed they all were owned by the King! But the colonists disagreed, and the Pine Tree Riot was the result.[331]

The *Appeal to Heaven Flag,* designed by George Washington for the first six naval vessels in 1775, has a pine tree on it. It is a declaration that trees are private property, and under God, we have a right to steward that property.[332]

It might help to explain the response of the colonists to the 300 British troops, under the command of Col. Leslie arriving at Salem on February 26, 1775. They arrived at Marblehead strategically on a Sunday, knowing the town was in church. They were coming to confiscate their arms.

Providentially, the colonists were alerted in church, and Pastor Barnard, stopping the service, went into the road. Col. Leslie demanded *"who are you and why are you blocking the road?"* He responded, *"I am Pastor Barnard, a minister of peace."*

Col. Leslie ordered the drawbridge to be lowered because the road was the "King's highway", several responded it was "private road" built by colonists. Bernard then offered a solution. Since the British wanted to keep their pride, and the colonists their rights, they agreed that the draw bridge would be lowered, the British would cross, march a few paces, and do an about face, leaving Salem![333]

The Bible was the source of ideas for our Declaration, but also for our Constitution. As the chart indicates below, among the ideas from the Bible placed into the Constitution, two of them were the poll tax and that our monetary system based on precious metals.

When the Constitution was ratified, there was no income tax, property tax or inheritance tax except as leftovers from the British colonial government.

Biblical Ideas Embedded in the original United States Constitution

• 5th Command – Ex. 20:8	• Sunday honored (I.7)
• Exodus 30:11-16	• Poll tax (I.2; I.8)
• Proverbs 11:1	• Metal based currency (I.8)
• Deuteronomy 17:16	• No standing army (I.8)
• Deuteronomy 17:15	• Natural-born Leader (II.1)
• Exodus 18:22	• Appellate justice (III.1)
• Exodus 18:21	• Judges term (III.1)
• Deuteronomy 4:1	• Law & Equity (III.2)
• Deuteronomy 21:2-3	• Justice is Local (IV.2)

From Private Property to Eminent Domain

Today, we think all our property belongs to the State. The Fifth Amendment to our Federal Constitution, however, like all the Bill of Rights, is a giant stop sign to the Federal Government not to interfere with State's rights. The "preamble" stated "Congress shall make no law."

The key phrase from the Fifth Amendment for our consideration is this,

> Nor shall private property be taken for public use, without just compensation.

This has now been re-interpreted, out of context, to mean "eminent domain" or permission to take anything as long as there is an excuse. But you will not find that phrase anywhere in our founding documents. But *you*, as a citizen, have eminent domain, not the government! It is part of the common law.

Justice Clarence Thomas, in *Keto v. City of New London,* June 23, 2005, wrote in his dissent;

> Long ago, William Blackstone wrote that 'the law of the land... postpones even public necessity to the sacred and inviolable rights of private property.'[334]

I agree with theologian R. J. Rushdoony when he writes;

> The doctrine of eminent domain is a basic but unexamined concept of civilization, an idea assumed without question by most people as a necessary evil. A simple definition... (of) the second edition of the Merriam-Webster dictionary... 'That superior dominion of the sovereign power over all the property within the state...' Eminent domain is thus an attribute of ultimate sovereignty, and therefore it is an attribute of divinity.[335]

Let us Remember the Meaning of our Flag

Consider the character qualities of the conscience, depicted in the original "Betsy Ross" flag of 13 stars and stripes. Charles Thomson, secretary of the Continental Congress[336], reported the significance of the colors:

> White signifies purity and innocence, Red, hardiness & valor, and Blue, the color of the Chief signifies vigilance, perseverance & justice.[337]

Let us remind ourselves and teach our children and grandchildren the qualities of purity, innocence, hardiness, valor, vigilance, perseverance and justice. All of these are embedded in the conscience when it is properly trained, beginning in the home.

Without conviction from within, followed by restraint, we have no hope as a nation.

George Washington stated; "Let the 13 stars (the original states) in a circle stand as a new constellation in the heavens."[338] You see, George Washington understood that God had given the United States a calling just as He has done every other nation. Our form of government, source of rights, and originally designed limited government of justice gives hope to others.

These are the character qualities that need restoring in the conscience of our citizens. They should be taught in all our schools, including our colleges, for that is the foundation for proper stewardship of property.

Let us remember that the phrase 'pursuit of happiness' in the Declaration means each of us has a right to pursue the acquisition of alodial property, free and clear of government taxation or interference.

Leading Idea – Protecting private property begins with the stewardship of the conscience so that pursuing happiness is being blessed with the fruit of one's labor

PART FOUR

The Significance of the Declaration

Chapter 12

SELF-PRESERVATION

*That to **secure** these rights, Governments are instituted among Men, deriving their just powers from the **consent** of the governed* – Declaration of Independence

Though the original Declaration has been preserved, and is kept under careful security and guard, rising and falling each day into a bomb-proof vault, it is sad to think that its ideas that gave birth to this nation have not been guarded with nearly the same care and protection.

We now turn our attention to an area of thought virtually neglected and ignored, but most basic – *the doctrine of self-preservation.*

Self-Preservation in the Bible

Edmund Burke, the famous orator and author who stood up for the Colonial cause during the Revolution in England, stated;

> There is but one law for all, namely, the law which governs all law, the law of our Creator, the law of humanity, justice, equity - the law of nature, and of nations.[339]

What is this one law that governs all law, called the law of nature, and also the law of nations. William Blackstone, writing in 1765, a famous jurist of England, and widely read by the founders of America, clearly articulated the definition of this Supreme law that had been understood and accepted for centuries:

> When the Supreme being formed the universe, and created matter out of nothing, he impressed certain principles upon that matter, from which it can never depart, and without which it would cease to be....

> Man, considered as a creature, must necessarily be subject to the laws of his creator, for he is entirely a dependent being.... This will of his maker is called the law of nature. For as God, when he created matter, and endued it with a principle of mobility, established certain rules for the perpetual direction of that motion; so, when he created man, and endued him with freewill to conduct himself in all parts of life, he laid down certain immutable laws of human nature, whereby that freewill is in some degree regulated and restrained, and gave him also the faculty of reason to discover the purport of those laws....
>
> This law of nature, being co-eval with mankind and dictated by God himself, is of course superior in obligation to any other. It is binding over all the globe, in all countries, and at all times: no human laws are of any validity, if contrary to this; and such of them as are valid derive all their force, and all their authority, mediately or immediately, from this original..."[340]

Blackstone goes on to say that because man's reason is blinded by sin and thus he needs an absolute guide in order to understand this law of nature that is binding on everyone. He relates that the Creator of the Universe did not leave man to simply grope about endeavoring to interpret the law of nature.

Instead, God gave him the law of revelation; clear doctrines from which to interpret the laws to which all are bound to obey. He states:

> The doctrines thus delivered we call the revealed or divine law, and they are to be found only in the holy Scriptures.... Upon these two foundations, the law of nature and the law of revelation, depend all human laws; that is to say, no human laws should be suffered to contradict these.[341]

Did the founders believe what Blackstone wrote in the mid 1700's? As we have seen, research has indicated that 34% of the quotes of our founders were taken directly from the Bible, over three times as much as any other source.

Also, other sources quoted by the founders (such as Montesquieu, Blackstone, Locke, Puffendorf, Vattel, etc.) quoted the Bible nearly 60% of the time as their original source for ideas![342] The Bible was certainly a trusted book at the time of our founding, and thus it is important to see if it supports the idea of *self-preservation*.

One of the cornerstones for the belief in the doctrine of self-preservation was the passage in Matthew's gospel, chapter 22, verses 37-40:

> Jesus said unto them, Thou shalt love the Lord thy God with all thy heart, and with all thy soul, and with all thy mind. This is the first and great commandment. And the second is like unto it. Thou shalt love thy neighbor as thyself. On these two commandments hang all the law and the prophets.

We are first obligated to obey God, but we are also commanded to love our neighbor *as we love ourself.* What does this mean? If you spend any quality time at all studying the Bible, you will see that it does not mean either self-idolatry on one hand, or self-annihilation on the other.

The Christian is enjoined to *deny himself* (see Matthew 16:24), not idolize himself. One of the foundational truths of Christianity is that of recognizing that your old life, or self life, *has been crucified with Christ*, and it is His life that now lives within you (see Galatians 2:20). Thus, self-preservation, and in the context above, loving oneself, is certainly not the idolatry of self.

It does not mean self-annihilation either. The Bible indicates that it is natural for a man to cherish his own life (see Ephesians 5:29). The

Bible indicates that each one of us ought to preserve and protect our own family before endeavoring to take care of another, (see 1st Timothy 5:8). We are exhorted to first take care of needs within our own church before endeavoring to reach a community, (see Galatians 6:10).

Are these statements of selfishness? No, they are simply stating priorities. The Bible implies such questions as these: How will you be able to help others if you are not at peace with yourself? If your own home is not governed well, you have less credibility to govern in a church. If one cannot manage his own private affairs, how can he be trusted to manage others' affairs?

We can see this principle playing out practically in politics. Usually someone doesn't run for President that has not governed a State, or large company that has enjoyed some success. Also, one doesn't usually try to become a State governor without the same experience of success in smaller areas.

In Luke 16:11-12, Jesus states:

> If you have not been faithful in the unrighteous mammon, who will commit to your trust the true riches? And if you have not been faithful in what is another man's, who will give you what is your own?

Taking care of our own finances (mammon) and being faithful to set priorities on paying our bills, will speak highly of being prepared through the good use of priorities to inherit true or lasting wealth (especially depicting of our spiritual values).

In like manner, if we cannot take care of what we borrow from another person, who will trust us with more? In other words, the doctrine of self-preservation is the set of priorities that keeps our lives in order so we can help others. If we don't preserve ourselves, we will become dependent on others.

In short, self-preservation is an extension of self-government, where the greatest concentration of government is in the heart of the individual, then the family, church, town and state. Only then will we be able to maintain independence at the national level.

Self-Preservation Identified in the Declaration

When the Declaration speaks of *securing rights,* and doing so *by the consent of the governed,* it speaks of the way our nation was to govern itself. As one individual said to me in Europe, "you folks wanted no taxation without representation, how do you now like taxation with representation?"

The Declaration stated clearly the opposition to having no representation in Parliament, and the reason was simple, *Parliament had overstepped its jurisdiction and ignored the colonial 'parliaments' already designated as places of local self-government.*

Thus, the Declaration of Independence clearly tells us how to preserve our nation's values, freedom and liberty. <u>We must remember that it is our responsibility to be active in self-government and making sure what is done at the town, state and national level is done by consent.</u>

Originating in Biblical law, and then articulated as English common law, Catholic canon law, and finally articulated by philosophers in Europe and America, this idea was clearly understood by the founders. The idea was that everyone, and subsequently each nation, had a right to ***self-identity.***

The right of ***self-government*** is here asserted. Everyone, and subsequently every nation, has the right to govern itself from within. This is an extension of self-preservation. No individual, and certainly no nation, has the right to usurp its jurisdiction and govern another without their consent.

Today, few Americans are involved in their local town, city or state government. Many races go unopposed, and towns that still exercise a form of local self-government have a hard time getting a quorum to do business. This is an example of losing our self-identity or neglecting self-preservation.

The History of Election Day in America

It was one of America's earliest holidays, starting around 1633. Observed annually, shops and schools were closed and everyone, dressed in their finest and gathered in the marketplace. As historian John Wingate Thornton wrote:

> The clergy were generally consulted by the civil authorities; and not infrequently the suggestions from the pulpit, on election days and other special occasions, were enacted into laws. The State was developed out of the Church.[343]

A parade would sometimes form, accompanied by the military, candidates for public office, and the clergy. They would go to the nearby church or meeting-house, pray and hear a sermon whose topics described the Biblical role of civil magistrates. The description of an election day service, once all were seated, is given by Edward Augustus Kendall in the Spring of 1807:

> The pulpit, or, as it is here called, the desk, was filled by three, if not four clergymen; a number which, by its form and dimensions, it was able to accommodate. Of these, one opened in prayer; another delivered a sermon; a third made a concluding prayer, and a fourth pronounced a benediction. Several hymns were sung; and, among others, an occasional one. The total number of singers was between forty and fifty. The sermon, as will be supposed, touched upon matters of government. When all was finished, the procession returned to the state house. The clergy, who walked, were about a hundred in number.[344]

Then, after a picnic lunch on the town green, the freemen who were qualified to vote would do so with often a 100% annual turnout. However, statistics show that as towns grew, but the qualifications for voting were held at a high standard, "the potential voters seemed to vary from about one-sixth to one-fiftieth of the population."[345]

Regardless of the small percentage of those qualified to vote, *they took the responsibility seriously.* Today, unfortunately, even though qualifications for voting are minimal, the number of people that turn out are still a much smaller percentage of those who are registered.

One of the reasons colonial citizens took voting so seriously was because of how precious a responsibility it was, hearing it from the pulpit and from "Election Day Sermons" but also understanding its reflection of the theology of "election" before God.

"You did not choose me, but I chose you" says Jesus in John 15:16 and coupled with the exhortation in Philippians 3:12 *"that I may lay hold of that for which Christ Jesus has also laid hold of me"* the doctrine of Election can be derived.

Each was to choose (elect) the ones perceived that God had chosen. It instantly makes voting a sanctified event before God and an exhortation to exercise one's duty to vote conscientiously based on the qualifications God Himself sets up for civil magistrates.

Thornton adds:

> The annual "Election Sermon" – a perpetual memorial, continued down through the generations from century to century – still bears witness that our fathers ever began their civil year and its responsibilities with an appeal to Heaven, and recognized Christian morality as the only basis of good laws.[346]

Voting in early America took the form of raising one's hand or voicing an assent. In some towns those who voted affirmatively would stand on one side of the room, while those voting in the negative would stand on the opposite side.

The Sheriff, often in charge of elections, would do the counting and discern the winner. Sometimes votes were tallied on a large white cloth for all to see as each individual made their decision. In New England voting tended to be more secret, utilizing the "corn and bean method." One placed corn in the bucket in favor of a candidate, or a bean against![347]

There were at least seven characteristics understood in early America, drawn from the Bible that informed the conscience regarding the casting of votes for a civil servant. These qualifications were frequent topics in Election Day sermons.

Exodus 18:21 – *"provide...such as... fear God, men of truth, hating covetousness"*

1. Fearing God – belief in God and eternal accountability
2. Truth – honest and upright in one's dealing with others
3. Hating covetousness – right motives, unwilling to take bribes and be "bought or sold"

Deuteronomy 1:13 – *"wise men, and understanding, and known among your tribes"*

4. Wisdom – making good judgments in negotiations without violating convictions and values
5. Understanding – practical desire to know the hardships facing people, a compassionate heart
6. Loyal citizen – a citizen of one's country, loyal to the unique values and culture of the nation

2nd Samuel 23:3 – *"He that rules over men must be just..."*

7. Justice – a desire to see that things are made right before God (righteousness) and the law

- Where a candidate stands on the moral issues of righteousness before God

- Where a candidate stands on protection of rights, security, defense, economic liberty, etc.

Justice and the protection of God-given rights is the main purpose of civil government (see Romans 13:1-7 as an example). A civil magistrate was considered a "minister" according to the Bible, to protect the citizen's religious and civil liberty along with their economic choices.[348]

A civil magistrate is also to defend the nation so that it remains independent, maintaining law and order so that it is a good environment for the free spread of the gospel (see 1st Timothy 2:1-5). In voting citizens gave their assent to what they believed to have been God's choice.[349]

There are no perfect candidates and no perfect voters. We vote our *conscience* for the *best* candidate. In a Republic like America, local races are seen as more significant since greater accountability is exercised. It is a travesty that so few people turn out to vote today for local town and state elections, waiting for the media to garner greater participation presidential elections only.

In a democratic republic, *we often get the government we resemble* (but by God's mercy not the one we deserve.) We know we will not get perfect justice on earth, but to refuse to vote is a sin of omission and to vote for corrupt candidates is a sin of commission.

Thus, we must choose the best candidate, (not necessarily a believer), knowing that God chooses, not perfect people, but those who stand for what is right though they may not be perfectly consistent.

Initially, property owners were the ones qualified, or freemen. This was to ensure that people had a vested interest in decisions affecting the land and its stewardship. Puritan New England restricted voting to males who were members of churches.

Over time, it was believed that some of these practices did not portray true equality and were not consistent with the Declaration of Independence. Voting qualifications have become more universal now, so that equality is respected in relation to race and sex.

Citizenship at the State and National levels remain as qualifications in the majority of States along with being at least the age of 18 in today's American society.

Since 1960, however, voting *participation* has changed significantly. The media has replaced the role of the family, church and local business owners as the most influential group getting individuals to perform their duty to vote intelligently.

In recent decades appearance on television and media "sound bites" have replaced an understanding of an individual's stand on their oath to the rule of law – the Constitution. The results have been devastating, with less than 50% of eligible voters participating on Election Day.

Electronic reporting prior to the close of the polls has not helped. The evangelical community is no better, however, with similar percentages of non-involvement. Many are not even registered to vote! *By default, we are allowing a small remnant who may have no interest in the rule of law to determine our future*! It is time to restore the expression of a righteous conscience in voting!

While the neglect of our responsibilities locally will have consequences such as rising taxes and isolation from our neighbors and the community we are to serve, it has larger and more difficult consequences at the national level.

What is the Law of Nations?

We read at the beginning of this chapter from William Blackstone's treatise in 1755; "There is but one law for all, namely, the law which governs all law, the law of our Creator, the law of humanity, justice, equity - the law of nature, and of nations."[350] We have heard of the "laws of nature and nature's God", but what is the "law of nations"

James Wilson, signer of both the Declaration and Constitution, an articulate writer and speaker from Pennsylvania, wrote clearly about the founders' philosophy of the law of nature and nations. The law of nations was simply the law of nature applied to nations, or the laws that apply to individuals being applied to nations internationally.

This code of ethical law among the nations had been reasoned out for several hundred years. Some of the more noteworthy scholars included Hugo Grotius, Samuel Pufendorf, and Emerc de Vattel. Wilson, a master of all three, commented succinctly on our topic of self-preservation:

> A state ought to attend to the preservation of its own existence... When a nation has a right, and is under an obligation to preserve itself and its members; it has, by a necessary consequence, a right to do everything, which, without injuring others, it can do, in order to accomplish and secure those objects...
>
> A nation ought to know itself. It ought to form a just estimate of its own situation, both with regard to itself and to its neighbors. It ought to learn the excellencies, and the blemishes likewise of its own constitution."[351]

Later under the leadership of John Quincy Adams, specific applications of the Law of Nations was applied in the Monroe Doctrine. One of the key principles of America's original foreign policy was "self-determination." A nation had the right, for its own self-preservation, to determine its destiny.[352]

The principle being debated in 1775 and 1776, and with which the colonists wrestled, as Wilson describes at the time, was England's violation of their self-preservation, the long-standing law of nature and law of nations. England would not let them define themselves as Englishmen with the same rights as those in Britain – nor could they have self-determination.

Thus, England violated the colonists *self-identity;* the rights inherent in their own charters.

The *Resolutions of the Stamp Act Congress*, October 19, 1765 stated:

> ...that his majesty's liege subjects in these colonies are entitled to all the inherent rights and privileges of his natural born subjects within the kingdom of Great Britain[353]

The *Declaration and Resolves of the First Continental Congress, October 14, 1774* stated:

> That the inhabitants of the English colonies in North America, by the immutable laws of nature, the principles of the English constitution; and the several charters or compacts, have the following RIGHTS... Resolved, that they are entitled to life, liberty and property; and they have never ceded to any foreign power whatever, a right to dispose of either without their consent. Resolved, that our ancestors, who first settled these colonies, were at the time of their emigration from the mother country, entitled to all the rights, liberties, and immunities of

> free and natural-born subjects, within the realm of England..."[354]

The colonists declared, through their representatives, that they were not allowed to govern themselves. This was an essential right of Englishmen that had been recognized for centuries, and clearly articulated in the *Magna Charta* of 1215, the *Petition of Right* in 1628, and the *English Bill of Rights* in 1689, all of which comprised England's constitution.

The charters of the colonies, upon their inception, had placed them under the King as subjects of England, but constitutionally under their own parliaments which were their respective legislatures in the various colonies.

When the parliament of England exercised jurisdiction over them in taxation, it was unconstitutional, and against their own English charters, as well as their rights and customs and Englishmen. It was, in essence, a violation of their self-preservation.

The colonists declared in their *Resolutions of the Stamp Act Congress*:

> It is inseparably essential to the freedom of a people, and the undoubted rights of Englishmen, that no taxes should be imposed on them, but with their own consent, given personally, or by their representatives... that the only representatives of the people of these colonies, are persons chosen therein by themselves; and that no taxes ever have been, or can be constitutionally imposed on them, but by their respective legislatures..."[355]

The *Declaration and Resolves of the First Continental Congress* declared:

> That the foundation of English liberty, and of all free government, is a right in the people to participate in their legislative council: and as the English colonists are not represented, and from their local and other circumstances, cannot properly be represented in the British parliament, they are entitled to a free and exclusive power of legislation in their several provincial legislatures..."[356]

The Colonies' debated their rights with the Crown for ten years, from 1765 to 1775. At stake was their right to self-preservation. If they said nothing, they would commit self-annihilation, or colonial suicide. In effect they would have been saying they were less than men, never mind less than Englishmen.

They were accused of being greedy, selfish, when insisting on their rights. Mr. Grenville, a member of parliament in the 1760's, stated in parliament that the Colonial resistance to the Stamp Act was foolish because the colonies were

> Children of their planting, and were nourished by their indulgence, and protected by their arms, until they had grown up to a good degree of strength and opulence.[357]

To which Colonel Barre rose and correctly replied:

> 'Children planted by your care!' No - your oppression planted them in America! They fled from your tyranny into a then uncultivated land, where they were exposed to all the hardships to which human nature is liable. 'They nourished by your indulgence!' No - they grew by your neglect! When you began to care about them, that care was exercised in sending persons to rule over them, whose behavior, on many occasions, has caused the blood of those sons of liberty to boil

> within them! 'They protected by your arms!' They have nobly taken up arms in your defence; have exerted their valour amidst their constant and laborious industry, for the defence of a country, the interior of which, while its frontiers were drenched in blood, has yielded all its little savings to your enlargement.[358]

In the *Declaration and Resolves of the First Continental Congress* in 1774, a further statement of defense against the usurpation of property was also given. It was declared that

> The keeping of a standing army in several of these colonies, in time of peace, without the consent of the legislature of that colony, in which such army is kept, is against law.[359]

This included the quartering of troops in peacetime, as well as unlawful searches and seizures without a warrant, and the rejection of the trial by a jury of one's local peers.

The culmination of these acts of tyranny from England was for the Colonists to declare the lawfulness of their last resort, the *armed defense of their rights and property.* Their *self-identity* had been challenged, and their liberty of *self-government* had been taken away.

With hostilities breaking out at Lexington and Concord, they realized they must either lay down their privately owned arms as demanded by the British or declare the lawful use of force in defense of their rights.

After careful deliberation, they chose the latter, and this position was made known through the publication of the *Declaration of the Causes and Necessity of Taking Up Arms*, written July 6, 1775.[360]

As we can see, one of the underlying premises for declaring independence was the right of the Colonies to ***self-preservation.*** The right to life, both individually and as a nation, is the right to preserve one's own identity. The right to liberty, individually and nationally, is the right of self-government. The right to property, or the pursuit of happiness, individually and nationally, is the right to protect that property through self-defense.

Listen to the warning of Patrick Henry in his reaction to the Resolutions of the Stamp Act Congress of 1764 that set the stage for the colonies' defense of their self-preservation:

> This (the document), brought on the war which finally separated the two countries and gave independence to ours. Whether this will prove a blessing or a curse, will depend upon the use our people make of the blessings, which a gracious God has bestowed upon us. If they are wise, they will be great and happy. If they are of a contrary character, they will be miserable. Righteousness alone can exalt them as a nation. Reader! Whoever thou art, remember this, and in thy sphere practice virtue thyself, and encourage it in others."[361]

Let us restore a sense of self-preservation, beginning in our individual hearts and lives, our homes, neighborhoods, towns, cities and states. Only then can we begin to see a change at the national level and restore the independence of our nation.

Leading Idea – Self-preservation is preparing to bless others by preserving our own integrity and resources, from local elections to foreign policy

Chapter 13

THE DECLARATION AND THE GREAT RESET

That whenever any Form of Government becomes destructive of these ends, it is the Right of the People to alter or to ***abolish it, and to institute new Government****, laying its foundation on such principles and organizing its powers in such form, as to them shall seem most likely to effect their Safety and Happiness.*
Declaration of Independence

The Declaration was a Great Reset

At the time of its signing, the Declaration of Independence was a "great reset."[362] As we have noted several times, most governments in recorded history prior to 1776 recognized few rights for people.[363] Our Declaration, however, proclaimed;

> We hold these truths to be self-evident, that all men are created equal, that they are endowed by their Creator with certain unalienable Rights, that among these are Life, Liberty and the pursuit of Happiness.

This presupposition that the God of the Bible gave unalienable rights directly to the individual shook the world!

Most nations were formed by war and conquest, but our birthright in 1776 was the defense of an idea! In essence, in context of Britain's attempt to force us under Parliament and "Crown Prerogative" (government-granted privileges) at the time, we reset our nation back to a critical premise from the book of Genesis, "…God created man in His own image."[364]

The Declaration was thus a reset, a unique restoration of the premise that God created mankind (male and female) in His image. A corollary of this premise is that though created in God's image, every man, woman and child has natural tendancies toward sin and evil. Sin is defined as the transgression of the law of God.

It should not surpise anyone today that individuals are capable of all kinds of evil unless restrained by law - thus no one can be trusted with total power. Though fallen, each individual has some capacity to understand self-evident truth, or what we call common grace.[365]

The fallenness of man produced the inequities existing at the time of the Declaration (such as racial slavery and the inequalities between male and female) but it was this premise of self-evident truth that would gradually and progressively check such a tendency for power and allow equal rights to be more consistently practiced.

In other words, the Declaration reset us on a firm foundation of a philosophy of government drawn from the pages of the Bible ahead of where we were living at the time. But this premise was not new, for it had been brought to America a century and a half earlier by the Pilgrims.

Another corollary of this premise is that God has given each individual rights of life, liberty and property, but it is our responsibility to protect and preserve them. Though many nations were inspired to revolt against their governments in the wake of our 1776 Declaration, few laid their revolution on the foundation of the idea of God-given rights.

The most notable example was the French Revolution of 1789. As we have seen, it declared freedom and equality, but without God, enthroning atheism and the power of the State as its foundation. The result? A worse tyranny under Napoleon than the one they revolted against.

Freedom and liberty from the hand of God as our Creator continued to inspire us for generations. But we now face a new reset which threatens to return to the old order that reacted so negatively to our Declaration back in 1776.

A New Global Reset on the Old Principles of Tyranny

An Israeli historian, Noah Yuval Harari, who lectures at the Hebrew University of Jerusalem and has written several books, has become the "voice of the Great Reset." He is an advisor at the World Economic Forum.

What is this "great reset" you might ask? *It is the resetting of Western Civilization in general, and the United States in particular, on a foundation of control by an external power other than the precepts of Biblical Christianity expressed in the Declaration.*

In his book, *Sapiens: A Brief History of Humankind* Harari writes,

> As far as we can tell, from a purely scientific viewpoint, human life has absolutely no meaning. Humans are the outcome of blind evolutionary processes that operate without goal or purpose.[366]

The Declaration of Independence rested on the fact that life does have meaning and a clear purpose. This is because the premise was rooted in biblical precepts. Our culture today is unfortunately ripe for the time Isaiah warned about in the 8th century BC;

> Woe to those who call evil good, and good evil; Who put darkness for light, and light for darkness; Who put bitter for sweet, and sweet for bitter![367]

Harari's re-write of the Declaration's pivotal phrase is telling.

> We hold these truths to be self-evident, that all men evolved differently, that they are born with certain mutable characteristics, and that among these are life and the pursuit of happiness.

He articulates his premise when he writes:

> We believe in a particular order not because it is objectively true, but because believing in it enables us to cooperate effectively and forge a better society;[368]

This is indeed a great reset, but one that will take us into the darkness of tyranny. It trades the objective truth of God giving unalienable rights to individuals for a select few (the powerful) to determine the extent of government granted privileges to forge a "better" society. Also, note that though life and happiness are listed, liberty is left out entirely.

In case you are wondering whether I am reading into Mr. Harari's worldview and his opposition to Christianity, he states his premises clearly when he writes,

> The Americans got the idea of equality from Christianity, which argues that every person has a divinely created soul, and that all souls are equal before God. However, if we do not believe in the Christian myths about God, creation and souls, what does it mean that all people are 'equal'? Evolution is based on difference, not on equality.[369]

No longer should we hold objective (absolute) truth. Instead, we are to hold to the shifting sand of popular opinion, most importantly the opinions of those who wish to be in control. It will return us to state sovereignty as opposed to the sovereignty of God.

Our God-given rights (whether life, liberty or property) that make us equal before the law would now become "mutable" and changeable characteristics as determined by others. It is a return to divisive tactics of the few to control the many and bring us all to the supposed goal of the Great Reset where we will "own nothing but be happy."[370]

To reject the truth of the Declaration that God has given us unalienable rights – life, liberty and property – is to reject the God of Christianity. The only other choice is the law of man which takes the varied forms of socialism, communism, fascism, racism and division. We must understand that in our day, across the globe, there are those who wish to put God on trial.

Yet, what kind of life will we have if we do so? Will rights be protected? Will they be defined? Are we better off with Critical Race Theory and social justice initiatives replacing the roots of Biblical justice that have historically been the foundation of the common law and American jurisprudence? Let's try something new, we are told.

Jesus gave us the way to discern ideas when he said,

> Beware of false prophets, who come to you in sheep's clothing, but inwardly they are ravenous wolves. You will know them by their fruits.[371]

There is not much new in the "great reset" except some new vocabulary. We have had nearly 5,000 years of recorded history to check out whether seeds of man-made "mutable" laws produce trees of liberty.

We have seen what a rejection of God produces. If you take just the last century, we have seen communism, Marxism, fascism, socialism and a host of other theories which are the same poison wrapped in new terminology produce tyranny, control and a loss of life, health and wealth. I would say that does not qualify these ideas for the hall of fame; but it does qualify them for the hall of shame!

The Original Meaning of the Declaration

But if you could go with me to peruse the many orations on the 4th of July that were given, especially in the first 50 years following the Declaration, you would find a different common theme.

You would find a rehearsal of the fact that America is unique, not because we are Americans, but because of the ideology defended in 1776; rights are unalienable because they come from God.

You would find all kinds of orators, from all kinds of backgrounds, from those that signed the document, to historians who rehearsed the primary sources, rehearsing the same ideas. Why?

They all feared there may come a day when the average American no longer understands where they liberty comes from and thus could be deceived when people come peddling "new ideas" that are really old ones of tyranny and control.

Take, for example, George Bancroft's fourth of July oration at Northampton, Massachusetts. Bancroft was a respected historian of the first order. A professor of Greek at Harvard, and a poet, he would later become one of the most celebrated authors of American history with his *History of the United States* published in 1834.

At only 26 years of age, on the Jubilee anniversary of the Declaration in 1826, he began his oration with this simple sentence – *"Our act of celebration begins with God."* He then goes on to say:

> To the eternal Providence on which states depend, and by whose infinite mercy they are prospered, the nation brings its

> homage and the tribute of its gratitude. From the omnipotent Power, who dwells in the unclouded serenity of Being without variableness – or shadow of change, we proceed as if from the Fountain of good – the Author of hope – the Source of order and justice – now that we assembly to commemorate the revolution, the independence, and the advancement of our country![372]

By honoring the God who gives rights, we appeal to a higher power than the whims of men and their desire for power and control! And we also agree with Professor Harari on this point, that Christianity is the author of equal rights. However, equality did not mean all people were the same, but that each one has the same objective value before God!

Ignorance leads to Global Statism

Most of the contemporary leaders in 1776 that opposed the Declaration did not understand unalienable rights or equality any more than those who oppose them today. The common form of government was centralized monarchy in 1776.

Today, ignorance tends to reign and thus many are unfamiliar with unalienable rights given by God and thus a basis for the rule of law. Governments, by unlawfully grabbing power, can take away those rights, but God still recognizes them.

You can foolishly give them away – if you murder, you have lost the right to life. If you steal, you lose some of your property. And if you take away another's freedom with no cause, you will lose yours.

The Great Reset is nothing new, for it is a return to the old order of government control from those in power and limited freedom of the individual all in the name of doing "what is best for us." The assumption is obvious – the common person is not smart enough, informed enough or astute enough to make decisions about their economic and health choices.

Let me give you an example. Harari's assertion that human happiness is merely chemical and biological, and that for our own good we must yield the imaginary human rights of the past to what is best for the community, is also nothing new.

In order to help my high school students understand the theory of communism and why the Bolsheviks overthrew the Russian monarchy in 1918, sending that nation into a darkness of 70 years that cost more than 70 million people their lives, I read to them from the 1936 leadership manual titled *Psychopolitics;* or what has come to be known as *The Soviet Art of Brainwashing.*

I think I need to read just a few quotes to let you know that as Ecclesiastes says, *"there is nothing new under the sun."*[373]

> Basically, man is an animal. He is an animal which has been given a civilized veneer... Man is already a colonial aggregation of cells, and to consider him an individual would be an error... sickness could be considered to be a disloyalty to the remaining organisms on the part of one organism... the individual must be directed from without to accomplish his exercise, education, and work... Goals of the State should be formulated by the State for the obedience and concurrence of the individuals within that State... On the subject of obedience itself, the most optimum obedience is unthinking obedience... Having no independent will of his own, Man is easily handled by stimulus-response mechanisms.[374]

I'll never forget the day that one of my students stopped me at this point and after raising her hand declared; *"if they really believe what they say about human beings, have they forgotten they are one also?*

If we have no will, no soul, and should be controlled, what about them?"

Yes, that is the irony of it all. Those who wish to force upon us a "great reset" for our own good don't disclose that they aren't part of the process. In effect, today's "great reset" is only for the benefit of those who are in control or who want to be in control.

It is for their good, not ours. But I digress, Goff goes on to disclose what he was taught in the 1930's as a communist activist here in the United States. The "enemy" of such a takeover is listed as scholars, youth leaders, athletes and above all – Christianity. The manual states:

> Nations which have high ethical tone are difficult to conquer… what they usually call spiritual integrity cannot be violated by duress… The first target is Man, himself. He must be degraded from a spiritual being to an animalistic reaction pattern…. The lying mechanisms of Christianity lead men to foolishly brave deeds… Thus, there must be no standing belief in the church, and the power of the church must be denied at every hand.[375]

There should be no shock that religious liberty is under assault today. People who believe in God, and in absolute values that don't change over time or within cultures and various races, are an obstacle to such a great reset.

A True Reset back to the Premises of the Declaration

Hillsdale College President Larry Arnn thinks that many of our challenges can be solved by going back to the original meaning of the Declaration. He writes,

> To "commemorate" is to remember together. It is time for us Americans to do that. It is not so hard. The Declaration is

> 1,350 words long. Its majesty is matched by its pithiness. It contains an entire account of the source, the purpose, and the manner of the government of the United States. In these three things is to be found the solution to our problems.[376]

In essence, we must return to the fundamental premises of the Declaration. What is more important, however, is to return, or more appropriately, *turn* to the God of the Declaration and that would be a reset in the right direction!

The greatest obstacle that all of those who wish to control us is not just the founding document of our nation, or the fact that more people are waking up. The greatest obstacle the globalist faces is God Himself!

I declare to you that there is a Great Reset coming that those who hunger for power should fear. It is the one God is orchestrating. Psalm 2 is one of the most amazing prophetic views of the perennial desire for leaders of nations to take over the world.

Verse 2 declares the fact that *"the kings of the earth set themselves, and the rulers take counsel together, against the Lord and against His anointed."* This has happened in every age, throughout history.

But the response of our Sovereign God is in verse 4; *"He who sits I the heavens shall laugh"* depicts the fact that it is folly to think that their great reset will be ultimately successful.

The Psalm tells us that nations are Christ's inheritance, and the Bible tells us that God is moving all of history toward the interests of His kingdom, though we just need to live long enough to see the victory o this come to pass. Darkness loses when each of us shines the light of truth, faith and confidence in its face.

My advice to those orchestrating what they think is the final Great Reset comes from verses 10-12;

> Be wise, O kings; be instructed, you judges of the earth, Serve the Lord with fear, and rejoice with trembling. Kiss the Son, lest He be angry, and you perish in the way, when His wrath is kindled but a little.

The solution is to pray for all those in authority – whoever they are – including those at the World Economic Forum, that they would realize who God is, repent, and "kiss the Son" so to speak.

The same solution is given to each of us as well. In fact, according to the Bible, *the repentance of the believer who has not lived as Christ wanted them to live, and the Church that has sat all too often on the sidelines with no strategy to pray for or and influence their culture, will be the precursor to seeing a world-wide awakening among the nations and its rulers.*

If you as a reader are willing, you can be part of God's Great Reset, putting our lives back on the foundation of our Creator and His Son, the Redeemer of mankind. If you don't know Him, you can ask His forgiveness, receive Christ as Lord, and you will be a part of the great advance of His Kingdom on earth "as it is in heaven."[377]

The modern Great Reset is no conspiracy theory. The leaders could not be clearer and are not hiding their goals or philosophy, and most important, they are serious. It is all out in plain view.

Just as the Declaration produced a reset in world history in 1776, an affirmation of the truth of the document, drawn from the Bible, can redirect our nation and other nations from the bottom-up. The God of the Bible is more serious than those in Davos, Switzerland.

Consider Dennis Peacocke's premise:

> This economic crisis is not a mere 'recession.' It is the beginning of a global reset which God will powerfully use to

> reorder systems, reinsert within the Christian community a love for people and the desire to serve and influence them with the values and principles of God's kingdom, and reveal a whole new set of global leaders who respond to a more fully integrated social order.[378]

God is working to *"set up a kingdom which shall never be destroyed."*[379] Though we may face difficult times ahead, like our Founders we must *mutually pledge to each other our Lives, our Fortunes, and our sacred Honor once again.*

Leading Idea – Today's global Reset offers centralized control as a solution to the nations, but that has been a failure throughout history. The nations need to reset on the ideas, drawn from the Bible, that empower individuals to demonstrate that unalienable rights and self-evident truth are what set people free.

Chapter 14

TYRANNY: UNFIT TO BE THE RULER OF A FREE PEOPLE

A Prince whose character is thus marked by every act which may define a Tyrant, is ***unfit to be the ruler of a free people.*** – Declaration of Independence

Introduction

You know that those who are considered rulers over the Gentiles lord it over them, and their great ones exercise authority over them. Yet it shall not be so among you; but whoever desires to become great among you shall be your servant. – Mark 10:42-43

As Jesus began the journey to Jerusalem to lay down His life on the cross in eternal payment for our sin, two of Jesus' disciples, James and John, inspired by their mother Salome, came to Jesus and said, *Teacher, we want You to do for us whatever we ask.* Jesus responded, *what do you want Me to do for you?*

Their response was, *Grant us that we may sit, one on Your right hand and the other on Your left, in Your glory.* Jesus told them that they did not understand what they were asking. Favors of royalty had no place in the Kingdom of God.[380]

Jesus clearly laid down two contrasting philosophies of government.[381] The word Gentile simply meant those desiring wisdom without consulting the revelation of God and the Scriptures laid down for our instruction. History has confirmed that the idea of earthly lordship, top-down elitist rule based on a sense of superiority, privilege and wealth, dominate most governments.[382]

As we have seen, the Bible appears to have been consulted more frequently than any other source among those called founders[383], and thus we have this unique phrase culminating at least 31 charges of tyranny against King George III that comprises over two-thirds of the Declaration.

So, we might ask, what does the Bible have to say about tyranny, and how was it defined at the time of our founding?

The Biblical Origin and Definition of Tyranny

Genesis 3:1-5 records the narrative in the garden of Eden between Satan, who is in the form of a serpent, and Eve. The serpent says, *has God indeed said, 'you shall not eat of every tree in the garden'?*

Eve responds to this doubt about the standard given by God by saying *we may eat the fruit of the trees of the garden; but of the fruit of the tree which is in the midst of the garden, you shall not eat it, nor shall you touch it, lest you die.*

God did not say you couldn't touch it, so she exaggerated it for effect. To which the serpent replied, *you will not surely die,* denying the consequences. Then the serpent concludes his argument by saying if she disobeys, *you will be like God, knowing good and evil.*

Though enticing, the result of Eve and Adam's disobedience would be determining for themselves what is right and wrong, but the result would be a loss of their liberty under the control of evil. This pattern has been repeated throughout history for every tyrant who has wanted control:

1. Exaggerate the problem beyond its reality
2. Claim the right to disobey what is just and then deny the consequences

3. Determine your own set of rules and lose control of your life to a budding tyrant

The results of this pattern, documented in Genesis 3, was *Adam blaming Eve, and Eve blaming the serpent* but with neither taking responsibility for their actions. *Pain and suffering would now accompany daily life,* and doing what is right would often be contested and require sacrifice.

Finally, *a desire to control one another* would begin a cycle of tyranny over others. The Hebrew word used for "rule" in Genesis 3:16 gives the meaning of utilizing manipulation and force in order to make the subject like the ruler.[384] That, my friends, is tyranny.

Thus, the Bible defines tyranny as sin arising from the heart to obtain an ***unjust control of another by manipulation or force***. Since tyranny begins within, there must be a change of heart to restrict its spread. Though it must be resisted, it can never be eradicated by external force alone.

It has been demonstrated historically that whenever we reject the notion of a Sovereign God and His rules, we accept a replacement, and most often it is civil government that assumes the role of God.

Noah Webster's 1828 dictionary is the standard for defining words at the time of our nation's formation. Also, he based his definitions on the meanings of their roots as they are use in Scripture. His definition of tyranny was:

> Arbitrary or despotic exercise of power; the exercise of power over subjects and others with a rigor not authorized by law or justice, or not requisite for the purposes of government. Hence tyranny is often synonymous with cruelty and oppression.[385]

But before we see how tyranny was addressed in the Declaration, we need to look at an unfamiliar founder, John Hancock.

John Hancock and Rev. Samuel Cooper

John Hancock, born in 1737, was 24 years of age when he witnessed the coronation of King George III (who was 22) on September 22, 1761, in London. Catherine, George's wife, was 17. Hancock had graduated from Harvard in 1754 and was on a business trip for his Uncle Thomas.

He was there when George II died in 1760, and he wrote his Uncle he hoped the delay of his return would be such that he could witness the coronation "as it is the grandest thing I shall ever meet with."[386]

The six hour coronation ceremony cost more than 6 million dollars in our money today. The crowded streets, crowns, regalia, with 42 singers, 105 musicians, feasts and fireworks, was a true celebration of royalty.[387]

In 1764, at 27 years of age, after the death of his Uncle, Hancock became one of the wealthiest men in America when he inherited the "House of Hancock." John was born in Braintree, but by the time he was 7 in 1744, he lost his father, the Rev. John Hancock.

Though raised in a godly home, his interests were in finances, so his mother sent him to live with his wealthy Uncle in Boston. After his death he moved into the Hancock mansion on top of Beacon Hill. Harlow Unger writes:

> Hancock loved his wealth. He reveled in it. He adored all the foppish trappings it could buy: the fashionable wigs, frilled shirts, silk and velvet jackets and breeches – and the shoes

> with silver or gold buckles that sparkled as he strode along Boston's Hancock Wharf... He owned Beacon Hill. His land covered its crest, and his was the only house there.[388]

Two individuals, separated by an ocean, who both loved wealth and prestige, were destined to be in direct opposition to one another on July 4, 1776. Two-thirds of the Declaration called King George III a tyrant, and the largest signature, three times bigger than any other, was that of John Hancock.[389]

John, who loved his wealth and the natural monopoly of trade in Boston, also wanted to avoid politics due to its negative consequences. John had married Dorothy Quincy the year before, so why would he put himself into conflict with the King of England?

What would cause him to be willing to lose two ships, the *Lydia* and *Liberty* to the British who asserted the Writs of Assistance of searching and seizing property without a warrant? What would have caused one who always wanted to avoid politics to become a Selectman and Legislator in the General Court, standing for liberty at the cost of his wealth?

The Sugar Act of 1764 was certainly a catalyst,[390] for this arbitrary tax would cost him dearly. However, I believe the real root for Hancock's maturing convictions to stand for liberty against tyranny was his faith.

I believe Hancock's change of demeanor was because of his rekindled faith. Samuel Cooper of Brattles Church in Boston was John Hancock's pastor. In his church were also Sam Adams, John Adams, James Bowdoin and Dr. Joseph Warren. Cooper virtually shepherded some of the most influential patriots of his time.[391]

He regularly corresponded with Benjamin Franklin on the events taking place in Boston.[392] Phyllis Wheatley, the African American poet whose freedom was purchased by members of the Old South Church in Boston, wrote a poetic eulogy of him upon his death in 1783.[393]

Cooper preached the inaugural sermon at the commencement of the Massachusetts State Constitution on October 25, 1780. Its title began *A Sermon preached before his Excellency John Hancock, Esq; Governour.* The admiration for which John Hancock had toward his Pastor is evident for the choice made on such an occasion.

The content of Cooper's sermon on this occasion is also interesting. It was likely a summary of the ideas and ideals Cooper had preached to his parishioners during the tumultuous time of the American Revolution.

> The characteristics of tyranny throughout history and particularly recorded in the Old Testament of the Bible;
>
> The unique government of Israel before she chose a King – a "republic" where the people are sovereign and function well only to the degree that they are virtuous before God; (please note that we were never considered a democracy – direct rule by the people – but always a representative republic under the rule of law)
>
> How the Massachusetts Constitution has been established on the independence of America and the nature of ancient Israel – a true republic.[394]

Samuel Cooper corresponded with Thomas Pownall[395], who was the former governor of the Province of Massachusetts Bay from 1757-1760. Pownhall also sat in the House of Commons from 1767 to 1780 in England. He opposed Parliamentary attempts to unjustly tax the colonists. He also supported the Revolutionary War and later advocated for trade barriers to be removed to have the newly established United States operate as an equal among the nations.

> John Adams wrote that "Pownall was the most constitutional and national Governor, in my opinion, who ever represented the crown in this province."[396]

Cooper was also able to preach the gospel without the political trappings that would turn the church into a revolutionary machine. He understood that the gospel works from within and tempers the believer in such a way as to be a servant rather than one who constantly attempts to find fault and bring change from without.

He had both Loyalists and Patriots sitting in his pews. He worked tirelessly for unity and peace among factions that differed. He worked for harmony by advocating civility of manners in disputes.

Of course, as the pressure intensified in the middle 1770's, those who left for England caused the congregation to be a unified target for British vengeance. Hancock, a man desiring to be out of the spotlight, was thrust on the stage at the perfect time with patriotic convictions inspired from his Pastor.

The convictions and resurging faith of John Hancock became apparent as President of the Continental Congress. In his Proclamation for a day of Fasting and Prayer on April 15, 1775, only a few days before the battles of Lexington and Concord, he wrote:

> In circumstances as Dark as these… All confidence must be withheld from the Means we use; and reposed only on that GOD who rules in the Armies of Heaven, and without whose Blessing the best human Counsels are but Foolishness – and all created Power Vanity. It is the Happiness of His Church that, when the Powers of Earth and Hell combine against it… that the Throne of Grace is of the easiest access and its Appeal thither is graciously invited by the Father of Mercies, who has assured it, that when his Children ask Bread he will not give them a Stone…[397]

The teachings of the Bible from Rev. Cooper, especially the teachings against tyranny, inspired John Hancock. The Bible warns against tyranny in ways that parallel the five ingredients of tyranny mentioned in the Declaration.

The 31 clauses of the Declaration written against the dictatorial conduct of King George III constitute two thirds of the entire document. They fall into five categories that were addressed consistently by the clergy and founders; (1) obstruction of justice, (2) military political bullying, (3) abuse of power, (4) chaos to increase control, and (5) the promotion of corruption.[398]

The Declaration is a Document Resisting Tyranny

(1) Obstruction of Justice

- Isaiah 1:17 - *seek justice, rebuke the oppressor, defend the fatherless, plead for the widow.*
- Clause 8 of the charges against King George III state that King George III *has obstructed the Administration of Justice by refusing his Assent to Laws for establishing Judiciary Powers.* In other words, the King refused to

acknowledge local courts, wanting justices dependent on the Crown in both their opinions and salary.

- William Blackstone wrote in 1753; "to bereave a man of life, or by violence to confiscate his estate, without accusation or trial, would be so gross and notorious an act of despotism, as must at once convey the alarm of tyranny throughout the whole kingdom."[399]

(2) <u>Military bullying of Civil Power</u>

- 1st Timothy 2:1-2 declares the purpose of civil law is to help us *lead a quiet and peaceable life.* This means civil powers are limited. They don't regulate the details of our lives.

- Clause 12 of the charges state; *He has affected to render the Military independent of and superior to the Civil Power.*

- Political bullying has been a trait of tyranny for centuries. The Military, if not checked by civil law, becomes a force for tyranny. Tyrannical forces can maintain their grip on a society by constantly advocating for war, because that brings them funds through their monopoly on warfare's industrial complex.

- James Madison wrote in 1795; "Of all the enemies to public liberty, war is, perhaps, the most to be dreaded, for it comprises and develops the germ of every other… no nation could preserve its freedom in the midst of continual warfare."[400]

(3) <u>Abuse of Power</u>

- Proverbs 29:2 states *when the righteous are in authority, the people rejoice, but when a wicked man rules, the people groan.*

- Clause 18 charges the King with *depriving us, in many cases, of the benefit of Trial by Jury.* The common law Jury was considered an essential part of liberty and government intervention to prevent a citizen of trying both the law and face was considered tyranny.
- John Locke writes in 1690 that tyranny is "the exercise of power beyond right."[401]

(4) Using chaos to gain Control

- Genesis 4:7 declares that God told Cain, *sin lies at the door, it's desire is for you, but you are to rule over it.* That sin was anger and violence. We can be angry and not sin, (Ephesians 4:26,) but the key is to conquer the rage on the inside so it can't be used to bring you under greater control.
- Clause 27 charges the King with *domestic insurrections among us.* A wicked ruler utilizes or promotes (through financing) chaos for an excuse to gain tyrannical control.
- Alexander Hamilton wrote in 1788; "Are not popular assemblies frequently subject to the impulses of rage, resentment, jealousy, avarice... and violent propensities? ...governed by a few individuals?"[402] His point was that government was necessary to bring order. A government that permits chaos for its own ends is obviously tyrannical.

(5) The Promotion of Corruption

- Isaiah 5:20 states; *Woe to those who call evil good, and good evil; who put darkness for light...* and Isaiah 10:1-2 says; *Woe to those who decree unrighteous decrees, who write misfortune, which they have prescribed to rob the needy of justice... that widows may be their prey.* These exhortations were given by the prophet to expose corruption in their civil leaders and call for justice!

- Clause 28 makes the charge that, *In every stage of these Oppressions We have Petitioned for Redress in the most humble terms: Our repeated Petitions have been answered only by repeated injury.* Corruption is a problem of the heart and character and thus when it is promoted and not just tolerated, it is tyranny.

- Baron de Montesquieu wrote in 1730; "No tyranny is more cruel than that which is practiced in the shadow of the law and with the trappings of justice."[403] When justice is corrupted the process appears to be there, but corruption pre-determines the outcome.

As part of Clause 28, nearing the conclusion of the final exposure of corruption in the Crown, Declaration stated, *A Prince, whose character is thus marked by every act which may define a Tyrant, is unfit to be the ruler of a free people!*

Today, governments around the world should take notice that in the Declaration, it is not just King George III, but any system that is characterized by such ingredients that is unfit to rule a people who know their rights are God-given and wish to defend their liberties!

The Declaration is a Document of Interposition

So, what does one do if such a tyranny is imposed upon them? What did the Colonists do? Well, first, they understood clearly the "doctrine of the lower magistrate" taught to them by the clergy and firmly rooted in Biblical theology.[404]

Essentially, the doctrine asserts that *direct resistance to a higher power is rebellion in the eyes of God.* Therefore, *only the lawfully instituted civil official (lower or lesser magistrate) can stand between the people and a tyrannical higher power.*

In Biblical terms, this means that one must demonstrate submission to God and His law more than merely resistance to evil (as James 4:7 exhorts).[405]

In the next chapter, we will illustrate the meaning and application of interposition as it is expressed in the Declaration.

On March 5, 1774, in his oration commemorating the Boston Massacre, John Hancock spoke at the Old South Church in Boston. Early in his oration he stated:

> Some boast of being friends to government; I am a friend to righteous government, to a government founded upon the principles of reason and justice; but I glory in publicly avowing my eternal enmity to tyranny.

He then closed with these words:

> I have the most animating confidence that the present noble struggle for liberty will terminate gloriously for America… …let us humbly commit our righteous cause to the great Lord of the universe, who loveth righteousness and hateth iniquity. And having secured the approbation of our hearts, by a faithful and unwearied discharge of our duty to our country, let us joyfully leave our concerns in the hands of him who raiseth up and putteth down the empires and kingdoms of the world as he pleases; and with cheerful submission to his sovereign will devoutly say, "Although the fig-tree shall not blossom, neither shall fruit be in the vines; the labor of the olive shall fail, and the field shall yield no meat; the flock shall be cut off from the fold, and there shall be no herd in the stalls; yet we will rejoice

in the Lord, we will joy in the God of our salvation.[406] (Habakkuk 3:17-18)

Leading Idea – It is time for the Nations to realize that tyranny, regardless of the color of its clothing, is unfit for people who long to be free. The Declaration of Independence offers an historic testimony in this regard.

Chapter 15

THE CAUSES AND NECESSITY OF TAKING UP ARMS

In every stage of these Oppressions We have ***Petitioned for Redress*** *in the most humble terms: Our repeated Petitions have been answered only by repeated injury.* – Declaration of Independence

The Biblical Doctrine of Interposition

Robert Robinson, in 1752, at 17 years old, came with a gang of his friends to disrupt a tent meeting in England where the revival preacher George Whitfield was speaking. But hearing Whitefield declare from Matthew 3:7: *"O generation of vipers, who hath warned you to flee from the wrath to come?"*

He later wrote that those "words sunk into my heart like lead in the water. I wept… and for weeks, I could think of little else." In 1755, only three years later, he found "full and free forgiveness through the precious blood of Jesus Christ."[407]

With a transformed heart, he would write the famous hymn, Come Thou Font of Every Blessing in 1757 when he was only 22 years old. One verse told his life story, "Jesus sought me when a stranger, wand'ring from the fold of God. He to rescue me from danger, interposed His precious blood."

The blood of Jesus had rescued his sinful heart by coming between the wrath of God on sin and his certain destiny in hell. Christianity calls this theology the ***atonement.*** It is the seminal definition of the word **interposition** – to come between two at odds to bring reconciliation.

God is Sovereign – perfectly righteous and holy (separate from sin). We are crippled by sin, desiring to set our own rules and get our own way. Even the good things we do cannot offset the guilt for our heart finds no rest in the pride of self. So what is the answer? It is the interposition of the blood of Jesus.

Jesus, the God-man, died on the cross – taking our punishment, but satisfying the requirements of the law to forgive sin – the shedding of blood. Just as Robert Robinson found out, Jesus is our mediator, and the one whose blood interposes between us (and our sin) and the holiness of God.

It is virtually impossible to fully understand the century of development of the ideas of liberty embraced by colonial America by the time of the Revolution without an understanding of biblical theology. Why would that be so, you might ask?

This is because the actions of the people and civil magistrates of that time were largely inspired and directed by the clergy who preached and applied their biblical theology to every area of life – and almost all the magistrates went to their churches.

The Historic Context of the Declaration of Independence

Today we often celebrate and interpret the Declaration of Independence outside its theological and historic context. But there would not have been a Declaration of Independence if there had not been *A Declaration Setting forth the Causes and Necessity of Their Taking Up Arms.*

Ratified by the Second Continental Congress on July 6, 1775, a full year before the more familiar one, it sets forth the reasoning for full separation while still hoping for reconciliation. It stands between the First Continental Congress of 1774 and the third one in 1776 which produced the Declaration of Independence.

Americans need to understand this document for it is based upon the *doctrine of interposition,* an application of biblical atonement which became the theological foundation for the lawful resistance to tyranny. It was understood that *lawful resistance* was approved by God, but lawless rebellion makes God our adversary.

Though distant from most American thought today, the *theological roots of interposition*, "the process of coming between a tyrant and the people," was clearly in the minds of civil magistrates at the time *because* of what they heard from the pulpits of colonial America.

Theologians of the Reformation faced this question, *when civil government in general and kings in particular overstep their bounds, how does God want us to respond?*

The Bible teaches that tyranny is *the unjust control of another through the means of manipulation or force* (Genesis 3).[408] As we noted in the last chapter, Noah Webster's 1828 dictionary, based on biblical words, defined tyranny as;

> Arbitrary or despotic exercise of power; the exercise of power over subjects and others with a rigor not authorized by law or justice, or not requisite for the purposes of government. Hence tyranny is often synonymous with cruelty and oppression.[409]

So how should people respond? Some proposed passivity, that martyrdom was the only option. Others proposed rebellion, taking the law into your own hands against established authority. But neither of these options were satisfactory responses according to the Bible.

The first option had been witnessed when martyrs died for their faith. Though an option for individuals facing no other option, there must also be a further way to lawfully resist evil. The second option of anarchy produced unfavorable results as well, for it lead to greater tyranny and control – the latter end being worse than the initial injustice.

The answer from the Bible to these opposite positions is the doctrine of interposition or the *lawful process by which one resists injustice and tyrannical government.*

It was in concert with the *Magna Charta* of 1215 when the Barons forced King John to sign this seminal document of rights.[410] It was articulated in John Calvin's *doctrine of the lower magistrate*. He wrote in 1536 that when a lower magistrate *connives* or conducts *nefarious perfidy* (wicked deception pretending to do the right thing but siding with tyranny),

> They fraudulently betray the liberty of the people, while knowing that, by the ordinance of God, they are its appointed guardians.[411]

After thousands of French Huguenots were slaughtered for their faith in 1572, *Vindiciae Contra Tyrannos* (Defense of liberty against tyrants) was written by Junius Brutus in 1579. He dealt with the question of *whether subjects are bound and ought to obey princes, if they command that which is against the law of God.*

He also dealt with the issue of *whether it be lawful to resist a prince who doth infringe the law of God; by whom, how, and how far it is lawful.* His conclusion? Only magistrates, inferior to the king, representing the people, can and should lawfully resist the King's tyrannical duties.[412]

Another example is Pastor Samuel Rutherford who wrote *Lex Rex* (the law is king) in 1644. Since God models his covenant with the people and the King, the King is answerable to God should he become a tyrant. Government is not our father, and neither is the king, the King is not above the law, ruling "of the people."

Thus, the steps of resistance to tyranny are to appeal, mediate through lower magisgtrates, flee, and as a last resort, defend oneself in resisting by force.[413] His views were consonant with John Knox, from Scotland, who wrote forcefully in the late 1500's in his stand against the practices of Queen Mary.

What were the sentiments of these and many other theologians of the Reformation? *Resistance to tyrannical rule is only permissible* *under* *authority – in personal self-defense or under the lesser magistrate.*

In other words, individuals must demonstrate submission at lower levels of authority to resist lawfully at higher levels. As we have noted, *interposition* was not a new concept. It was articulated clearly in the Old Testament and affirmed by Jesus in the New Testament.

When Egypt commanded Hebrew midwives to kill their male children, they interposed themselves, deceived the government, and *"God dealt well with the midwives"* (Exodus 1:20). When Queen Athaliah seized the throne of Judah by force and overstepped her jurisdiction, Jehoiada interposed as a lower magistrate and restrained her (2nd Kings 11).

When Uzziah as a civil magistrate attempted to burn incense as a priest, overstepping his bounds, Azariah interposed as a lower magistrate, and God struck Uzziah with leprosy (2nd Chr. 26). In all these cases, *fearing God meant demonstrating submission to Him under law so that we might not resist tyranny directly, incurring His wrath.*[414]

Resistance to tyrants through mediation – the lower magistrate – is a process, a progression of smaller steps until the last resort is reached, and even then, only entered cautiously and under counsel and under authority.

Consider the historic example of the German Magdeburg Confession of 1550. The magistrates of Magdeburg applied the biblical theology of making a distinction between "patient forbearance" of injustice and defensive resistance to outright tyranny. They, in fact, articulated four levels of injustice in their application of the doctrine of interposition.

The first might be called *not excessively atrocious.* All people and hence governments "have their own vices and sins, by which, either knowingly or wantonly, they sometimes do injuries, not excessively atrocious, but remediable."[415] To revolt at such offenses would be to cause unnecessary strife.

The second might be called *the lawless tyrant.* These were "atrocious and notorious injuries."[416] This is where a magistrate violates his own oath. These more atrocious violations of the law most people will understand that they are not bound to obey and are willing to suffer the consequences.

The third level might be called *the coercive tyrant.* This means that individuals can no longer tolerate such injustice. The line here can be difficult and requires "accurate and true judgment."[417] Here interposition is required, and the lesser magistrate should stand up to the higher official who is abusing the law.

Finally, the fourth can be called *the persecutor of God.*

> Tyrants begin to be so made that they persecute with guile and arms, not so much the persons of the inferior magistrates and their subjects, as their right itself... and that they persecute God, the author of right in persons, not by any sudden and momentary fury, but with a deliberate and persistent attempt to destroy good works for all posterity.[418]

The Declaration of Independence identifies at least five areas of tyranny practiced by King George II as seen in the previous chapter. If we identify them by clauses, they could be put in the following categories:

- Cl 1-10 - <u>Obstruction of justice</u> – oppression of people
- Cl 11-15 - <u>Military use of Civil law</u> – political bullying
- Cl 16-22 - <u>Abuse of power</u> – unlawful control beyond one's jurisdiction (authority)
- Cl 23-27 - <u>Inciting violence/chaos</u> - to gain more control...
- Cl 28-31 - <u>Promotion of corruption</u> – evil is now classified as good[419]

Steps for Lawful Resistance in Interposition

The Declaration stated that:

> Prudence, indeed, will dictate that Governments long established should not be changed for light and transient causes; and accordingly all experience hath shown, that mankind are more disposed to suffer, while evils are sufferable, than to right themselves by abolishing the forms to which they are accustomed. But when a long train of abuses and usurpations, pursuing invariably the same Object evinces a design to reduce them under absolute Despotism, it is their right, it is their duty, to throw off such Government, and to

> provide new Guards for their future security. Such has been the patient sufferance of these Colonies; and such is now the necessity which constrains them to alter their former Systems of Government.

It is obvious from the historic example of Magdeburg that those who wrote this Confession were attempting to inspire the lesser magistrate to stand up to the tyrant so that the people would not have to do so directly and violate the Scriptures.

Rebellion produces anarchy which in turn brings upon a people greater evil. This is seen throughout history. Thus, both the theology of resistance, and the civil examples that followed it, reveal a *slow progression* of resistance, with the last and final resort a call to arms.

James 4:7 depicts this truth by stating "Submit to God. Resist the devil and he will flee from you." The degree to which we walk in humility, acknowledging God, submitting our temper, emotions, and will under His control, is the degree to which we will be able to resist evil properly without bringing a great evil upon us as a result.

Remember, ***the attitude and actions we pursue to correct a wrong will also be used to enact the solution.***

The greatest fear of the clergy and the civil magistrates who attended their churches was that if the colonies did not resist lawfully, the Supreme Sovereign of the Universe would be their adversary. There is no way you can win a war when God opposes you!

It is interesting to note that just prior to the document under examination, George Washington was appointed by the same Continental Congress to be the commander of the Army. What many do not realize but is relevant to the point we are making, is the humility in which Washington accepted this position. He stated:

> Mr. President, Tho' I am truly sensible of the high Honour done me in this Appointment, yet I feel great distress, from a consciousness that my abilities & Military experience may not

> be equal to the extensive & important Trust: However, as the Congress desire it I will enter upon the momentous duty, & exert every power I Possess In their service & for the Support of the glorious Cause: I beg they will accept my most cordial thanks for this distinguished testimony of their Approbation… As to pay, Sir, I beg leave to Assure the Congress that as no pecuniary consideration could have tempted me to have accepted this Arduous employment at the expense of my domestic ease & happi⟨ness⟩ I do not wish to make any profit from it: I will keep an exact Account of my expenses.. that is all I desire.[420]

Note that Washington agreed to serve only *under* the civil authority of Congress. Humility is a trait that rarely exists unless the individual sees themselves under the Sovereignty of God. Washington's humility was coupled with his fear and respect for God. His initial orders to the newly formed army, interestingly on July 4, 1775, were discipline and honor of God:

> It is required and expected that exact discipline be observed, and due Subordination prevail thro' the whole Army, as a Failure in these most essential points must necessarily produce extreme Hazard, Disorder and Confusion; and end in shameful disappointment and disgrace. The General most earnestly requires, and expects, a due observance of those articles of war, established for the Government of the army, which forbid profane cursing, swearing & drunkenness; And in like manner requires & expects, of all Officers, and Soldiers, not engaged on actual duty, a punctual attendance on divine service, to implore the blessings of heaven upon the means used for our safety and defense.[421]

The Second Continental Congress justified the taking up of arms, noting that the British army "made an unprovoked assault on the inhabitants of... Lexington."[422] Pastor Jonas Clarke, an eyewitness, documented that the British fired first in his one-year anniversary sermon of April 19, 1776. This was also confirmed by many legal depositions.[423]

The Second Continental Congress declared that *"Our forefathers, inhabitants of the island of Great-Britain, left their native land, to seek on these shores a residence for civil and **religious freedom**."*[424]

The place where religious freedom exists, which determines the quality of civil liberty, is the condition of the heart. Just as the physical condition of the heart is vital to remain healthy, so the condition of our spiritual heart is vital as well.

Jesus, in the sermon on the Mount, defined what it meant to be free internally when He said, *"Every tree is known by its fruit... a good man out of the good treasure of his heart brings forth good; and an evil man out of the evil treasure of his heart brings forth evil."*[425] In other words, the condition of the heart is the source of good and evil.

So, the place to begin in resisting evil is in the heart. I have good news today, for Jesus cleanses hearts and it is by His power alone that transforms them, for as Jesus said, *"the Kingdom of God is at hand. Repent, and believe in the gospel."*[426] Due to Jesus' sacrifice, we can invite Him in, and He will cleanse it and make it a new source of good more powerful than the evil.

Avoid Conflict if at all possible

The Bible teaches plainly that resistance to evil begins in our hearts, it does not begin externally. A heart cleansed of sin and walking in freedom of guilt is the root of religious liberty. When facing conflicts in life and culture, however, Jesus stated in Matthew 5:38-41 that we are not to make minor offenses major ones, but instead "turn the other cheek," ***avoiding conflict.***

The Second Continental Congress declared that, in violation of their written charters, Parliament has "undertaken to give and grant our money without consent, though we have ever exercised an exclusive right to dispose of our own property."[427]

From 1660 to 1764, Parliament passed laws restricting navigation and economic productivity without the consent of colonial assemblies as required by law. Whatever the colonies produced, Parliament wanted to control – a few examples are the *Navigation Acts* of 1660, 1663 and 1696; the *Woolen Act* (1699); *Hat Act* (1732); *Molasses Act* (1733); *Iron Act* (1750); *Revenue Act* (1764). The colonies turned the other cheek on these except to avoid the negative consequences.

Appeal to Authority

Jesus stated in Matthew 18:15-18 that when conflicts occur, another step is to ***appeal*** to authority peacefully (privately) to attempt a restoration of relationships. Congress stated that *We for ten years* (1764-1774) *incessantly and ineffectually besieged the throne as supplicants; we reasoned, we remonstrated with parliament, in the most mild and decent language.*[428] All this was to no avail during this ten years that have been dubbed "the constitutional debate period."

Take steps for Civil Redress

A further step, in the spirit of Matthew 18, of calling more witnesses, in response to royal Governors dissolving colonial assemblies (miniature parliaments,) *A Congress of delegates from the United Colonies was assembled at Philadelphia*[429] (called the First Continental Congress.) This was the election of new lower magistrates, for the purpose of ***civil redress***. Acts 25:11 indicates that Paul the Apostle, as a Roman citizen, appealed in this way utilizing lawful interposition.

Boycott

In addition, the First Continental Congress in 1774 enacted a further peaceful measure of resistance, the economic ***boycott***. Jesus taught that this was a proper action in Matthew 10:14 when he indicated that if a city or village does treats you improperly, you can *shake off the dust of your feet.* This was the middle eastern form of boycotting, refusing to do business with those who treat you unjustly. The Congress stated;

> We have pursued every temperate, every respectful measure; we have even proceeded to break off our commercial intercourse with our fellow-subjects, as the last peaceable admonition, that our attachment to no nation on earth should supplant our attachment to liberty.[430]

Resist by Force

Though Jesus explained to his disciples that they were not to fight to keep him from being crucified, he made it clear that there would come a time when *he who has no sword, let him sell his garment and buy one* (Luke 22:36.) In other words, a last resort when no other is possible, is ***resistance by force*** but again, only when justified as self-defense.

Having followed these peaceful steps of resistance – or *submissive disobedience* to unrighteous and unlawful commands, over a period of a hundred and fifteen years, from 1660 to 1775, the document states that the;

> unprovoked assault… commenced by the British troops… butchered our countrymen… burnt Charlestown… our ships are vessels are seized… we are reduced to the alternative of choosing an unconditional surrender to the tyranny of irritated ministers, or resistance by force.[431]

It is important to note that long before the conflict of the English Colonies with her Crown and Parliament, theologians and others had recognized that in certain cases, a pre-emptive strike is warranted as a form of self-defense.

In the context of Just War Theory, three criteria are given in the context of preemptive strikes, especially in today's world of nuclear weapons and terrorism.

First, *the immediacy of the threat.* There must be clear intentions from the enemy.

Second, *the credibility of the intelligence* that indicates preparedness to attack from consistent actions must be confirmed.

Third, *the failure of diplomatic attempts* to alleviate such a need.[432]

Even with all of these cautions, the strike, if enacted justly, would have to target military and their industrial facilities, not civilians.

The July 6, 1775 Document In Context

In the case of the Colonies, the very context of the July 6, 1775 document we are examining made it clear that Britain was conducting the preemptive strike. On July 5, just prior to this declaration, the "Olive Branch" petition, prepared by John Dickinson, was submitted to Parliament.

On August 23, "the day Penn was to have presented the petition to Lord Dartmouth, King George III issued a proclamation of rebellion."[433] This was in response to the battle of Bunker Hill. He declared that the colonies were now traitors.[434]

Then, the "Prohibitory Act" was given December 22, 1775; severing the colonies completely. John Adams wrote that this;

> throws the thirteen colonies out of the royal protection, levels all distinctions, and makes us independent in spite of our supplications and entreaties... It may be fortunate that the act of independency should come from the British Parliament rather than the American Congress.[435]

In summary, then, the Declaration of Independence is a document of <u>interposition</u>, clearly stating that the colonies were justified in taking the final step as a last resort, severing the relationship with Great Britain, which, as John Adams wrote, had already occurred.

The clear preparation for the Declaration, however, was the document drafted a year before by the Second Continental Congress in 1775. It articulated the steps already taken that would show to the world that the colonies were not acting in anarchy or outright rebellion. It is this historic context that is often left out of today's discussions.

The federal constitution, ratified in 1789, also had clear boundaries of jurisdiction that would curb abuses by any of the three branches if they overstepped their bounds. In addition to horizontal interposition among the branches, interposition was imbedded vertically in relation to States, counties and the national government.

Counties were formed to protect the people from State encroachment. States were to interpose against federal encroachment as well. And most importantly, *only the Congress can declare war.* It is only a multitude of counselors, as representatives of the people, that can authorize the use of force, except in immediate self-defense.

The most underused Amendment of interposition at the national level is the 10th Amendment to the Bill of Rights. It states;

> The powers not delegated to the United States by the Constitution, nor prohibited by it to the states, are reserved to the states respectively, or to the people.

The earlier editions of Black's Law Dictionary confirmed it applies to interposition,

> The concept is based on the 10th Amendment of the Constitution of the United States reserving to the states powers not delegated to the United States.[436]

My point is simple. The Bible has been used for generations to give a priority to the process by which we ought to preserve peace and order when we disagree or have civil discourse. This is true neighbor to neighbor, as well as in the differences we all have with one another politically.

If we silence our conscience, or allow public policy to do so, we surrender by omission. If we use the tools of anarchy, as is often the case today, we simply label others an enemy, before even hearing their reasoning.

We need to reject these extremes and begin by following the concepts of interposition, beginning with civil and respectful discussion - at the local level.

After John Adams stood and read a letter from his wife Abigail about the battle of Bunker Hill, the serious tone of the Second Continental Congress was felt. Even though there was the sliver of hope for reconciliation in this document, it was clear that the Congress echoed the views of the clergy, for only a few days later, on July 20, the Congress called a day of fasting and prayer, and a sermon was preached entitled, *Defensive War in a Just Cause Sinless!*[437]

The document closed with some powerful words that lead to a greater understanding of the Declaration written a year later:

> Our cause is just... Our internal resources are great, and if necessary, foreign assistance is undoubtedly attainable. We gratefully acknowledge, as signal instances of the Divine favor towards us, that his Providence would not permit us to be called into this controversy, until we were grown up to present strength, had been previously exercised in warlike operation, and possessed of the means of defending ourselves. With hearts fortified with these animating reflections, we most solemnly, before God and the world, declare, that, exerting the utmost energy of those powers, which our beneficent Creator hath graciously bestowed upon us, the arms we have been compelled by our enemies to assume, we will, in defiance of every hazard, with unabating firmness and perseverance, employ for the preservation of our liberties; being with one mind resolved to die freemen rather than to live slaves.

> …we mean not to dissolve that union which has so long and so happily subsisted between us, and which we sincerely wish to see restored. Necessity has not yet drive us into that desperate measure… We have not raised armies with ambitious designs of separating from Great-Britain, and establishing independent states. We fight not for glory or for conquest. We exhibit to mankind the remarkable spectacle of a people attached by unprovoked enemies, without any imputation or even suspicion of offense….
>
> In our own native land, in defense of the freedom that is our birthright, and which we ever enjoyed till the late violation of it – for the protection of our property, acquired solely by the honest industry of our fore-fathers and ourselves, against violence actually offered, we have taken up arms. We shall lay them down when hostilities shall cease on the part of the aggressors, and all danger of their being renewed shall be removed, but not before.
>
> With a humble confidence in the mercies of the supreme and impartial Judge and Ruler of the Universe, we most devoutly implore his divine goodness to protect us happily through this great conflict, to dispose our adversaries to reconciliation on reasonable terms, and thereby to resolve the empire from the calamities of civil war.[438]

The Declaration, a year later, would close in a similar way, calling upon God in humility, to;

> Appeal to the Supreme Judge of the world, and with a firm reliance of Divine Providence, mutually pledge to each other our Lives, Fortunes and our sacred Honor!

Leading Idea – The severance of a personal covenant or national separation should be conducted so that the final step is the end of a process of interposition

PART FIVE

The Price and Influence of the Declaration

Chapter 16

SIGNING THE DECLARATION

We, therefore, the Representatives of the united States of America, in General Congress, Assembled, appealing to the Supreme Judge of the world for the rectitude of our intentions, do, in the Name, and by Authority of the good People of these Colonies, solemnly publish and declare, That these United Colonies are, and of Right ought to be Free and Independent States
Declaration of Independence

The Doctrine of Confession

If you confess with your mouth the Lord Jesus and believe in your heart that God has raised Him from the dead, you will be saved. For with the heart one believes unto righteousness, and with the mouth confession is made unto salvation. – Romans 10:9-10

The Scriptures affirm that belief in the heart on the inside and confession with the mouth externally completes the declaration that one is converted in Christ. Though this is not a legalistic rule as to how and when this must occur, *it establishes the fact that there is a need to declare what one believes.*

This declaration, and salvation, constitutes a written signature, so to speak. Consider Luke 10:20 where Jesus tells the disciplines that the greatest joy is not what you do on earth, but that "your names are written in heaven." A confession of Christ on earth affirms a written signature in heaven.

Revelation 3:5 declares that those who believe and whose names are written in the Book of Life will be confessed by Jesus before the Father and His angels! And Revelation 21:27 declares that "only those who are written in the Lamb's Book of Life" will be honored in heaven.

My point is this: *open confession about what we believe in our hearts has blessed consequences for eternity. However, it also means there can be a price to pay on earth.*

As 2nd Timothy 3:10-12 declares;

> But you have carefully followed my doctrine, manner of life, purpose, faith, longsuffering, love, perseverance, persecutions, afflictions, which happened to me at Antioch, at Iconium, at Lystra – what persecutions I endured. And out of them all the Lord delivered me. Yes, and all who desire to live godly in Christ Jesus will suffer persecution.

When Paul the Apostle, writer of most of the books in the New Testament, confessed Christ openly, he paid a price for doing so. Once declaring his position as a believer, *many others were inspired to do so.* This is a great consequence.

However, as he notes in this passage, he encountered all kinds of opposition – persecution – for his faith. It has always caused a healthy fear of God in many before they openly confess their faith. There is good reason to make sure you confess what you truly believe.

Think of it this way. Paul did not say you simply know my confession. He said you know my "manner of life" or how I lived it out before you. Not all of us will encounter the same intensity of persecution, of course, but we will all encounter some opposition.

The Initial Signing of the Declaration – July 4, 1776

As it is in heaven as the Scriptures declare, so it will be on earth.[439] Names written in heaven are one thing, but signatures on earth are another. Those who affixed their signatures to the Declaration of

Independence paid a dear price for doing so once their names were published in London.[440]

Stephen McDowell has written:

> The delegates went on to approve the Declaration of Independence. After the announcement of the vote, silence moved over the Congress as the men contemplated the magnitude of what they had just done. Some wept openly, while others bowed in prayer.[441]

John Hancock

Only two signatures appeared on the original Dunlap document printed the night of July 4th. The first was John Hancock, the largest and probably now the most famous. McDowell continues:

> After signing the Declaration with unusually large writing, the President of the Continental Congress, John Hancock, broke the silence as he declared 'His majesty can now read my name without glasses. And he can double the price on my head.'[442]

Hancock, as we have seen in the last chapter, signed his name as a public opponent of the policies of King George III whom he had witnessed at his coronation many years before.

Charles Thomson

The only other signature on the official copy of the Declaration on July 4 was Charles Thomson, secretary of the Continental Congress. On July 19, 1783, John Jay who would become Chief Justice of the first Supreme Court in 1789, wrote Charles Thomson, saying this:

No Person in the World is so perfectly acquainted with the Rise, Conduct, and Conclusion of the American Revolution, as yourself...[443]

The reason for this sentiment was that he was the only secretary of the Continental Congress for all of its 15 years. He kept the minutes, both public and secret, and his notes became the archives of the nation. His duties included being the Secretary of the Senate, and the Clerk of the House of Representatives.

Thomson's name meant integrity and truth. His judgment was respected in every factual dispute. He helped the Continental Congress retain respect from the people due to his honest reports. As MacArthur has written;

His reputation was such that his reports were in great demand. When a Congressional paper appeared containing his signature the expression was frequently heard, 'Here comes the truth.'[444]

George Washington wrote a letter to Charles Thomson on July 24, 1789 as President and said:

The present age does so much justice to the unsullied reputation with which you have always conducted yourself in the execution of the duties of your Office, and Posterity will find your Name so honorably connected with the verification of such a multitude of astonishing facts, that my single suffrage would add little to the illustration of your merits... your Services have been important, as your patriotism was distinguished; and enjoy that best of all rewards, the consciousness of having done your duty well.[445]

Charles was also an opponent of slavery. He would write to Thomas Jefferson in 1785:

> It grieves me to the soul that there should be such just grounds for your apprehensions respecting the irritation that will be produced in the Southern States by what you have said of slavery. However, I would not have you discouraged. This is a cancer we must get rid of. It is a blot on our character that must be wiped out. If it cannot be done by religion, reason, and philosophy, confident I am that it will be one day by blood.[446]

Thomson was also a good friend of the Natives. At age 29 he describes an experience he had:

> In the year 1757, happening to be present at a treaty held at Easton, in the State of Pennsylvania, with the Indians, who were commonly distinguished by the name of Delaware, for the purpose of making peace, and having by a concurrence of circumstances, gained the confidence of the Indians who came to treat, I was admitted into their council, and obliged to enter deep into their policies and investigate their claims.
>
> This led me to inquire touching the state of this nation, and to examine all the treaties and conferences held with them from the first settlement of the province; and having in your following attended another treaty with the same at which were present the chiefs of the Six Nations, and still retaining the confidence of the Delawares, and being by a solemn act adopted into their nation and called to assist in their councils, I had an opportunity of presenting any inquiries, and gaining some knowledge of their internal policy, customs, and manners.[447]

Ben Franklin published Thomson's book "An Enquiry into the causes of the alienation of the Delaware and Shawanese Indians from the British Interest" in 1759 in London.[448]

Thomson's Great Seal and Bible Translation

It was Charles Thomson whose idea for the Great Seal of the United States was confirmed by the Continental Congress. MacArthur writes:

> So important was the Great Seal that on Day One – July 4, 1776 – Congress appointed Benjamin Franklin, John Adams, and Thomas Jefferson to begin the design process that would later involve two other committees.[449]

Franklin, Jefferson and Adams all desired representations of the Israelites crossing the Red Sea and the Anglo-Saxons being a "guardian of freedom" over the common law. But, as Skousen comments:

> Congress did not immediately adopt any official seal, and as time went by other committees were appointed. Eventually Congress adopted a similar simpler seal.[450]

The idea that Franklin may have desired to have the turkey as a symbol instead of the eagle comes from a letter to his daughter in 1784, but it "was more a critique of the eagle than a serious proposal to elevate the turkey."[451]

It was Thomson's work that was approved. MacArthur gives the actual description of the final Seal in Thompson's words on June 12, 1783:

> The shield (scutcheon) is composed of thirteen strips that represent the several states joined into one solid compact, supporting the chief (top section of the shield) which unites the whole and represents Congress. The strips are kept closely united by the chief and the chief depends upon that union and the strength result from it. The motto *E Pluribus Unum* (out of many, one) alludes to this union. The shield is born on the breast of an American Eagle without any other supporters to denote that the United States of America ought to rely on their own virtue.
>
> The olive branch and arrows denote the power of peace and war which is exclusively vested in Congress. The constellation of thirteen stars denotes a new state taking its place and rank among other sovereign powers. The pyramid signifies strength and duration. The Eye over it and the motto *Annuit Coeptis* (He favors our undertakings) allude to the many signal interpositions of providence in favor of the American cause. The date 1776 underneath is that of the Declaration of Independence and the words *Novus Ordo Seclorum* (A New Order of the Ages) under it signify the beginning of the new American Era, which commences from that date.[452]

Probably the greatest achievement of this signer of the Declaration was his translation of the Scriptures. As the Museum of the Bible declares:

> The Thomson Bible was the first translation of the Septuagint published in English and the first Bible printed by a woman in the United States.[453]

The woman was Jane Aitken, daughter of Robert Aitken who had published the first English Bible after the Declaration at the request of the Continental Congress in 1782.[454] He spent almost twenty years translating the Greek Septuagint into English and then sold it in 1808 with four thousand four volume sets. His work was used in later translations due to its accuracy.[455]

The Official Signing on August 2, 1776

The official signing took place a month later August 2nd. Why? Other than Hancock and Thomson, all the others wanted to make sure they signed an engrossed copy.

Some of those who voted for independence on July 2nd could not be there a month later and some who signed in August were not present to vote a month earlier. In fact, the actual group whose signatures are at the bottom of the official document had never been in the same room at the same time!

Though we have few records of what was said by the delegates in August, McDowell writes that the consensus over time has been, but can't be proven;

> Adding to the solemnity of the tense moment, Hancock said 'We must be unanimous; there must be no pulling different ways; we must all hang together.' Benjamin Franklin responded in his characteristic wit, 'Yes we must indeed all hang together, or most assuredly we shall hang separately!'[456]

We must remember that a war was going on, and thus there was still much pressure regarding the eventual publishing of the names on a Declaration considered to be treasonous by Britain.

My focus to close this chapter, however, will be on the penman of the American Revolution, Samuel Adams. His speech at the official signing has been passed down to us and highlights the philosophy and significance of this document better than I am able. Not known for his eloquence, his speech is worth highlighting for its significance and meaning.

> We are now on this continent, to the astonishment of the world, three millions of souls united in one cause. We have large armies, well disciplined and appointed, with commanders inferior to none in military skill, and superior in activity and zeal. We are furnished with arsenals and stores beyond our most sanguine expectations, and foreign nations are waiting to crown our success by their alliances. There are instances of, I would say, an almost astonishing Providence in our favor; our success has staggered our enemies, and almost given faith to infidels; so we may truly say it is not our own arm which has saved us.
>
> The hand of Heaven appears to have led us on to be, perhaps, humble instruments and means in the great providential dispensation, which is completing. We have fled from the political Sodom; let us not look back, lest we perish and become a monument of infamy and derision to the world... We have no other alternative than independence, or the most ignominious and galling servitude. The legions of our enemies thicken on our plains; desolation and death mark their bloody career; whilst the mangled corpses of our countrymen seem to cry out to us as a voice from Heaven.

Remember that this oration occurred in 1776, when the contest was far from decided. In fact, it appeared that the colonies were unable to defend themselves, losing contest after contest. He continued:

> Courage, then, my countrymen! Our contest is not only whether we ourselves shall be free, but whether there shall be left to mankind an asylum on earth, for civil and religious liberty!

He concluded his oration with these words:

> Go on, then, in your generous enterprise, with gratitude to Heaven for past success and confidence of it in the future. For my own part, I ask no greater blessing than to share with you the common danger and common glory. If I have a wish dearer to my soul than that my ashes may be mingled with those of a Warren and a Montgomery, it is that these American States may never cease to be free and independent."

Early in his oration Adams articulated his most important point. Here he states something every American should ponder in our day. Were the framers (including Samuel Adams) aware of the momentous significance of what was happening in 1776? Consider and ponder this paragraph from Sam Adams at the official signing.

> We have explored the temple of royalty, and found that the idol we have bowed down to, has eyes which see not, and ears that hear not our prayers, and a heart like that of nether millstone. We have this day restored the Sovereign, to whom alone men ought to be obedient. He reigns in heaven, and with a propitious eye beholds his subjects assuming that freedom of thought, and dignity of self direction which He bestowed on them. **From the rising to the setting sun, may His Kingdom come**![457] (emphasis added)

Leading Idea – The signing of the Declaration was one of great solemnity as it has been throughout history when leaders take a public stand for liberty on threats of treason and death

Chapter 17

THE SACRIFICE OF THE DECLARATION

And for the support of this Declaration, with a firm reliance on the protection of divine Providence, ***we mutually pledge to each other our Lives, our Fortunes and our sacred Honor***
Declaration of Independence

The Price of Liberty

And he (Job) said: Naked I came from my mother's womb, and naked shall I return there. The Lord gave, and the Lord has taken away; Blessed be the name of the Lord – Job 1:21

...all who desire to live godly in Christ Jesus will suffer persecution. – 2nd Timothy 3:12

The story of Job is legendary in the Bible. A righteous man, living at the time of Abraham, was allowed by God to be tested, and lost all he had. Even his wife told him he should curse God and die. But his famous words recorded in chapter 1 are telling, "the Lord gave, and the Lord has taken away. Blessed be the name of the Lord."

The determination to stand for a cause, (in Job's case a righteous testimony of maintaining a relationship with both God and others), when tested to an extreme, makes a massive influence.

The last chapter of Job (42:12) states, "now the Lord blessed the latter days of Job more than his beginning." The most influential individuals are not those with money, fame and property. Job had all of that. The Bible emphasizes the attitude of the heart and character of an individual is what brings the greatest blessing.

Saul had it all as well. He had fame, power and with it, persecuted the early Church in its first three years. God allowed it all to be stripped away, and Saul (whose name was changed to Paul) traded the power for a walk with God. It took years to restore relationships with the leaders whom he had opposed.

Scholar Bart Ehrman has documented that the persecution endured by Paul and his subsequent travel of more than 10,000 miles, caused him to be "the most significant convert of all time."[458] As Ecclesiastes 7:8 states, "the end of a thing is better than its beginning; the patient in spirit is better than the proud in spirit."

Give me liberty or give me death!
Patrick Henry – March 23, 1775

St. John's Church in Henrico Parish was the only building large enough to hold the convention on March 20. But delegate Patrick Henry almost never gave his most famous speech. About two weeks before March 23, 1775, wife Sarah had passed away after an awful mental illness where she had to be restrained from hurting herself. Henry was devastated.

Henry was absent when he was elected a delegate to that 2nd Virginia Convention. His grief was so great he confided with his physician that he was "a distraught old man."[459]

A sorrowful and grieving Henry drew from the well of conviction for liberty. Patrick Henry rehearsed all his convictions and more in the speech that was later heralded as *"perhaps the greatest political speech in American history."*[460] He closed his speech on the 23rd of March 1775 with these stirring words;

> We shall not fight our battles alone. There is a just God who presides over the destinies of nations, and who will raise up friends to fight our battles for us. The battle sir, is not to the strong alone; it is to the vigilant, the active, the brave... Is life so dear, or peace so sweet, as to be purchased at the price of chains and slavery? Forbid it, Almighty God! I know not what course others may take, but as for me, give me liberty, or give me death![461]

Hearing Patrick Henry was George Mason, Thomas Jefferson, and George Washington among others – and all were stirred and impacted. As David Vaughn wrote,

> The convention sat in stunned silence, as if they had heard the voice of heaven, 'for Henry had called them to the bar of judgment.'[462]

All great men and women who make a massive influence for the improvement of humanity and especially for the securing of liberty pay a price to do so. Though Henry would not be a delegate at the signing of the Declaration, his words still rang in the hearts of those who had heard or read it.

When John Trumbull returned to America in 1817 after many years abroad, he was commissioned by Congress to paint four large murals to be placed in the newly finished Capitol Rotunda. His father,

Jonathan Trumbull, had been Governor of Connecticut during the War for Independence.

Trumbull, who served under George Washington as his aide-to-camp, had made sketches of many of our Founders from his firsthand acquaintances. When he went to England after the war, he studied under the renowned Benjamin West.

In the famous painting above (hung in the Capitol in 1826), Trumbull depicts the Committee of five bringing forth their first draft of the Declaration of Independence on June 28, 1776. The painting shows 42 of the 56 signers because he was not able to obtain likenesses for all of them. He included some who debated in Independence Hall but for one reason or another did not sign it.[463]

The room he chose was more like Carpenter's Hall, not the room where the document was actually signed. The men sitting in the room were never in the same room with each other because they had to flee for their lives and were not all elected to Congress at future sessions.

So, if the purpose of the painting was not the depiction of an actual historic event, what was its purpose? By 1818 when this painting was commissioned it was well known to John Trumbull that many of the individuals who signed the Declaration had sacrificed on account of their signature.

Bensing Lossing wrote in the Introduction of his book *Lives of the Signers of the Declaration* in 1848;

> The signing of that instrument was a solemn act, and required great firmness and patriotism in those who committed it. It was treason against the home government, yet perfect allegiance to the law of right. It subjected those who signed it

> to the danger of an ignominious death, yet it entitled them to the profound reverence of a disenthralled people.[464]

Of the 56 delegates who eventually signed the Declaration; five were captured, tortured and killed, twelve had their homes ransacked and burned, two lost their sons and two more had their sons captured, nine fought and died from wounds, and the remaining individuals were fugitives and fled for their lives.

Though the late Rush Limbaugh often spoke honorably about his father Rush, Sr., he became famous when his son published his Dad's oratory essay, *The Americans who Risked Everthing* in his Limbaugh Letter of November 21, 2018. Rush, Sr. declared:

> On July 4, 1776, the Declaration of Independence was adopted. There were no trumpets blown. No one stood and cheered... What kind of men were the 56 signers who adopted the Declaration of Independence and who, by their signing, committed an act of treason against the crown? To each of you, the names Franklin, Adams, Hancock and Jefferson are almost as familiar as household words. Most of us, however, know nothing of the other signers. Who were they? What happened to them? Ben Franklin was the only really old man. Eighteen were under 40; three were in their 20s. Of the 56 almost half – 24 – were judges and lawyers. Eleven were merchants, nine were landowners and farmers, and the remaining 12 were doctors, ministers, and politicians.
>
> With only a few exceptions, such as Samuel Adams of Massachusetts, these were men of substantial property. All but two had families. The vast majority were men of education and standing in their communities. They had economic security as few men had in the 18th century. Each had more to lose from revolution than he had to gain by it... These men knew what they risked. The penalty for treason was death by hanging. And remember, a great British fleet was

> already at anchor in New York Harbor... They were sober men. There were no dreamy-eyed intellectuals or draft card burners here. They were far from hot-eyed fanatics yammering for an explosion... It was principle, not property, that had brought these men to Philadelphia.[465]

Ezra Taft Benson in his treatise *This Nation Shall Endure,* writes:

> Two of the signers would become presidents of the United States – Thomas Jefferson... and John Adams. Two – John Adams and Benjamin Harrison – would be fathers of future presidents. Another, Elbridge Gerry, was vice-president under James Madison.[466]

Historian M. E. Bradford documents the religious affiliation of those who signed the Constitution. Perhaps their faith in God, rooted in the Scriptures was the true root of their convictions that they would price for in the cause of liberty.

> ...With no more than five exceptions (and perhaps no more than three), they were orthodox members of one of the established Christian communions; approximately twenty-nine Anglicans, sixteen to eighteen Calvinists, two Methodists two Lutherans, two Roman Catholics, one lapsed Quaker and sometime-Anglican, and one open Deist – Dr. Franklin, who attended every kind of Christian worship, called for public prayer, and contributed to all denominations.[467]

Though there are too many stories to tell in this short chapter, a few are worth remembering, especially those less known signers who paid a price for their signatures.

William Ellery of Newport, Rhode Island was 48 years old on August 2nd when the official signing of the Declaration took place. The National Constitution Center writes:

> On July 10, he wrote to his brother Benjamin that "We have lived to see a Period which a few years ago no human forecast could have imagined – to see these Colonies shake off and declare themselves independent of a State which they once gloried to call Parent…' Ten days later, still proud of Congress for its radical action, he wrote to Rev. Ezra Stiles, President of Yale College, saying that Americans would accept no accommodations Britain might offer to preserve the union of colonies and Mother County. 'The door is shut,' he said, 'We have been driven into a Declaration of Independency & must forget our former love of our British brethren. The Sword must determine our quarrel.'
>
> On August 2 William Ellery joined other members of Congress in signing the Declaration of Independence penned by Thomas Jefferson. Ellery recognized the historic nature of the day. 'I was determined to see how they all looked as they signed what might be their death warrant, I place myself beside the Secretary Charles Thomson and eyed each closely as he affixed each name to the document.' He was proud to note that 'Undaunted resolution was displayed in every countenance.'[468]

When the British invaded Newport, they "wreaked their resentment against Mr. Ellery, by burning his dwelling house, and depredating on his property."[469] He, however, remained in Congress. His testimony was truly amazing, for he served as collector of customs for the port of Newport for 30 years, under the Washington, Adams, Jefferson and Madison administrations. As historian N. Dwight writes:

> He read his Bible much, and from its contents, of which as a Divine Revelation, he was a firm believer, he derived his support and confidence in all the adversities of this life, and his hope of happiness in the life to come… (He died) on the 15th of February, 1820, in the ninety-third year of his age.[470]

John Morton of Pennsylvania was 51 when he anguished over what to do when the Declaration was debated. He was the swing vote between the State's five delegates. Finally, on July 2nd he voted for Independence. He then signed the document on August 2nd. When he got home, his friends, relatives and neighbors turned against him. The anguish at such a cross weighed heavily upon him.

He had written the previous June, "I hope Time will manifest to the World that a steady Perseverance in the Cause of Freedom will triumph over all the deep lay'd Schemes of Tyrrany." He died of tuberculosis in early April, 1777, at 52 years of age. His wife, Ann, after the battle of Brandywine in 1777, had to flee across the Delaware with her nine chilren but all her husband's papers from decades of public service were lost.[471]

Caesar Rodney of Delaware, at 47, had facial cancer and in deep pain but was the deciding vote for his State as well. He left his sickbed at midnight, rode all night on horseback through a severe storm. He got there just in time to cast the deciding vote. His doctors told him he must go to Europe to get treatment. He would not leave his country at such a crucial time and it cost him his life. A grateful Delaware has forever honored Rodney with their statue of him on horseback.[472]

Thomas McKeane, at 42 years of age, was not present on August 2nd for the official signing due to the fact that he was a military officer and on duty. He signed it sometime in October at a later date like other delegates at various times.[473] In a letter to John Adams, written November 8, 1779, he wrote;

> I know, I too have had my full share of the anxieties cares and troubles attending the present war. For sometime I was obliged to act as President of the Delaware State and as Chief Justice of this. General Howe had just landed Aug. 1777 at the head of Elk River, when I undertook to discharge those two great trusts. The consequence was to be hunted like a fox by the enemy and envied by those who ought to have been my friends. I was obliged to remove my family five times in a few months, and at last fixed them in a little Log house on the banks of the Susquehanna above an hundred miles from this; but safety was not to be found there, for they were soon obliged to remove again, occasioned by the incursions of the Indians.[474]

John Hart was one of the five delegates from New Jersey. He was one of the oldest delegates at 65 years of age. When the British came to Trenton they settled near his home and while his wife was on her deathbed, Hessian soldiers destroyed his grist mills and property and he and his 13 children had to flee. He became a fugitive. When he returned home in broken health, his wife had died and his children were gone. He died in 1779.[475]

Richard Stockton was also a delegate from New Jersey. He was 45 at the time of dthe signing. He had been successful in bringing Rev. John Witherspoon from Scotland to America. He served in the Provincial Assembly of New Jersey, and in 1774 was appointed to the Supreme Court of the State. He initially proposed conciliatory measures between the Colonies and the King but the Monarch of England would have none of it.

After signing the Declaration, Stockton was sent on an expedition to New York to help in the War. When coming back to New Jersey to protect his family, he was dragged from his bed by loyalists and turned over to the British. When he refused to sign a document to receive a pardon, retaining his oath to the American militia, he was put in irons and treated brutally in prison. [476]

The four New York delegates lost it all. ***William Floyd*** (at 41) was exiled from his home for seven years and was ruined financially. 63 year old ***Francis Lewis'*** home was ransacked and burned, and his wife was carried away prisoner, dying a few weeks later. ***Robert Morris*** (at 42) had to flee his home for seven years. ***Philip Livingston*** (60) never went home again for his estate became a British hospital. He gave it all away to finance the Revolution.[477]

Thomas Nelson, Jr., *signed* the Declaration as a delegate of Virginia at 37 years of age. After signing, he became commanding General of the Lower Virginia Militia. He then became Governor of Virginia and was with General Washington at the siege of Yorktown that ended the war. Just after the bombardment began, Nelson told Washington that he thought the British generals would probably occupy his home since it was the finest in town. He offered to fire the first canon shot which entered his own living room, killing some of the British officers. A wealthy man, he died bankrupt, and his home was destroyed.[478]

I encourage the reader to look up the lives of those who signed the Declaration and read "the rest of their stories." As Rush Limbaugh, Sr. concluded his 2018 essay:

> And, finally, there is the New Jersey signer, Abraham Clark.

He gave two sons to the officer corps in the Revolutionary Army. They were captured and sent to that infamous British prison hulk afloat in New York Harbor known as the hell ship Jersey, where 11,000 American captives were to die. The younger Clarks were treated with a special brutality because of their father. One was put in solitary and given no food. With the end almost in sight, with the war almost won, no one could have blamed Abraham Clark for acceding to the British request when they offered him his sons' lives if he would recant and come out for the King and Parliament. The utter despair in this man's heart, the anguish in his very soul, must reach out to each one of us down through 200 years with his answer: "No."

The 56 signers of the Declaration Of Independence proved by their every deed that they made no idle boast when they composed the most magnificent curtain line in history. "And for the support of this Declaration with a firm reliance on the protection of divine providence, we mutually pledge to each other our lives, our fortunes, and our sacred honor.[479]

A Lesson of Fulfilling their Mutual Pledge and Relying on God's Providence

In 1776 the Declaration was ratified and then signed during a dismal year for liberty. New York City had been taken and Washington had to retreat (miraculously) from Long Island just to keep from from losing his army. The invasion of Canada failed. Only the victories of Trenton and Princeton held a sliver of hope. And in 1777 the Americans had been driven out of New York and New Jersey.

On September 11, 1777, Washington lost the Battle of Brandywine in Delaware (200 died, 500 wounded, 400 captured); then the Paoli massacre in Pennsylvania (claiming another 300 lives and 100 captured). The British then forced Congress out of Philadelphia, capturing the city on September 26, 1777.

John Adams wrote; "the prospect is chilling, on every side: gloomy, dark, melancholy, and dispiriting."

Only twenty members of Congress gathered in York, Pennslvania. The Congress considered giving up, for the cause appeared lost. Sam Adams rose and said these inspiring words:

> 'Gentlemen', said he, 'your spirits appear oppressed with the weight of the public calamities. Your sadness of countenance reveals your disquietude. A patriot may grieve at the distress of his country. But he will never despair of the commonwealth.
>
> Our affairs, it is said, are desperate! If this be our language, they are indeed. If we wear long faces, long faces will become fashionable. The eyes of the people are upon us. The tone of their feelings is regulated by ours. If we despond, public confidence is destroyed, the people will no longer yield their support to a hopeless contest, and American liberty is no more. But we are not driven to such narrow straits. Though fortune has been unpropitious, our condition is not desperate. Our burdens, though grievous, can be borne. Our losses, though great, can be retrieved. Through the darkness which shrouds our prospects the ark of safety is visible. Despondency becomes not the dignity of our cause, nor the character of those who are its supporters.
>
> Let us awaken then, and evince a different spirit - a spirit that shall inspire the people with confidence in themselves and in us - a spirit that will encourage them to persevere in this glorious struggle, until their rights and liberties shall be established on a rock. We have proclaimed to the world our determination 'to die freemen, rather than to live slaves.' We have appealed to Heaven for the justice of our cause, and in Heaven have we placed our trust. Numerous have been the manifestations of God's providence in sustaining us. In the

> gloomy period of adversity, we have had 'our cloud by day and pillar of fire by night.' We have been reduced to distress, and the arm of Omnipotence has raised us up. Let us still rely in humble confidence on Him who is mighty to save. Good tidings will soon arrive. We shall never be abandoned by Heaven while we act worthy of its aid and protection.[480]

The "good news" did come for at that time the battles of Saratoga and the surrender of the entire northern British army were taking place! Upon hearing of the victories, Adams proposed that Congress set aside a day of Thanksgiving for the answered prayers and on December 18, 1777 it was declared:

> …with one heart and one voice… together with their sincere acknowledgements and offerings, they may join the penitent confession of their manifold sins, whereby they had forfeithed every favour, and their humble and earnest supplication that it may please God, through the merits of Jesus Christ, mercifully to forgive and blot them out of remembrance… under the providence of Almighty God, to secure for these United States the greatest of all human blessings, independence and peace… and enlargement of that kingdom which consisteth 'in righteousness, peace and joy in the Holy Ghost.[481]

Rus Walton, writing in his *Letter from Plymouth Rock* in 1981, stated;

> So deeply were they committed to the principles that were the bedrock of the Declaration, so intensely were they given to the cause of liberty under God, that they willingly – enthusiastically – voted for and signed that document. <u>They signed for their countrymen.</u> <u>They signed for us!</u>

To those who will take the time to study its wonder and ponder its message, it comes clear <u>it is as much a Declaration of Dependence upon the Lord God as it is a Declaration of Independence from Civil Tyranny.[482]</u>

Leading Idea – Those who signed the Declaration did so at great cost for future Americans, but they also inspired signers for the nations yet to embrace true liberty

Chapter 18

THE LEGACY OF THE DECLARATION

A decent respect to the opinions of mankind requires that they should declare the causes which impel them to the separation... ***let facts be submitted to a candid world***
Declaration of Independence

The Liberty Bell and the Declaration

And ye shall hallow the fiftieth year, and ***proclaim liberty throughout all the land unto all the inhabitants thereof****: it shall be a jubilee unto you; and ye shall return every man unto his possession, and ye shall return every man unto his family*
Leviticus 25:10

If you are a student of history, you know that the middle part of this verse is inscribved on what has come to be known as the Liberty Bell. It was carved into the Bell in 1751 by a London Bell Foundry. It was then installed into the State House in Philadelphia to call the Legislature into session.

It cracked when it first rung in 1751 and it could not be repaired. Why would a Scriptural reference from ancient Israel about the year of Jubilee be carved into a bell in Philadelphia?

What did the State Legislature have to do with the fiftieth year of release, that returned all property to its original owners, released all servants and slaves, and forgave all debt acquired during the previous 49 years?

The year of Jubilee is a foreshadowing of spiritual and natural liberty whose origin rests in the God of the Bible. When Jesus came to the earth as the visible image of an invisible God, He died on the cross for our sins, freeing us from the captivity and debt of sin and restoring us to the "promised land" of victorious living.

Jesus was the fulfillment of the Year of Jubilee. Sin is the origin of all evil and is reflected in all forms of tyranny on earth. The internal freedom from sin will, when expressed, curb tyrants and evil oppression on the outside for religious liberty is the best to bring a good quality of civil liberty.

The rights of conscience gives rise to the civil liberty in a nation. The National Park Service in Pennsylvania writes;

> Speaker of the Pennsylvania Assembly Isaac Norris chose this inscription for the State House bell in 1751, possibly to commemorate the 50th anniversary of William Penn's 1701 Charter of Privileges which granted religious liberties and political self-government to the people of Pennsylvania.

Penn's Charter reads;

> BECAUSE no People can be truly happy, though under the greatest Enjoyment of Civil Liberties, if abridged of the Freedom of their Consciences… And Almighty God being the only Lord of Conscience… no Person or Persons, inhabiting in this Province or Territories, who shall confess and acknowledge One almighty God, the Creator, Upholder and Ruler of the World; and profess him or themselves obliged to live quietly under the Civil Government, shall be in any Case molested or prejudiced, in his or their Person or Estate, because of his or their conscientious Persuasion or Practice…
>
> AND that all Persons who also profess to believe in Jesus Christ, the Savior of the World, shall be capable (notwithstanding their other Persuasions and Practices in Point of Conscience and Religion) to serve this Government in any Capacity…[483]

You will note that the Charter for Pennsylvania is clearly built on the foundation of the God of the Bible. You will also note that liberty of conscience is central to its first clause. Furthermore, the protection of religious liberty is a prerequisite for the protection of civil liberty.

These are the same seminal ideas that the Declaration rests on, among others. There is an ideological link between the foundation of Pennsylvania and the foundation of America as denoted in the Declaration of Independence. In 1683 Penn wrote:

> I do not find a model in the world that time, place, and some singular emergencies have not necessarily altered, nor is it easy to frame a civil government that shall serve all places alike. I know what is said by the several admirers of monarchy, aristocracy, and democracy, which are the rule of the one, a few, and many, and are the three common ideas of government when men discourse on that subject.
>
> But I choose to solve the controversy with this small distinction, and it belongs to all three, - any government is free to the people under it (whatever be the frame) where the laws rule and the people are a party to those laws; and more than this is tyranny, oligarchy, or confusion... Liberty without obedience is confusion, and obedience without liberty is slavery.[484]

In a sense, the Liberty Bell is inseparably linked with the main idea of the Declaration, drawn from the anniversary of Penn's charter that illustrates his wisdom.

Ponder Penn's last sentence – *liberty without obedience is confusion.* In other words, if people can do anything they want, it is anarchy, for only liberty under law empowers people to be free.

The other part of his sentence is also significant – *obedience without liberty is slavery.* It matters what kind of law, for if the source does not empower the people, it protects the power of government and is slavery. That is why the Bible says it should be the balance – the "law of liberty." (James 1:25; 2:12)

The Liberty Bell rang on July the 8th to summon citizens to hear the Declaration of Independence being read in Pennsylvania.[485] It was read throughout the colonies to the joy of the people!

The Declaration is Unique

David Armitage, professor of history at Harvard University has noted;

> No American document has had a greater global impact than the Declaration of Independence. It has been fundamental to American history longer than any other text because it was the first to use the name "the United States of America": in this sense, the Declaration was the birth certificate of the American nation.
>
> It enshrined what came to be seen as the most succinct and memorable statement of the ideals on which that nation was founded: the rights to life, liberty, and the pursuit of happiness; the consent of the governed; and resistance to tyranny. And, as the first successful declaration of independence in world history, its example helped to inspire countless movements for independence, self-determination, and revolution after 1776.[486]

Note that Professor Armitage says that it has had such a global impact because it is unique. And what makes it so unique? It had *the most succinct and memorable statement of the ideals on which that nation was founded.* And what were those ideals? He lists rights to life, liberty, pursuit of happiness, consent of the governed, and resistance to tyranny.

The Laws of Nature and Nature's God – or the law of nature and the law of God as we saw in chapter 2. If a nation bases their nation's laws on the law of nature (Creator) and the law of God (Redeemer) it will thrive in empowering individuals to liberty.

Rights of life, liberty and the pursuit of happiness (property) endowed by the Creator – unalienable rights that are given by God and cannot be taken away by any government. Unalienable rights are given to individuals, and they empower families, businesses, churches and civil governments to stay within their God designed jurisdictions.

Rights are secured by government – the purpose of government in every sphere of jurisdiction is to protect rights, not provide them. It is not the purpose of government to force equality from the outside, but to empower people to express their liberty of diversity from the inside.

Governments operate by the consent of the governed – the protection of God-given rights is secured by government at all levels from the self-governed individual, family, business, church and state by *consent* (or permission) of their representatives in each sphere.

People have a right to change their government after "a long train of abuse" by following the steps of lawful resistance to tyranny – or interposition. Built into this process is the understanding that internal fortitude and self-control must be the focus so that a government can change from the bottom-up, with the last resort being a call to self-defense and forceful resistance.

At all levels of society, we must embrace a firm reliance on the Protection of Divine Providence to ultimately get the government He has designed for our nation. A declaration of the source of our rights must ultimately be on of dependence on God more than merely resisting evil and corruption.

The Declaration is Submitted to a Candid World

The Declaration was never intended by the delegates to apply only to the United States. If so, they would only have published it among themselves and Great Britain. They knew that the ideas expressed in it were universal and could be implemented anywhere there were enough people with the character and integrity to support self-government for the purpose of empowering liberty.

On the fiftieth anniversary of the Declaration, in 1826, both John Adams (at 90 years of age) and Thomas Jefferson (at 83) died. It shocked the nation and caused them to reconsider the Declaration's meaning. Jefferson is reported to have said weeks before he died that the Declaration was;

> An instrument... pregnant with our own and the fate of the world.[487]

Professor Armitage explains how the Declaration's influence began to spread;

> The other powers of the earth were naturally curious about what the Declaration said. By August 1776, news of American independence and copies of the Declaration itself had reached London, Edinburgh, and Dublin, as well as the Dutch Republic and Austria. By the fall of that year, Danish, Italian, Swiss, and Polish readers had heard the news and many could now read the Declaration in their own language as translations appeared across Europe. ...One of its most enthusiastic admirers was the nineteenth-century Hungarian nationalist, Lajos Kossuth: for him, the Declaration was nothing less than 'the noblest, happiest page in mankind's history.'[488]

The Declaration goes International - Treaty of Watertown with the Mi'kmaq Nation

Claimed to be the first international treaty between the United States and another sovereign nation immediately after and inspired by the Declaration of Independence, it took place on July 19, 1776. It is an excellent example of how the Declaration inspired a friendly peace treaty with Native Americans.

> …15 days after the signing of the Declaration of Independence, between the Provincial Council of Massachusetts, empowered by the Continental Congress to act on behalf of all 13 colonies, and the delegates of the Mi'kmaq and Maliseet First Nations. This treaty, with wording taken directly from the Declaration is the sister document and stands alone as the true vessel of sovereignty of the United States of America.
>
> It was at General George Washington's direct request that this treaty of peace, friendship and military alliance be consummated, thereby recognizing the crucial role that indigenous nations might play in the colonist' struggle for freedom and independence from England. As James Bowdoin, the president of the Massachusetts Council stated, 'the United States now forms a long and strong chain, and it is made longer and stronger by our brethren, the Mi'kmaq Tribes joining with us; and may Almighty God never suffer this chain be broken.'[489]

The Rebuttals to the Declaration

The people who read the Declaration around the world loved it, but those with power that did not want to diffuse it were terrified of its words, scrambling to maintain the status quo. Loyalist Governor Hutchinson (who had been Governor of Massachusetts) offered a rebuttal noting "the absurdity of making the governed to be governors."[490]

John Lind from England was hired to publish *An Answer to the Declaration of the American Congress*. It was over 100 pages long. In it, Lind begins with the premise;

> It would become the dignity of an insulted Sovereign to descend to altercation with revolted subjects. This would be to recognize that equality and independence, to which subjects, persisting in revolt, cannot fail to pretend.[491]

King George III in England ignored the writings of the Continental Congress, but the Declaration got his attention and the result was that he believed the Colonies had no right to leave, though he had already effectively severed his relationship with them six months prior.

Jeremy Bentham, the European "father of the welfare state" who wrote his own *Short Review of the Declaration,* refuting the concept of natural rights, stated;

> They attempt to establish a theory of Government… that is subversive of every actual or imaginable kind of Government.

When discussing the assertion that all men are created equal, he wrote;

> This surely is a new discovery.

He asserted that no government has ever acknowledged unalienable rights for;

> Here they have laid the axe to the root of all Government… They are about to change a government… which have always subsisted, which must continue to subsist, wherever Government has subsisted, or can subsist.[492]

The rebuttals rested on the presupposition that the ideas in our Declaration are perposterous – independence and equality - because they have not existed in the majority of governments on the earth. In essene, the rebuttal states that the power exercised in centralized, top-down government cannot be difused since it would threaten the way things have been done in the past!

Though times have changed, the attacks on the notion of God-given rights and self-government have not. The arguments are the same, for the very idea of calling on the God of the Universe, as revealed in the Bible, for the *individual* to get rights from Him rather than government, "lays the axe to the root."

But it was the "right to revolution" (changing a government), stated in the Declaration, that put fear in all the monarchies of Europe. True it was, that there is always a tendency for humanity to go from one extreme to the other, for if all colonies revolted, we would tend to move toward anarchy.

The lessons of history are hard to ignore. *The fruit of a revolution reveals which set of ideas were the seeds of their resistance.* The source of liberty will always determine its quality.[493]

The most common misconception taken from the Declaration by other countries wanting its quality of liberty was simply copying the words but leaving out one key concept – God. By doing so, they rejected His jurisdictional way of bringing forth His rule – bottom-up beginning with the individual. Others deliberately deceived the populace. No better example of this was the French Revolution.

The French Revolution

The French Revolution of 1789 was said to be inspired by the Declaration, but its declaration of human rights left out the crucial source of those rights – *God.* If God does not grant the rights, then government is the source and freedom will by consequence be limited and if left unchecked – eliminated.

Consider Gary DeMar's brief critique of the French Revolution as an example:

> Revolutions generally do not turn out well. (The American Revolution was not a revolution but a war for independence. There was no uprising of the people but a joining of 13 individual governments to defend their sovereignty.) Think French Revolution.
>
> The French Revolution is still celebrated in France and is often compared to our War for Independence. "Bastille Day" is celebrated on July 14th as a national holiday. Festivities and official ceremonies are held all over France. It is also celebrated in Belgium, Hungary, South Africa (naturally), the United Kingdom, and in more than 50 cities across the United States.
>
> The murdering mobs that attacked the nearly empty Bastille (at the time of the siege there were only seven non-political prisoners) believed their actions were for a better France, similar to what today political revolutionaries have in mind. The storming of the Bastille was a catalyst for what became known as the reign of terror. "French society underwent an epic transformation as feudal, aristocratic and religious privileges evaporated under a sustained assault from left-wing political groups and the masses on the streets." How bad was it?
>
> Internally, popular sentiments radicalized the Revolution significantly, culminating in the rise of Maximilien Robespierre and the Jacobins and virtual dictatorship by the Committee of Public Safety during the Reign of Terror from 1793 until 1794 during which between 16,000 and 40,000 people were killed.
>
> Did you get that? Between 16,000 and 40,000 French citizens were killed for a better France. Consider the following:

Ordered by the king [Louis XVI] to surrender, more than 600 Swiss guards were savagely murdered. The mobs ripped them to shreds and mutilated their corpses. "Women, lost to all sense of shame," said one surviving witness, "were committing the most indecent mutilations on the dead bodies from which they tore pieces of flesh and carried them off in triumph." Children played kickball with the guards' heads. Every living thing in the Tuileries [royal palace in Paris] was butchered or thrown from the windows by the hooligans. Women were raped before being hacked to death.

The Jacobin club . . . demanded that the piles of rotting, defiled corpses surrounding the Tuileries be left to putrefy in the street for days afterward as a warning to the people of the power of the extreme left.

This bestial attack, it was later decreed, would be celebrated every year as "the festival of the unity and indivisibility of the republic." It would be as if families across America delighted in the annual TV special "A Manson Family Christmas." ((Ann Coulter, *Demonic: How the Liberal Mob is Endangering America* (New York: Crown Publishing Group, 2011), 107.))

In time, the just cause of the revolutionary mobs got out of hand, and people began to notice. "During the Reign of Terror, extreme efforts of de-Christianization ensued, including the imprisonment and massacre of priests and destruction of churches and religious images throughout France. An effort was made to replace the Catholic Church altogether, with civic festivals replacing religious ones. The establishment of the Cult of Reason was the final step of radical de-Christianization."

It was at this point that the people became disillusioned with the revolutionary ways of the radicals, but not before more atrocities were committed for the salvation of the people and the nation. As revolutionary leader Jean-Paul Marat declared, "Let the blood of the traitors flow! That is the only way to save the country."

> Once the mob starts down the road of violence to justify the first "just cause," there is no way to stop the radical remedy because there's always one more thing that needs to be changed. They already had killed tens of thousands, what's ten thousand more?[494]

Not all revolutions are equal. The root can be discerned in time through the fruit.

Other Revolutions inspired by our Declaration

The nations in Central and South America, inspired by our Declaration, copied its contents along with our Constitution, expecting to get stability and order, as well as good government, from the documents alone. They soon found out that the words were not the *source* of liberty, but instead the *fruit of it.* Here are some others;

> The *Manifesto of the Province of Flanders* in 1790, the Haitian Revolution (1804), Venezuelan (1811), Granada (1811), Argentine (1816), Chilean (1818), Costa Rica, El Salvador, Guatemala, Honduras, Mexico, Nicaragua and Peru (1821), Bolivia and Uruguay (1825), Ecuador (1830), Colombia (1831), New Zealand (1835), Paraguay (1842), Dominican Republic (1844), Liberia (1847), Hungary (1849)[495]

Though some of the words from our Declaration were quoted, the meanings were often ignored or changed, God and His law was left out, and the results exchanged one form of tyranny for another.

European Communist Revolutions

The European revolutions of 1848 never quoted our Declaration. Inspired by the *Communist Manifesto* of Karl Marx, these revolts focused on overthrowing government itself.[496] The result was the reign of an all-powerful State.

The ideas in our Declaration, drawn from the laws of nature and nature's God give unalienable rights to the *individual* and thus bind down the civil government's power by the chains of a written Constitution. When the chains are forged on people rather than the government, the ideas in our Declaration are either being ignored or their meanings revised.

Twentieth and Twenty-first Century Revolutions

The Declaration inspired the break-up of the Ottoman Empire, the Austria-Hungry Empire, the independence of Czechoslovakia, Vietnam and virtually 70 other revolts between 1945 and 1979 alone. The 21st century has seen uprisings in the streets of Europe and America similar to what was seen in the revolts following the Communist Manifesto. But what quality of liberty are they seeking?

As constitutional attorney Herb Titus has written:

> Since the beginning of the 20th century, mankind has observed the lawless consequences of revolutionary wars. The Bolshevik revolution in Russia and the post-World War II revolutions in China and Cuba produced totalitarian regimes which by raw power took away the people's lives, liberties, and properties. Why? The Communist revolutions, like the French revolution before them, were not governed by the law of God. To the contrary, these revolutions were inspired by men who rejected both God and His Law.
>
> America's revolution stands apart. It was governed by God's law and, therefore, restored the rule of law and enlarged the liberty of the people. Today, many Americans are placing this great heritage in danger, because they refuse to submit to the 'laws of nature and of nature's God' that governed the nation's

> founders. Unless America is restored to its Christian heritage, the lawlessness that plagues this great land will continue to increase, and the Declaration's legacy of life, liberty, and the pursuit of happiness will be lost.[497]

We must remember that *the source of liberty determines its quality.* There is always hope when there is a God in heaven whose desire is to the bring a measure of His kingdom to earth. Yet, we must also remember that God's judgment on evil helps along that path.

Thomas Jefferson wrote in 1785 in reference to the evils of slavery;

> Can the liberties of a nation be secure when we remove their only firm basis, a conviction in the minds of the people, that these liberties are the gift of God? That they are not to be violated but with His wrath? Indeed, I tremble for my country, when I reflect that God is just; that His justice cannot sleep forever; that a revolution of the wheel of fortune, a change of situation, is among possible events; that it may become probable by supernatural interference! The Almighty has no attribute which can take side with us in that event.[498]

So, is the Declaration of Independence relevant today? We believe it is for all the reasons we have given. If we desire to leave a legacy of liberty to our children and grandchildren, *we need to make sure the foundation that sustains it is understood and passed on!*

John Adams wrote to his wife Abigil in 1777;

> *Posterity! You will never know, how much it cost the present Generation, to preserve your Freedom! I hope you will make a good Use of it.*[499]

Leading Idea – The ideas in the Declaration transcend America. Any nation can utilize them if they are willing to express and apply them by empowering individuals to practice them in the jurisdictions where they have influence.

Epilogue – a Testimony from Posterity

What Faith, Family and Freedom Mean to Me

Jonathan Jehle

Faith. Family. Freedom. This popular mantra is often linked to conservative values. But what do these words truly mean?

A scene from one of my favorite movies comes from Indiana Jones and the Last Crusade: Indiana stands at the edge of a vast chasm with no visible bridge to the other side. In order to get across and save his father, he must make a "leap of faith." The concept is straightforward. He has to step forward in belief, even though nothing appears to support him. It's a powerful visual metaphor, yet it only hints at the deeper reality of Biblical faith.

Biblical faith isn't blind; it is confident trust in God and reliance on His promises, even when the path isn't visible. Faith is paramount. As Hebrews 11:6 states, "without faith it is impossible to please [God], for whoever would draw near to God must believe that he exists and that he rewards those who seek him." Our ultimate hope rests in faith in God, not in any politician, party, or even our nation.

The family is the cornerstone of a thriving society. The Bible teaches that the family models how a nation should function. The home serves as the first school for practicing righteousness, citizenship, and self-government. Our faith's values are lived out and transmitted through the family. When families grow weak or are broken, disorder inevitably spreads throughout society.

A memorable moment from Braveheart captures the essence of true freedom. Near the film's climax, as William Wallace faces execution, he cries out "Freedom!" with his final breath. What makes this scene iconic isn't just the declaration, but the deep faith and conviction behind it. It was built through every conscious decision, sacrifice, and belief in something greater than personal comfort or immediate gain.

It's easy to ring the bells of liberty or shout in the streets for a cause, but such displays often ring hollow and fade. True freedom isn't merely the ability to do whatever we want; it is rooted in submission to something bigger than ourselves. Faith in God brings responsibility to obey His Word, which in turn produces genuine personal liberty. When a society first acknowledges its Creator, people of every race and religion can flourish under the protection of that freedom.

One of the most profound principles I've learned from both private education and Biblical teaching is the idea of self-government. Simply put: the more internal control we exercise, the less external control is needed. Biblical self-government means allowing God to rule our hearts, which leads to voluntary obedience and authentic freedom. When individuals lack this internal restraint, societies drift toward heavier external regulations to preserve order. We must first learn to govern ourselves from within. Then, we can effectively govern our families, and in turn, build and sustain a strong, stable society.

That is what faith, family, and freedom mean to me.

Appendix A
About the Author: Dr. Paul Jehle

Paul Jehle graduated from Barrington College with a major in Mathematics and a minor in Biblical studies in 1975. He then received a PHD and Doctorate in Education from Whitefield Theological Seminary in 1992 and 1994.

Paul was introduced to the Pilgrim Story by John G. Talcott, Jr. in historic Plymouth in 1975. John opened his primary source library to Paul who began researching the history of Plymouth. John introduced Paul to the work of the Foundation for American Christian Education the same year and began his study of America's Christian heritage. He subsequently became a member of several historic societies (Pilgrim Hall, Old Colony Club, Plimoth-Patuxet Museums, to name a few).

Paul began his hobby of giving historic tours in costume in 1978 when he began researching the history and meaning of The National Monument to the Forefathers. He was soon introduced to Rus Walton, Executive Director of the Plymouth Rock Foundation and joined its board in 1988 as Education Director.

He was part of the 1989 centennial committee of Forefathers Monument, the 375th celebration in 1995 and was a member of Plymouth 400, Inc. for 2020 for Plymouth. He now serves the town of Plymouth in several capacities, and as historic consultant for America's Hometown Thanksgiving Celebration and its annual event in Plymouth the weekend prior to Thanksgiving.

Dr. Jehle served as youth pastor at the New Testament Church in 1977, founded the New Testament Christian School in 1980, and became Senior Pastor of the Church in 1988. He has since become President of the Plymouth Rock Foundation. He lives with his wife, Charlene, in Sagamore Beach, MA, and has two children; Jonathan (who married Rebecca and they have four children) and Shauna (who married Asad Moosa.) Paul believes that one's faith should be expressed through loving service in one's community as an example of sustaining religious and civil liberty.

Appendix B
A Prayer for the United States of America
(that can be adapted as a prayer for any nation)

As the Creator, you, O Lord, caused the nation of America to be born, resting on universal principles of equality, unalienable rights of life, liberty and property – to pursue happiness and enjoy the fruits of our labor. It was a promise beyond our achievement, but You reminded us of this pledge, and at times we repented, and continually we seek to move toward such a goal.

All those in our nation, of every race, culture and creed, are made in your image, and have the same rights given by you. Let us pledge allegiance to you, as our chief Legislator, Captain and Judge, to "do justly, love mercy, and walk humbly with our God."

The nations are in turmoil because of those who take counsel against you, O Lord, to persecute your people, and break asunder their bonds of unity. You, however, have set your King, the Redeemer of Mankind, Jesus Christ, "on your holy hill of Zion."

Help us take our responsibility as the Church to live out our faith and exercise liberty under law as individuals, families, and among our neighbors, towns and states, treating people with kindness and respect, bringing unity as children of your creation.

We trust you, that your promise, Father, given to your Son will be fulfilled for you said; "Ask of me, and I will give you your inheritance, and the ends of the earth for Your possession." Let us do our part in serving you that you, Lord Jesus, might inherit the nations as promised by the Father and empowered by the Spirit.

May you enable us to flourish in the spheres where we have influence, our homes, places of employment, and neighborhoods. May you judge evil, remove corrupt rulers, and lead us to fulfill your prayer that "your kingdom would come, and your will would be done, on earth as it is in heaven" in Christ's name, Amen.
(Malachi 6:8; Psalm 2; Matthew 6:10)

Selected Bibliography

Allen, Scott, *Why Social Justice is not Biblical Justice,* Credo House Publishers, 2020

Amos, Gary, *Defending the Declaration,* Wolgemuth & Hyatt, 1989

Baldwin, Alice, *The New England Clergy and the American Revolution*, Frederick Unger Publishing, 1928

Barton, David., *Psalm 139 – The Bible, the Founding Fathers, and Abortion.,* www.wallbuilders.com; 2012

Batten, Don; Ham, Ken, Wieland, Carl, *One Blood: the Biblical Answer to Racism,* Master Books, 1999

Beck, Paul, Jr., *The Life of George Washington,* American Sunday School Union, Philadelphia, 1832

Beeke, Joel R., editor, *ForeRunner of the Great Awakening,* Sermons by Theodorus Jacobus Frelinghuysen (1691-1747), Eerdmans, 2000.

Beliles, Mark, and Newcombe, Jerry, *Thomas Jefferson and the God Who Gave Us Liberty,* Morgan James, 2026

Bemis, Samuel Flagg, *John Quincy Adams and the Foundations of American Foreign Policy,* Alfred A. Knopf, 1950

Butterfield, L. H., Editor, *Adams Family Correspondence, Volume I – December 1761-May 1776,* Belknap press, 1963

Black's Law Dictionary, Fourth Edition (1961-1967)

Blackstone, William, *Commentaries on the Laws of England,* Volume I, University of Chicago Press, 1765

Bowen, Catherine Drinker, *John Adams and the American Revolution*, Little, Brown and Company, Boston, 1950

Bradford, M.E., *A Worthy Company*, Plymouth Rock Foundation, 1982 – www.plymrock.org

Brooks, Pat, *The Return of the Puritans,* New Puritan Library, 1976

Bushman, Richard L., editor, *The Great Awakening: Documents on the Revival of Religion, 1740-1745,* Institute of Early American History and Culture by the University of North Carolina Press, 1970

Calvin, John, *Institutes of the Christian Religion,* Eerdmans Publishing Company, 1989

Carter, Robert III, *A Man Named Robert: Lessons from the life of America's First Great Emancipator,* Cartier and Beaufort Press, 2022

Chappell, Rev. F. L., *The Great Awakening of 1740,* American Baptist Publication Society, 1903.

Cole, Darrel, *When God Says War is Right,* Waterbrook Press, 2002

Colvin, Matthew, article and translation of the Magdeburg Confession, 1550

DeMar, Gary, *God and Government, Volume 1,* American Vision, 1982

DeMar, Gary, *Historical Revisionism,* American Vision Press, 2009

DeMar, Gary, *The Case for America's Christian History,* American Vision Press, 2009.

Dexter, Henry Martin, *The Congregationalism of the Last Three Hundred Years*, New York, 1880

De Tocqueville, Alexis, *Democracy in America,* Vintage Books, Volumes 1 and 2, 1990.

Eidsmoe, John, *Christianity and the Constitution: The Faith of our Founding Fathers,* Baker Book House, 1987

Eidsmoe, John, *God and Caesar: Biblical Faith and Political Action,* Wipf and Stock Publishers, 1997.

Eidsmoe, John, *The Doctrine of Interposition in Christian Theology*, Plymouth Rock Foundation, Volume 24, Issue 1, February 2001.

Eidsmoe, John, *Historical and Theological Foundations of Law,* American Vision Press, Volumes I-III, 2011.

Erhman, Bart D., *The Triumph of Christianity,* Simon and Schuster, 2018

Federer, William, editor; *America's God and Country Encyclopedia of Quotations*

Federer, William J., *Change to Chains, 6,000 Year Quest for Control,* Amerisearch, Inc., 2011

Federer, William J., *Who is the King in America?* Amerisearch, Inc., 2018.

Fiske, John, *Beginnings of New England of the Puritan Theocracy in Its Relation to Civil and Religious Liberty*, Houghton Mifflin and Company, 1889

Fithian, Philip Vickers, *Journal and Letters: A Plantation Tutor of the Old Dominion, 1773-1774,* University Press of Virginia, 1957.

Founders Online – www.archives.gov

Fugate, Robert E., *Toward a Theology of Taxation,* Lord of the Nations, 2012

Galloway, Charles P., *Christianity and the American Commonwealth,* 1898, republished by American Vision, 2005

Gilman, Theodore, *Rev. Jonas Clark, Pastor of the Church at Lexington during the Revolution, Leader of Revolutionary Thought,* New York Society of the Order of the Founders and Patriots of America, 1911

Goen, C.C., *Broken Churches, Broken Nation,* Mercer University Press, 1985

Goff, Kenneth, *The Soviet Art of Brainwashing,* 1936-1939.

Green, Harry Clinton and Mary Wolcott, *The Pioneer Mothers of America,* in three volumes, 1912, excerpts republished by Wallbuilders in 1997. – www.wallbuilders.com

Hall, David W., *The Legacy of John Calvin: His Influence on the Modern World,* P & R Publishing, 2008.

Hall, Verna, editor, *The Christian History of the American Revolution: Consider and Ponder*, Foundation for American Christian Education, 1976 – www.face.net.

Hall, Verna., editor, *The Christian History of the Constitution of the United States: Christian Self-Government*, Foundation for American Christian Education, San Francisco, 1966 – www.face.net

Hardinge, Leslie, *The Celtic Church in Britain,* London, 1972

Headley, J. T., *The Chaplains and Clergy of the Revolution,* originally published 1864, republished by Barristers' Inn.

Hosmer, James K., *Samuel Adams: American Statesman*, Riverside Press, Cambridge, 1885

House, Wayne, H., editor, *The Christian and American Law,* Kregel Publications, 1998

Howard, John A., *Christianity: Lifeblood of America's Free Society (1620-1945),* Summit Press, 2008.

Hyneman, Charles S., Lutz, Donald S., *American Political Writing during the Founding Era,* Volumes I and II, 1983.

Jehle, Paul, *Go Ye Therefore and Teach All Nations, Volumes I-2,* Plymouth Rock Foundation, 2006.

Jehle, Paul, *Journey of Faith: Why the Pilgrims Came,* Plymouth Rock Foundation, 2020.

Jehle, Paul, *Spiritual Warfare: the Salem Witch Trials of 1692,* Heritage Institute Ministries, 1992.

Johnston, Jeremiah, *Unanswered, Lasting Truth for Trending Questions*, Whitaker House, 2015

Johnston, Jeremiah, *Unimaginable: What would our World be Like without Christianity*, Bethany House, 2017

Jones, Archie, *Christian Principles in the Articles of Confederation,* Plymouth Rock Foundation, 1991

Jones, Archie, *Thomas Jefferson: The Man & The Myth,* Plymouth Rock Foundation, 1998 – www.plymrock.org.

Kelley, Kate, *Election Day: An American Holiday, An American History,* ASJA Press, 2008

Ketcham, Ralph, *The Anti-Federalist Papers and the Constitutional Convention Debates,* 1986

Kuyper, Abraham, *Christianity: A Total World and Life System,* Plymouth Rock Foundation, 1996.

Leslie's Retreat from the Historical Collections of the Essex Institute, Volume 27, July, 1880

Leeming, Rev. J. R., *Stephen Langton: Hero of Magna Charta,* London, 1915

Levy, Andrew, *The First Emancipator: Slavery, Religion, and the Quiet Revolution of Robert Carter,* Random House, 2005.

Limbauh, Rush, Sr., *The Americans who Risked Everything,* November 21, 2018

Lossing, Benson, *Lives of the Signers of the Declaration of Independence,* 1848, republished by Wallbuilders, 1995, - www.wallbuilders.com.

Love, William DeLoss, *The Fast and Thanksgiving Days of New England,* Houghton-Mifflin Company, 1895

McCullough, David, *John Adams,* Simon and Schuster, 2001.

McCullough, David, *1776,* Simon & Schuster, 2005.

McDowell, Stephen, *Apostle of Liberty: The World-Changing Leadership of George Washington*, Cumberland House, 2007

McDowell, Stephen, *The Bible: America's Source of Law and Liberty,* Providence Foundation, 2015.

McDowell, Stephen, *The Bible, Slavery and America's Founders,* Providence Foundation, 2003

McDurmon, Joel, *The Problem of Slavery in Christian America*, American Vision Press, 2017

Mill, John Stuart., *On Liberty*, 1859, re-published by The Classics of Liberty Library, 1992,

Morris, Benjamin, *The Christian Life and Character of the Civil Institutions of the United States*, originally published in 1864, republished by American Vision, 2007

Nelson, E., *The Hebrew Republic*, Harvard Press, 2010

Newcombe, Jerry, *The Book that Made America,* Nordskog Publishing, 2009.

Peacocke, Dennis, *On the Destiny of Nations: Resolving our Economic Crisis,* Rebuild, 2012

Perry, Richard L., editor, *Sources of Our Liberties*, William S. Hein & Co., 1990

Prince, Derek, *Changing History through Prayer and Fasting,* Fleming H. Revell, 1973

Robertson, G., *The Tyrannicide Brief,* Pantheon Books, 2005

Rushdoony, R. J., *The Institutes of Biblical Law,* The Craig Press, 1973

Rushdoony, R. J., *The Myth of Over-Population,* Craig Press, 1969

Rutherford, Rev. Samuel, *Lex Rex,* 1644, republished by Sprinkle Publications, 1982, Harrisonburg, Virginia

Sandoz, Ellis, editor, *Political Sermons of the American Founding Era: 1730-1805,* Volumes I and II, Liberty Fund, 1998

Skousen, Cleon., *The Making of America*, National Center for Constitutional Studies, Washington, D.C., 1985

Spalding Matthew, *The Founder's Almanac,* The Heritage Foundation, 2002.

Sparks, Jared, *The Works of Benjamin Franklin*, Boston: Tappan, Whittemore, and Mason, 1840

Stoll, Ira., *Samuel Adams: A Life,* Simon and Schuster, 2008

Stout, Harry, *The Divine Dramatist: George Whitefield and the Rise of Modern Evangelism*, Eerdmans Publishing, 1991.

Stout, Harry, *The New England Soul*, Oxford University Press, New York, 1986

Stratton, Eugene Aubrey, *Plymouth Colony Its History and People: 1620-1691,* Ancestry Publishing, 1986

Swanson, Mary-Elaine, *The Education of James Madison,* Hoffman Center, 1992.

Thornton, J. Wingate, *The Pulpit of the American Revolution,* 1860

Titus, Herbert, *God, Man, and Law: The Biblical Principles,* Institute in Basic Life Principles, 1994

Titus, Herbert, *The Declaration of Independence: The Christian Legacy,* Titus Publications, 1995

Thomas, Hugh., *The Slave Trade,* Simon and Schuster, 1997

Trueman, Carl R., *Strange New World*, Crossway, 2022

Tocqueville, Alexis de, *Democracy in America,* Alfred A Knopf, 1972 – in two volumes.

Unger, Harlow Giles, *John Hancock: Merchant King and American Patriot,* John Wiley & Sons, 2000

Vaughn, David. J., *Give Me Liberty,* Cumberland House, 1997

Walton, Rus, *Before there was a Declaration of Independence, there were Committees of Correspondence*, Plymouth Rock Foundation, 1988 – www.plymrock.org

Walton, Rus, *Biblical Solutions to Contemporary Problems: A Handbook,* Plymouth Rock Foundation, 1988 – www.plymrock.org.

Waters, Thomas Franklin, and Felton, Mrs. Eunice Whitney Farley, *Two Ipswich Patriots*, Publication of the Ipswich Historical Society, volume xxvi, 1927

Webster, Daniel, *The Great Speeches and Orations of Daniel Webster,* Little Brown and Company, 1879.

Webster, Noah, *An American Dictionary of the English Language,* 1828, facsimile edition republished by the Foundation for American Christian Education – www.face.net

West, Thomas G., *Vindicating the Founders: Race, Sex, Class, and Justice in the Origins of America,* Rowman & Littlefield Publishers, 1997.

Whitefield, George, *Sermons* – in three Volumes, Pietan Publications, 1994.

Wilson, Douglas, *God Is: How Christianity Explains Everything,* American Vision Press, 2008

Wilson, Douglas, *The Deluded Atheist, A response to Richard Dawkins' The God Delusion,* American Vision Press, 2008

Wines, Rev. E. C., *The Roots of the American Republic,* Plymouth Rock Foundation, 1997.

Winters, Brent, *Excellence of the Common Law,* 2008.

Wise, John, *A Vindication of the Government of New England Churches*, printed in Boston, 1717, republished by Kessinger Publishing

Wood, Gordon, *World Socialist Web Site,* www.wsws.org for Wood's letter on the 1619 Project of December 21, 2019.

Endnotes

Chapter 1

1. Titus, Herbert, God, Man, and Law: The Biblical Principles, Institute in Basic Life Principles, 1994, p. 65.
2. Mayhew, Jonathan, A Discourse Concerning Unlimited Submission and Non-Resistance to the Higher Powers, January 30, 1750, sermon preached in Boston.
3. Ibid.
4. Ibid.
5. Foljambe, Rev. S. W., January 5, 1876 – "The Hand of God in American History", as quoted in Hall, Verna, editor, The Christian History of the American Revolution: Consider and Ponder, pages 46-47 – www.face.net.
6. General Orders, 2 July, 1776, Founders Online.
7. Bowen, Catherine Drinker, John Adams and the American Revolution, Little, Brown and Company, Boston, 1950, page 217 and source notes on page 620.
8. Stout, Harry S., The New England Soul, Oxford University Press, New York, 1986, pages 3-10 where Stout documents that the average individual in New England alone listened to almost 7,000 sermons totaling fifteen thousand hours of concentrated listening in their lifetime. These sermons covered every fundamental principle later written in the Declaration of Independence.
9. Perry, Richard L., editor, Sources of Our Liberties, William S. Hein & Co., 1990, page 44 where the original charter of Virginia in 1606 declared that all inhabitants and their successors "shall have all liberties, franchises, and Immunities" of Englishmen. This is an example that could prove true for all the original thirteen colonies.
10. See Bowen, pages 204-205 for a detailed explanation of the difference in viewpoints here expressed.
11. Ibid., pages 205-213.
12. Ibid., pages 214-215.
13. The diary of John Adams on James Otis speech of 1761.
14. From John Adams to William Tudor, Sr., 29 March 1817, Founders online.
15. Bowen, page 210.
16. Hall, Verna., editor, The Christian History of the Constitution of the United States: Christian Self-Government, Foundation for American Christian Education, San Francisco, 1966, page 328 where Richard Frothingham's Rise of the Republic of the United States (1890) is quoted.
17. Sources of Our Liberties, pages 287-288.
18. Ibid., page 299.
19. Bowen, page 579.
20. Ibid., page 583.
21. Ibid., pages 594-595.
22. Ibid., page 595.

23. Webster, Daniel, The Great Speeches and Orations of Daniel Webster, "Adams and Jefferson" – Faneuil Hall, Boston, August 2nd, 1826, pages 168-170.
24. Bowen, page 596.
25. Ibid., page 596-597.
26. Ibid., pages 598-599; 606-607.
27. Ibid., pages 600-601.
28. Ibid., page 602.
29. Ibid., pages 602n.
30. Skousen, Cleon., The Making of America, National Center for Constitutional Studies, Washington, D.C., 1985, pages 32-33.
31. Hosmer, James K., Samuel Adams: American Statesman, Riverside Press, Cambridge, 1885, page 349.
32. Ibid., page 349.

Chapter 2

33. See The God Delusion - Wikipedia. (Dawkins, Richard (2006). The God Delusion. Boston: Houghton Mifflin. p. 406.)
34. Dawkins, page 31, as quoted in Wilson, Douglas, The Deluded Atheist, A response to Richard Dawkins' The God Delusion, American Vision Press, 2008, page 16.
35. Webster, Noah, An American Dictionary of the English Language, 1828, facsimile edition republished by the Foundation for American Christian Education – www.face.net; see Websters 1828 - Webster's Dictionary 1828 - Evolution.,
36. See EVOLUTION Definition & Meaning | Dictionary.com.
37. Dawkins, pages 40 and 41, as quoted in Wilson, page 18.
38. Wilson, Deluded Atheist, pgs. 18-19.
39. Wilson, Douglas, God Is: How Christianity Explains Everything, American Vision Press, 2008, page 7.
40. Ibid., p. 8.
41. See Bradford, M.E., A Worthy Company, Plymouth Rock Foundation, 1982, where he documents that the vast majority of the delegates who signed the Constitution were members of evangelical denominations at the time – www.plymrock.org.
42. See chapter 17 for a more comprehensive discussion of the sacrifice exhibited by those who signed the Declaration.
43. Blackstone, William, Commentaries on the Laws of England, Volume I, University of Chicago Press, 1765, pgs. 38-39.
44. Ibid., page 42.
45. Amos, Gary, Defending the Declaration, Wolgemuth & Hyatt, 1989, page 86.
46. Skousen, The Making of America, pages 182-183.
47. See chapter 7 for a comprehensive discussion of the meaning of equality as it is used in the Declaration.

48. Amos, Gary, Defending the Declaration, page 104.
49. See chapters 10, 11 and 12 for a more comprehensive articulation of these three unalienable rights.
50. See chapter 13 for a comprehensive look at the characteristics of tyranny of England over her Colonies.
51. The Constitution of the Commonwealth of Massachusetts, Preamble,
52. Plymouth Rock Foundation is now led by the author of this work – see www.plymrock.org.
53. How America Got Its Declaration of Independence, article on-line.
54. Ibid.
55. John Adams to Thomas Jefferson, 28 June 1813 – Founders online.
56. Definitive Peace Treaty between the United States and Great Britain – Founders online.

Chapter 3

57. Calvin, John, Institutes of the Christian Religion, Eerdmans Publishing Company, 1989, Chapter II, Section 1, page 40.
58. Wells, W. V., Life of Samuel Adams, as quoted in Hall, Verna, Christian History of the Constitution: Christian Self-Government, p. 363
59. Jehle, Paul, Restoring the Christian Committees of Correspondence, Proclaim Liberty Newsletter, Heritage Institute Ministries, Vol. 2, Issue 2, April-June, 1992, p. 4.
60. Hall, Verna, The Christian History of the Constitution of the United States, pages 365-370 where Samuel Adams 'Rights of the Colonists' treatise is located.
61. Ibid., pages 365, 367, 368.
62. Calvin Coolidge's Speech on the Occasion of the One Hundred and Fiftieth Anniversary of the Declaration of Independence, July 5, 1926, Philadelphia, Pennsylvania – online.
63. Thomas Jefferson to Richard Henry Lee, May 8, 1825 - Founders online.
64. Baldwin, Alice, The New England Clergy and the American Revolution, Frederick Unger Publishing, 1928, page xii.
65. Stout, page 4.
66. Galloway, Charles P., Christianity and the American Commonwealth, 1898, republished by American Vision, 2005, p. 116
67. John Adams to Timothy Pickering, August 6, 1822 - Founders online.
68. Hall, CHOC, pages 365-370.
69. Thornton, J. Wingate, The Pulpit of the American Revolution, 1860, as quoted in The Christian History of the Constitution of the United States of America: Christian Self-Government, F.A.C.E., 1966, page 372.
70. See 1st Timothy 2:1-5; 3:4
71. Matthew 28:18-20; Ephesians 4:11-16; Matthew 5:13-16.
72. Fiske, John, Beginnings of New England of the Puritan Theocracy in Its Relation to Civil and Religious Liberty, Houghton Mifflin and Company, 1889, page 302.

73. Waters, Thomas Franklin, and Felton, Mrs. Eunice Whitney Farley, Two Ipswich Patriots, Publication of the Ipswich Historical Society, volume xxvi, 1927.
74. THE Declaration, Of the Gentlemen, Merchants, and Inhabitants of BOSTON, and the Country Adjacent. April 18th. 1689.
75. Fiske, Beginnings, pages 301-304.
76. See The "Birthplace of American Independence" – Historic Ipswich Seal.
77. Waters and Felton, Two Ipswich Patriots.
78. Ibid.
79. Dexter, Henry Martin, The Congregationalism of the Last Three Hundred Years, New York, 1880, as quoted in The Christian History of the American Revolution: Consider and Ponder, F.A.C.E., 1976, page 100.
80. Psalm 19 is an example of this, with the first 6 verses reveal God as Creator, and the rest articulate revealed law.
81. Wise, John, A Vindication of the Government of New England Churches, printed in Boston, 1717, republished by Kessinger Publishing, page 37.
82. Ibid., page 42.
83. Ibid., page 61.
84. Ibid., page 44.
85. See the book Wines, E.C., The Roots of the Republic, where excerpts from the 1861 original work are reprinted by the Plymouth Rock Foundation, 1997 – www.plymrock.org.
86. See 1st Samuel 8.
87. Bushman, Richard L., editor, The Great Awakening: Documents on the Revival of Religion, 1740-1745, Institute of Early American History and Culture by the University of North Carolina Press, 1970, pages xi-xii.
88. Cooke, Tony, Highlights from Whitefield's Journal, 1740-1745, Tony Cooke Ministries - Highlights from Whitefield's Journal (1740-1745) by Tony Cooke | Tony Cooke Ministries
89. Stout, Harry, The Divine Dramatist: George Whitefield and the Rise of Modern Evangelism, Eerdmans Publishing, 1991, p. xiv, 5.
90. Beeke, Joel R., Editor, Forerunner of the Great Awakening; Sermons by Theodorus Jacobus Frelinghuysen (1691-1747), Eerdmans Publishing, 2000, p. vii.
91. Ibid., pages xi-xiii.
92. Winslow, Ola Elizabeth, Jonathan Edwards (1703-1758): A Biography, Macmillan Company, 1940, p. 34 and 45.
93. Hansen, Chadwick, Witchcraft at Salem, George Brazilier, 1969, pages 210 and 215.
94. Jehle, Paul, Spiritual Warfare: The Salem Witch Trials of 1692, Heritage Institute Ministries, Volume 3, Issues 3-4, 1992, pages 41-42.
95. Morgan, George, The True Patrick Henry, Lippincott, 1929, p. 57.
96. Stoll, pages 20-21.
97. Ibid., page 21.
98. Ibid., page 50.

99. Beliles, Mark, and Newcombe, Jerry, *Thomas Jefferson and the God Who Gave Us Liberty,* Morgan James, 2026, page 160.

Chapter 4

100. Adams, Samuel, January 9, 1769 article in the Boston Gazette, as quoted in Hall, Verna, page 38.
101. Blackstone, William, Commentaries on the Laws of England, 1755, as quoted in The Christian History of the United States Constitution: Christian Self-Government, compiled by Verna Hall, 1966, page 141. – www.face.net.
102. Ibid., p. 143.
103. Skousen, Cleon, The Making of America, National Center for Constitutional Studies, pages 53-61.
104. Hardinge, Leslie, The Celtic Church in Britain, London, 1972, pages 49-50.
105. See The Original Catholic Encyclopedia on Stephen Langton - Stephen Langton | Catholic Answers Encyclopedia - online.
106. Leeming, Rev. J. R., Stephen Langton: Hero of Magna Charta, London, 1915, page 72.
107. See Hall, Verna, who compiles excerpts from Magna Charta, pages 37-41.
108. Ibid., page 40.
109. See chapter 15 for more information on George III's Prohibition Bill in December of 1775.
110. Hall, page 38.

Chapter 5

111. See Federer, William J., Change to Chains, 6,000 Year Quest for Control, Amerisearch, Inc., 2011.
112. Rushdoony, R. J., The Institutes of Biblical Law, The Craig Press, 1973, page 10 and 11.
113. John Quincy Adams oration of July 4, 1837 – wallbuilders.com.
114. Bradford, William, Of Plimoth Plantation, edited by Samuel Eliot Morison, Alfred A. Knopf, 1989, page 75.
115. Ibid, page 9.
116. Ibid., page 370.
117. Titus, Herb., The Mayflower Compact: Seedbed for the American Constitutional Republic, Plymouth Rock Foundation's E-news, Plymouth Rock Foundation, www.plymrock.org, November, 2013.
118. Stratton, Eugene Aubrey, Plymouth Colony Its History and People: 1620-1691, Ancestry Publishing, 1986, pages 373-374.
119. Robertson, G., The Tyrannicide Brief, Pantheon Books, 2005, page 191.
120. Ibid., page 192.
121. Nelson, E., The Hebrew Republic, Harvard Press, 2010, pages 2, 3 and 6.
122. Eidsmoe, John, The Mayflower Compact, America's Charter of Government - Col. John Eidsmoe: The Mayflower Compact — America's charter of government – online.

Chapter 6

123. Jones, Archie, Christian Principles in the Articles of Confederation, Plymouth Rock Foundation, 1991, p. 5.
124. See Lee Resolution (1776) | National Archives.
125. Sources of our Liberties, pgs. 272-289.
126. Ibid., pgs. 290-300.
127. See Chapter 15 for a deeper explanation of interposition.
128. Eidsmoe, John, *Historical and Theological Foundations of Law,* Volume I, Ancient Wisdom, American Vision Press, 2011, p. 215.
129. Eidsmoe, John, *The Iroquois Confederacy and the American Republic,* Plymouth Rock Foundation Newsletter, Vol. 30, Issues 3-4, 2007.
130. *Ibid.*
131. Jones, p. 5.
132. See The John Dickinson Draft of the Articles of Confederation – The Panorama – online.
133. Jones, p. 5.
134. BC, AD, CE, and BCE: Meanings and Differences Explained – Calendar – online.
135. Jones, pages 13-27.
136. The State Debate papers, along with the Federalist Papers (letters written in newspapers by James Madison, John Jay and Alexander Hamilton), provide the best commentary on the original intention of the clauses of our present constitution.
137. Article VII.
138. James Madison to Robert Hayne, 3 April, 1830 – Founders online.
139. See chapter 14 for an explanation of self-preservation as it relates to the nature of the Declaration of Independence.
140. Skousen, Cleon, The Making of America, p. 230.
141. Ibid, pages 206-207.
142. Ibid., p. 390, taken from Norton, Thomas James, Undermining the Constitution: A History of Lawless Government, New York: Devid-Adair Co., 1950, p. 188.
143. Ketcham, Ralph, The Anti-Federalist Papers and the Constitutional Convention Debates, 1986, Speech of Patrick Henry June 5, 1788, page 199.
144. Wilson, James, Of the Law of Nations, as quoted in Hall, Verna, The Christian History of the Constitution of the United States: Christian Self-Government with Union, F.A.C.E., 1962, p. 221. – www.face.net.
145. Allen, Dr. William, Best Friends: The Declaration and the Constitution, Plymouth Rock Foundation Newsletter, Volume 28, Issues 1-2, January-April, 2005.

Chapter 7

146. Word #120 from Strong's Exhaustive Concordance of the Bible, by James Strong, MacDonald Publishing Company.
147. See the New Living Translation of the Bible as an example.
148. See Amos, Gary, Defending the Declaration, Wolgemuth & Hyatt, 1989, page 106, documenting J.I. Packer's reasoning.
149. See McDowell, Stephen, The Bible, Slavery and America's Founders, Providence Foundation, 2003, page 2.
150. Spurgeon, Charles, Spurgeon's Verse Expositions of the Bible – www.truthaccordingtoscripture.com.
151. Johnston, Jeremiah, Unimaginable: What would our World be Like without Christianity, Bethany House, 2017, page 52.
152. Ibid., pages 52,57.
153. Ibid., page 57.
154. See Galatians 4:4.
155. See 1st John 2:29 which states both truths in the same verse, "if you know that He is righteous (born again), you know that everyone that practices righteousness is born of him" (in other words their lives progressively match their profession).
156. Gray, Derwin, and Viola, Frank., The Race Card of the Early Christians – What they can teach us Today, page 1.
157. Johnston, page 52.
158. See https://wallbuilders.com/faqs/
159. See https://chicago.suntimes.com/2019/9/10/20859458/fact-check-declaration-independence-slaves-trumbull-painting-arlen-parsa
160. Wood, Gordon, World Socialist Web Site, www.wsws.org for Wood's letter on the 1619 Project of December 21, 2019.
161. Quoted from J. L. Bell, Blogspot Sunday, January 11, 2009 - Boston 1775: Samuel Adams and Slavery: The Private Man
162. Bowen, Catherine Drinker, John Adams and the American Revolution, pages 600-601.
163. McCullough, David, John Adams, p. 104
164. Ibid., p. 103-104.
165. Ketcham, The Anti-Federalist Papers and the Constitutional Convention Debates, pages 161-162.
166. See https://www.nlnrac.org/american/declaration-of-independence/primary-source-documents/dred-scott-decision
167. Butterfield, L. H., Editor, Adams Family Correspondence, Volume I – December 1761-May 1776, Belknap press, 1963, Letter from John Adams to Abigail Adams, March 31, 1776, page 370.
168. Ibid., page 382.
169. John Adams to John Taylor, April 19, 1814 – Founders online.
170. Webster, Noah., An American Dictionary of the English Language, published in facsimile edition by the Foundation for American Christian Education, 1967, under Right, n., #5 and #10 definitions.
171. King, Martin Luther, Jr. I have a Dream Speech, August 28, 1963 – available on-line.

172. Wood, Gordon, see
https://chicago.suntimes.com/2019/9/10/20859458/fact-check-declaration-independence-slaves-trumbull-painting-arlen-parsa
173. De Tocqueville, Alexis, Democracy in America, Chapter 17 - DeTocqueville - Democracy in America.pdf

Chapter 8

174. Levy, Andrew, The First Emancipator: Slavery, Religion, and the Quiet Revolution of Robert Carter, Random House, 2005.
175. The contents of this chapter, in an abbreviated form, was published as an E-Newsletter by the Plymouth Rock Foundation, July, 2017.
176. See Luke 17:20-21 where Jesus tells the Pharisees that the kingdom of God comes not from the outside from external forces, but primarily from within the hearts of individuals.
177. See Tickets & Passes - Colonial Williamsburg.
178. Levy, p. 6.
179. See "Nomini Hall Slave Legacy" - see History of the Carter Family – Nomini Hall Slave Legacy
180. Levy, p. 11, 13.
181. "History of the Carter Family" – online.
182. Levy, p. 15.
183. Ibid., pages 21-22.
184. Ibid., p. 19.
185. Ibid., pages 28-29.
186. Ibid., pages 29-30.
187. Ibid., p. 27.
188. Ibid., pgs. 47-51.
189. Fithian, Philip Vickers, Journals & Letters 1773-1774, University Press of Virginia, 1957, pages 84-85.
190. Ibid., pages 72-73.
191. Levy, p. 75.
192. Ibid., p. 80. – taken from Romans 7:9.
193. Levy, p. 139.
194. Levy, p. 81.
195. Levy, p. 98.
196. Ibid., p. xvii.
197. Ibid., pgs 111-120, 125.
198. West, Thomas G., Vindicating the Founders, Rowman & Littlefield Publishers, Inc., 1997, page 5.
199. Ibid., p. 6.
200. Ibid., p. 7.
201. Northwest Ordinance (1787) | National Archives
202. Ibid., pgs. 136-139.
203. Ibid., page 144.
204. Ibid., p. xiii.

205. Ibid., p. 139.
206. West, p. 11.
207. Carter, Robert III, A Man Named Robert: Lessons from the life of America's First Great Emancipator, Cartier and Beaufort Press, 2022, pages 37-38.

Chapter 9

208. See Rushdoony, R. J., The Myth of Over-Population, Craig Press, 1969 where among other things, he demonstrates that over-population due to centralized government is the real issue, not the number of people on the planet.
209. Locke, John, Of the State of Nature, Of Civil Government, Book II, Chapter X, as quoted in Hall, Verna, The Christian History of the American Revolution: Christian Self-Government, page 58 – www.face.net.
210. Amos, pages 106-107.
211. Locke, in CHOC, www.face.net, p. 61.
212. Allen, Scott, Why Social Justice is not Biblical Justice, Credo House Publishers, 2020, page 43.
213. Trueman, Carl R., Strange New World, Crossway, 2022, pages 34-35.
214. *Ibid.,* page 35.
215. Wiser, Dan, Culture of Death: The Troubling Rise of Assisted Suicide and Euthanasia, 2024 – available on-line.
216. Walton, Rus., Biblical Solutions to Contemporary Problems, Plymouth Rock Foundation, 1989, pages 18-19.
217. Supreme Court case 410 U.S. 113 (1973).
218. U.S. Abortion Statistics By Year (1973-Current) - Christian Life Resources
219. See the recent Pew Research Study at https://www.pewresearch.org/fact-tank/2022/06/24/what-the-data-says-about-abortion-in-the-u-s-2/
220. Titus, Herb, The Forecast, Volume 3, Issue 5, "Roe v. Wade", 1996.
221. Supreme Court case 60 U.S. at 407.
222. See https://teachingamericanhistory.org/document/speech-on-the-dred-scott-decision/
223. Titus, page 6.
224. Ibid., pages 4-5.
225. See http://ww1.antiochian.org/node/16956.
226. Tertullian, Apology 9.8.
227. Blackstone, Sir William, Commentaries on the Laws of England (1771), Vol. 1, pages 129-130.
228. See https://publishing.cdlib.org/ucpressebooks/view?docId=ft967nb5z5&chunk.id=d0e195&toc.id=&brand=ucpress
229. See https://www.lifeissues.net/writers/tay/tay_03foundingfather.html
230. "Lectures on Law," Ch. 12, p. 597 in The Works of James Wilson. ed. Robert G. McCloskey (1967)
231. Barton, David., Psalm 139 – The Bible, the Founding Fathers, and Abortion., wallbuilders.com; 2012.

232. See https://www.supremecourt.gov/opinions/21pdf/19-1392_6j37.pdf - pages 9-10 (Alito, pgs. 1-2)
233. See https://www.axios.com/2022/05/14/abortion-state-laws-bans-roe-supreme-court
234. "From John Adams to Massachusetts Militia, 11 October 1798," Founders Online, National Archives.
235. Johnston, Jeremiah, Unanswered, Lasting Truth for Trending Questions, Whitaker House, 2015, page 107.
236. *Ibid.,* p. 107.
237. See D.L. Moody - I cannot preach on hell unless I preach with...
238. See Corrie ten Boom on God's Presence in Dark Times - HavenToday.org.
239. See Matthew 5:21-22.
240. See Ephesians 4:15 exhorting us, as a matter of spiritual maturity, to speak the truth in love.

Chapter 10

241. Gesenius, H.W.F., Hebrew-Chaldee Lexicon to the Old Testament, pages 473-474, word #4390 in Strong's. The implication of this word is not to re-fill as in re-populate (from a pre-Adamic race or "gap theory" of creation). It appears, in its breadth, to fill empty space with actions of men and women, to complete, hence, the thought of productivity and technology.
242. See Genesis 4 when all sorts of vocations were introduced, from iron to instruments, from the freedom to produce.
243. See Jehle, Paul, Go Ye Therefore and Teach All Nations, Volume I: Philosophy and Vision, Plymouth Rock Foundation, 2006, pages 115-116 for a more discussion of what it might mean to fill the earth with the productivity and technology of inventions by discovering God's creation laws and utilizing them to serve others.
244. See Rushdoony, R. J. The Institutes of Biblical Law, The Craig Press, 1973, page 219, expanding the command from the commentary of John Calvin.
245. Federer, William, Ancient Israel Inspired the Right of the People to Keep and Bear Arms, American Minute, March 2, 2022.
246. Ibid.
247. Cole, Darrel, When God Says War is Right, Waterbrook Press, 2002, page 43.
248. Thayer's Greek-English Lexicon of the New Testament, Baker Book House, 1977, page 204.
249. See Galatians 5:16-18; and Ist John 3:4-6.
250. Galatians 5:13 states that "you have been called unto liberty, only use not liberty for an occasion to the flesh, but by love serve one another." Liberty is not license to do what you want.
251. See Galatians 5:14-15 which indicates that lawlessness leads to being consumed (dominated by) one another.
252. Webster, Noah., 1828 Dictionary.
253. Webster, Noah., History of the United States, 1835, page 273.

254. Webster, Noah, Value of the Bible and Excellence of the Christian Religion, 1834, republished by the Foundation for American Christian Education, 1988, page 99.
255. See, for the year 2021; https://www.opendoorsusa.org/christian-persecution/
256. See https://www.monticello.org/research-education/thomas-jefferson-encyclopedia/virginia-statute-religious-freedom/
257. See DeMar, Gary, God and Government, Volume I, American Vision, 1998.
258. Schaff, Philip, Church and State in the United States, 1888, as quoted in The Christian History of the Constitution of the United States: Self-Government with Union, compiled by Verna Hall, Foundation for American Christian Education, 1962, pages 38-39.
259. See https://www.monticello.org/research-education/thomas-jefferson-encyclopedia/virginia-statute-religious-freedom/
260. Story, Joseph, A Familiar Exposition of the Constitution of the United States, Regnery Gateway, Inc., 1986, page 314.
261. See DeBouer, Louis, Lord of the Conscience, published by Plymouth Rock Foundation, for a detailed explanation of religious liberty at the state and eventually the federal level that birthed the First Amendment and Religious Liberty.
262. De Toqueville, Alexis, Democracy in America, Vintage Books, 1990, Volume I, pages 305-306.
263. See Malachi 4:5-6 where the final prophet declares that through generational transfer blessing is given to the earth rather than a curse when "he shall turn the heart of the fathers to the children, and the children to their fathers."
264. Titus, Herb., The Forecast, July 1, 1994, The Establishment Clause: Education, page 6.
265. See https://www.monticello.org/research-education/thomas-jefferson-encyclopedia/virginia-statute-religious-freedom/
266. See https://face.net/wp-content/uploads/2018/11/The-Christian-Roots-of-Our-Constitution-Verna-Hall.pdf, page 4.
267. See https://face.net/wp-content/uploads/2018/11/The-Christian-Roots-of-Our-Constitution-Verna-Hall.pdf, page 6.
268. Schaff, Philip, Church and State in the United States, 1888, as quoted in The Christian History of the Constitution of the United States: Self-Government with Union, compiled by Verna Hall, Foundation for American Christian Education, 1962, page 40.
269. De Toqueville, Alexis, Democracy in America, Volume I, Vintage Books, 1990, p 308, 306.
270. Schaff, pages 38-39.
271. Stout, Harry, The New England Soul, Oxford University Press, 1986, pages 3-4.
272. Ibid., page 7.

273. Stout, Harry., The New England Soul, Oxford University Press, 1986., page 16.
274. Ibid., page 16.
275. See chapter 15 for a more in-depth look the doctrine of interposition.
276. Stout, The New England Soul, pages 3-4, 7-8 where he documents that the average church-goer heard 7,000 sermons in a lifetime and thematically when government demanded unlimited submission, lawful resistance was imperative.
277. Hart, Levi., Liberty Described and Recommended: in a Sermon Preached to the Corporation of Freemen in Farmington, Hartford, 1775, American Political Writing during the Founding Era, 1760-1805, Volume I, Liberty Press, 1983, page 312.
278. Mill, John Stuart., On Liberty, 1859, re-published by The Classics of Liberty Library, 1992, pages 21-22.
279. See Jehle, Paul, The Pilgrims and the Defense of Liberty, Plymouth Rock Foundation E-News, June, 2020, and The Establishment of the Citizen Militia: Plymouth, 1621, Plymouth Rock Foundation E-News, February, 2021.
280. See Daniel 9:2-3; Joel 1:16; 2:16-17 and 2nd Chronicles 7:14 as examples.
281. See James 4:6-8 as a recipe for dealing with evil. Our focus must first be on submission to God rather than resistance.
282. See Genesis 1:28 and the author's explanation of the nature of liberty replenishing the earth with man's creativity in honor of God in his work Go Ye Therefore and Teach All Nations, Volume I, Plymouth Rock Foundation, 2006, pages 115-116.
283. Prince, Derek, Changing History through Prayer and Fasting, Fleming H. Revell, 1973, page 132.
284. Lechford, Thomas, Plain Dealing or News from New England, 1867, as quoted in Love, William DeLoss, The Fast and Thanksgiving Days of New England, Houghton-Mifflin Company, 1895, pages 240-241.
285. See Jehle, Paul, Spiritual War: the Salem Witch Trials of 1692, Heritage Institute Ministries, 1992.
286. Love, William DeLoss, The Fast and Thanksgiving Days of New England, Houghton-Mifflin Company, 1895.
287. https://wallbuilders.com/chw/lessons/lesson-3-american-revolution-original/
288. Bancroft, George, History of the United States, page 295.
289. Sources of our Liberties, where the Resolutions of the Stamp Act Congress (October, 1765) declared that England had violated their own written Charters in having Parliament tax them, the Declarations and Resolves of the First Continental Congress (October, 1774) reiterated the rights of life, liberty and property as God-given, the Declaration of the Causes and Necessity of Taking up Arms (July, 1775) carefully laid out the right of self-defense, American Bar Association, 1978, pages 261-300.
290. Bancroft, page 291.
291. See https://wallbuilders.com/sermon-battle-of-lexington-1776/
292. See https://www.nationalguard.mil/Resources/Image-Gallery/Historical-Paintings/Heritage-Series/Stand-Your-Ground/

293. See https://www.lexingtonminutemen.com/the-minute-man-oath.html.
294. Gilman, Theodore, Rev. Jonas Clark, Pastor of the Church at Lexington during the Revolution, Leader of Revolutionary Thought, New York Society of the Order of the Founders and Patriots of America, 1911, page 10.
295. Ibid., page 11.
296. Clark, Jonas, The Fate of Blood-thirsty Oppressors, and God's tender Care for his distressed People, April 19, 1776, The Noah Webster Library, printed by Powars and Willis, 1776, page 6.
297. https://www.nationaldayofprayer.org/history_of_prayer_in_america
298. Clark, page 6.
299. Ibid., pages 6-7, 11-13.
300. https://christianheritagefellowship.com/june-12-1775-first-congressional-fasting-and-prayer-proclamation/
301. See https://revive1775.com/patriots-day-geo-varney/
302. Matthew 6:10.

Chapter 11

303. Eidsmoe, John, Christianity and the Constitution, Baker Academic, 1987, pages 51-53.
304. Amos, Gary, Defending the Declaration, Wolgemuth & Hyatt, Publishers, Inc., 1989, page 107.
305. See Walton, Rus, Fundamentals for American Christians, Volume I, Plymouth Rock Foundation, 1979, pages 25-45 for an excellent treatise on the "dominion mandate." This is also covered by Paul Jehle's teaching on this classic course, FACS, available at www.plymrock.org.
306. Exodus 20:15,17.
307. See Jefferson's own words as to why he was pressed by the committee to be the primary penman of the Declaration. https://www.archives.gov/founding-docs/declaration-history#:~:text=case%20for%20independence.-,The%20Committee%20of%20Five,southerner%2C%20Thomas%20Jefferson%20of%20Virginia.
308. https://www.monticello.org/research-education/thomas-jefferson-encyclopedia/pursuit-happiness/
309. Part the First, Article I – Massachusetts State Constitution – online.
310. Amos, page 120.
311. See Numbers 18:21-28 which is the Lord's Tithe for the Levites; Deuteronomy 12:6-7, 17-18 where the festive tithe went for the great feasts – Passover, Pentecost, and Tabernacles; and finally; Deuteronomy 14:27-29, for those in need. See Rushdoony, R. J., Institutes of Biblical Law, the Craig Press, 1973, pages 52-53.
312. See Rushdoony, R. J., Tithing and Dominion, for fuller explanation of this premise.
313. See Exodus 30:11-16, as well as Fugate, Robert, Toward a Theology of Taxation, Lord of the Nations, 2012.

314. See Leviticus 25:1-13. The year of Jubilee allowed family generational dynasties, preserving the right of families to gain wealth. Every 50 years a Jubilee was called. It returned land to the original owners, released all slaves, and for our purposes today, it also released debt slaves in addition to giving rest to the land. Loans would be figured based on the upcoming Jubilee, and it kept debt from accumulating beyond one generation.
315. Matthew 12:35
316. Webster, Noah, An American Dictionary of the English Language, 1828, published in facsimile by The Foundation for American Christian Education, 1967. – www.face.net.
317. Blackstone, William, Commentaries on the Laws of England, Book 2, chapter 7, as quoted in Landholding in England, Chapter 1 - https://en.wikisource.org/wiki/Landholding_in_England/Chapter_1
318. See https://thelawdictionary.org/?s=allodial
319. See 1st Samuel 8.
320. Amos, pages 111-115.
321. Skousen, Cleon, pages 41-61.
322. Landholding in England - online.
323. Hardinge, Leslie, The Celtic Church in Britain, London, 1972; and Witley Stokes, ed., The Tripartite Life of Patrick, II, 300 where Stokes states; "This synthesis, of the old Brehon Laws and the regulations of the Old Testament, throws light on the practices of the ancient Irish Christians, and hence of the Celtic Church. It probably goes back for its inspiration to the old law book, Liber ex Lege Moisi. Wherever Patrick established a church he was believed to have left a copy of "the books of the Law and the Books of the Gospel"
324. See Jehle, Paul, The Significance of Magna Charta, Plymouth Rock Foundation, 2015; a two-part audio teaching that documents the fact that the colonies attempted to restore the original English liberties under King Alfred - www.plymrock.org.
325. Locke, John, Second Treatise on Government, 1790, chapter IX – Of the Ends of Political Society and Government, see https://press-pubs.uchicago.edu/founders/documents/v1ch16s3.html
326. Madison, James, 1792; The Papers of James Madison. Edited by William T. Hutchinson et al. Chicago and London: University of Chicago Press, 1962--77 (vols. 1--10); Charlottesville: University Press of Virginia, 1977, as quoted in The Founders Constitution - https://press-pubs.uchicago.edu/founders/documents/v1ch16s23.html.
327. The Virginia Declaration of Rights | National Archives – online.
328. Webster, Noah, An American Dictionary of the English Language, published in 1828, republished by the Foundation for American Christian Education, 1967, see www.face.net.
329. Bancroft, George, History of the United States of America, from chapter XIV, Self-Government in Massachusetts, p. 283.
330. See Jefferson, Thomas, A Summary View of the Rights of British America, 1772; https://avalon.law.yale.edu/18th_century/jeffsumm.asp

331. See New England Historical Society – Pine Tree Riot – online.
332. See, as an example, David Barton's explanation of this flag - https://wallbuilders.com/an-appeal-to-heaven-flag/
333. See "Leslie's Retreat" from the Historical Collections of the Essex Institute, Volume 27, July, 1880, page 191.
334. See https://www.law.cornell.edu/supct/html/04-108.ZD1.html
335. See https://chalcedon.edu/resources/articles/eminent-domain
336. https://www.amphilsoc.org/blog/musings-manuscripts-testament-thomson#:~:text=Through%20his%20pioneering%20biblical%20translations,to%20translate%20the%20New%20Testament.
337. https://www.healingfield.org/education/
338.
https://www.ushistory.org/betsy/#:~:text=Why%20are%20the%20stars%20in,new%20constellation%20in%20the%20heavens.%22

Chapter 12

339. Burke, Edmund, in the Impeachment of Warren Hastings, May 28, 1794, as quoted in America's God and Country Encyclopedia of Quotations, edited by William J. Federer, FAME Publishing, Inc., 1994, page 82.
340. Blackstone, William, Commentaries on the Laws of England, Volume I, 1765, reprinted by University of Chicago Press, 1979, pages 38-41.
341. Ibid., page 42.
342. Federer, William, editor; America's God and Country Encyclopedia of Quotations, pages 48-49.
343. Thornton, John Wingate, The Pulpit of the American Revolution, published 1860, as quoted in the Intercessors for America newsletter of November, 1994, written by John G. Talcott, Jr., titled "Election Days in Early America."
344. Kendall, Edward Augustus, Travels through the Northern Parts of the United States in the Years 1807-1808, as published in the Providential Perspective, Vol. 9, No. 3, August, 1994 – www.providenefoundation.com
345. Kelley, Kate, Election Day: An American Holiday, An American History, ASJA Press, 2008, p. 10.
346. McDowell, Stephen, Election Day in Early America, quoting Thornton in its Volume 9, Number 3, August, 1994 newsletter, published by the Providence Foundation – www.providencefoundation.com
347. Kelley, pages 5-7.
348. See Walton, Rus, On Selecting Those who Represent Us, April, 1980 newsletter of the Plymouth Rock Foundation – www.plymrock.org.
349. See Burnet, Matthias, whose Election Sermon of May 12, 1803 noted many of these qualities, published in the Providential Perspective, Vol. 9, No. 4, October 1994 – www.providencefoundation.com.
350. Burke, Edmund, in the Impeachment of Warren Hastings, May 28, 1794, as quoted in America's God and Country Encyclopedia of Quotations, edited by William J. Federer, FAME Publihing, Inc., 1994, page 82.

351. Wilson, "Of the Law of Nations" - Lectures on Law 1790-91, from the "Christian History of the Constitution of the United States; Self-Government with Union," quoted on page 223.
352. Bemis, Samuel Flagg, John Quincy Adams and the Foundations of American Foreign Policy, Alfred A. Knopf, 1950, p. 568.
353. Resolutions of the Stamp Act Congress, October 19, 1765, reproduced in the Sources of Our Liberties, American Bar Foundation, 1978, page 270.
354. Declaration and Resolves of the First Continental Congress, October 14, 1774; Ibid., page 287.
355. Resolutions of the Stamp Act Congress, October 19, 1765, Ibid., page 270.
356. Sources, Declaration and Resolves, page 287.
357. Beck, Paul, Jr., The Life of George Washington, American Sunday School Union, Philadelphia, 1832, as quoted on p.47.
358. Ibid., as quoted on page 47.
359. Declaration and Resolves of the First Continental Congress, reprinted in Sources, page 289.
360. See chapter 15 for a more in-depth discussion of this document and its meaning of interposition.
361. Henry, William Wirt., Patrick Henry - Life, Correspondence and Speeches, NY: Burt Franklin, 1969, Volume I, pages 91-93., as quoted in America's God and Country Encyclopedia of Quotations, p.289.

Chapter 13

362. This chapter and its general contents was given as an oration at New Testament Church's Christian Heritage Sunday on July 3, 2022.
363. See From Change to Chains by Bill Federer (2011).
364. Genesis 1:27.
365. See Amos, Gary., Defending the Declaration, Wolgemuth & Hyatt Publishers, Inc., 1989, pages 75-77. See also Romans 2:14-15 as well as Locke's Essay on Human Understanding, from Amos, pages 93, 95 to see how Locke (well-read by the Founders) used the understanding of creation and the fall to discern the origin of God-given rights and self-evident truth.
366. Harari, as quoted in DeMar, Gary, "Human Life has absolutely No Meaning", American Vision, March 24, 2022, p. 1
367. Isaiah 5:20.
368. Harari, Yuval Noah, Sapiens: A Brief History of Humankind, HarperCollins, 2015, page 110.
369. Ibid., page 109.
370. Schwab, Klaus declared this goal at the Davos, Switzerland meeting of the Great Reset in June of 2020.
371. Matthew 7:15-16.
372. Bancroft, George, Fourth of July Oration, July 4, 1826 in Northampton, Massachusetts, as quoted in Hawken, Henry, Trumpets of Glory: Fourth of July Orations, 1786-1861, Salmon Brook Historical Society, 1976, pages 81-82.
373. Ecclesiastes 1:9.

374. Goff, Kenneth, a former member of the Communist Party from 1936-1939, and who writes in the forward This manual of the Communist Party should be in the hands of every loyal American, that they may be alerted to the fact that it is not always by armies and guns that a nation is conquered." – The Soviet Art of Brainwashing, p. 5, 8, 17, 33, 35.
375. Ibid., pages 42, 43, 44.
376. Arn, Larry, Today's Firestorm and the Declaration, Imprimis, Hillsdale College, November, 2025 - Today's Firestorm and the Declaration - Imprimis.
377. Matthew 6:10.
378. Peacocke, Dennis, On the Destiny of Nations: Resolving our Economic Crisis, Rebuild, 2012, page 15.
379. Daniel 2:44.

Chapter 14

380. See Matthew 20:20-28 and Mark 10:35-45 to gain the context of this story.
381. The general contents of this chapter was originally given as an oration at New Testament Church's Christian Heritage Sunday on June 30, 2024.
382. See from Change to Chains by Bill Federer (2011).
383. Eidsmoe, John, Christianity and the Constitution, Baker Academic, 1987, pages 51-53.
384. See Genesius Hebrew-Chaldee Lexicon to the Old Testament, Baker Book House, 1979, page 517 where word #4910 and #4911 as used in Strong's Concordance are given amplification.
385. Webster, Noah, An American Dictionary of the English Language, 1828, republished by the Foundation for American Christian Education, www.face.net, 1967.
386. Unger, Harlow Giles, John Hancock: Merchant King and American Patriot, John Wiley & Sons, 2000, page 58.
387. See "Coronation of George III and Charlotte"; https://en.wikipedia.org/wiki/Coronation_of_George_III_and_Charlotte#:~:text =The%20coronation%20of%20George%20III,Chapel%20Royal%2C%20St%20 James's%20Palace.
388. Unger, page 1.
389. See John Hancock's Signature: Size Does Matter - Brian D. Colwell online.
390. Charles River Editors, American Legends: The Life of John Hancock, charlesrivereditors.com, p. 6.
391. See https://en.wikipedia.org/wiki/Samuel_Cooper_(clergyman)
392. See https://www.masshist.org/2012/juniper/assets/ed-curricula/blackington_samuel_cooper_documents.pdf
393. https://www.masshist.org/database/viewer.php?item_id=781
394. https://www.consource.org/document/a-sermon-on-the-day-of-the-commencement-of-the-constitution-by-samuel-cooper-1780-10-25/
395. Letters of Samuel Cooper to Thomas Pownell, 1769-1777, The American Historical Review, Jan., 1903, Vol. 8, No. 2 (Jan – 1903), pp. 301-330, Oxford University Press.

396. https://en.wikipedia.org/wiki/Thomas_Pownall
397. https://www.loc.gov/resource/rbpe.03800700/?st=text
398. See Charles Edel's commentary - https://www.ussc.edu.au/a-tyrant-is-unfit-to-be-the-ruler-of-a-free-people
399. Blackstone, William, Commentaries on the Laws of England, Volume I - https://oll.libertyfund.org/quotes/sir-william-blackstone-provides-a-strong-defence-of-personal-liberty-and-concludes-that-to-secretly-hurry-a-man-to-prison-is-a-dangerous-engine-of-arbitrary-government-1753
400. Madison, James, Letters and Writings of James Madison, 1795.
401. Locke, John, Second Treatise of Government, 1690.
402. Hamilton, Alexander, Federalist #6 - https://avalon.law.yale.edu/18th_century/fed06.asp
403. See https://harpers.org/2010/05/montesquieu-tyranny-in-the-shadow-of-the-law/
404. See the author's treatise on "Interposition", a series of four lectures plus the accompanying notes on "interposition"; www.plymrock.org.
405. See the next chapter, 15, that will articulate in greater depth how this doctrine was applied by the colonists.
406. See https://www.famous-trials.com/massacre/200-oration

Chapter 15

407. The Story Behind: Come Thou Fount of Every Blessing.
408. Jehle, Paul, Tyranny: Unfit to be the Ruler of a Free People, The New Testament Church, June 30, 2024, pages 1-2 where the biblical definition is derived from Genesis 1-3.
409. Webster, Noah, 1828 Dictionary - www.face.net.
410. See chapter 4 for how the Declaration relates to Magna Charta.
411. Calvin, John, Institutes of the Christian Religion, Eerdmans Publishing, 1989, Book 4, pages 674-675.
412. A Defense of Liberty Against Tyrants | Natural Law, Natural Rights, and American Constitutionalism.
413. Rutherford, Rev. Samuel, Lex Rex, 1644, republished by Sprinkle Publications, 1982, Harrisonburg, Virginia.
414. Jehle, Paul, Whom Shall we Obey? – published by the New Testament Church, July, 2020.
415. Colvin, Matthew, article and translation of the Magdeburg Confession, 1550 - 4 Levels of Injustice: Knowing When to Suffer Patiently and When to Resist - Into Your Hands LLC
416. Ibid.
417. Ibid.
418. Ibid.
419. See the oration by Paul Jehle, Tyranny: Unfit to the be the Ruler of a Free People, June 30, 2024, www.tntchurch.net.
420. Founders Online; Address to the Continental Congress, 16 June 1775
421. Founders Online; General Orders, 4 July 1775.

422. Perry, Richard L., Cooper, John C., editors; Sources of our Liberties, American Bar Foundation, 1978, Ch. XX, page 298.
423. Clarke, Jonas, The Battle of Lexington: A Sermon and Eyewitness, April 19, 1776 – Nordskog Publishing, 2007.
424. Sources, p. 295.
425. Luke 6 :44-46.
426. Mark 1:15
427. Sources, p. 296.
428. Ibid, p. 297.
429. Ibid., p. 297
430. Ibid., p. 297.
431. Ibid., p. 298, 299.
432. Understanding the Rationale for Preemptive Strikes in Policy - Total Military Insight - online.
433. Sources of our Liberties, p. 293-294.
434. Proclamation of Rebellion, King George III, Text, Primary Source Document.
435. From John Adams to Horatio Gates, 23 March 1776
436. Black's Law Dictionary, Fourth Edition (1961-1967) – definition of Interposition.
437. Jones, Rev. David, Defensive War in a Just Cause Sinless, Fast Day Sermon on July 20, 1775, Philadelphia, reprinted in The Christian History of the American Revolution: Consider and Ponder, Foundation for American Christian Education, 1976, pages 536-543, www.face.net.
438. Ibid. pgs. 299-300.

Chapter 16

439. Matthew 6:10.
440. See the next chapter (17) where some of what the delegates went through as a sacrifice is given.
441. McDowell, Stephen, What Really Happened on July 4th, Providential Perspective, Vol. 27, No. 2, June 2013, p. 1.
442. Ibid., p. 1 - McDowell notes that there is discrepancy regarding the exact wording of what Hancock said, but the sentiment is clear. In his footnote he writes "This quote is in Robert Flood, Men who Shaped America, Chicago, 1968, p. 276. Another records Hancock said: 'There, I guess King George will be able to read that' (The Annals of America, Vol. 2, Chicago: Encyclopedia Britannica, 1968, p. 449)
443. See John Jay to Charles Thomson, 19 July 1783.
444. MacArthur, John D., Charles Thomson – Principal Designer of the Great Seal, 2013 - Charles Thomson, Principal Designer of America's Great Seal.
445. See George Washington to Charles Thomson, 24 July 1789
446. MacArthur, p. 2.
447. Ibid., p. 2.

448. See - An enquiry into the causes of the alienation of the Delaware and Shawanese Indians from the British interest : and into the measures taken for recovering their friendship ... Together with the remarkable Journal of Christian French ... : Thomson, Charles, 1729-1824 : Free Download, Borrow, and Streaming : Internet Archive
449. MacArthur - Overview of the Great Seal of the United States – online.
450. Skousen, Cleon, pages 32-33.
451. Why Did Ben Franklin Favor the Turkey Over the Eagle for America's National Bird? – online.
452. Official 1782 Explanation' of the Great Seal of the United States – online.
453. Home | Museum of the Bible – online.
454. Journals of Congress, September 1782, pages 468-469. (Library of Congress) – online.
455. Thomson's Translation Explained – online.
456. McDowell, p., 1.
457. Samuel Adams Heritage Society – online.

Chapter 17

458. Erhman, Bart D., The Triumph of Christianity, Simon and Schuster, 2018, p. 72.
459. Vaughn, David. J., Give Me Liberty, Cumberland House, 1997, p. 75.
460. Ibid., p. 80.
461. Ibid., pages 80-85.
462. Ibid., p. 85.
463. Declaration of Independence | Architect of the Capitol
464. Lossing, Benson, Lives of the Signers of the Declaration of Independence, 1848, republished by Wallbuilders, 1995, p. 11 – www.wallbuilders.com.
465. Limbaugh, Rush, Sr., The Americans who Risked Everything, November 21, 2018. - My Father's Speech: The Americans Who Risked Everything – online.
466. The Signers of the Declaration of Independence - Ezra Taft Benson
467. Bradford, M.E., A Worthy Company, Plymouth Rock Foundation, 1982, p. viii – ix. – www.plymrock.org
468. William Ellery | Constitution Center.
469. Dwight., Lives of the Signers of the Declaration of Independence, New York, 1852, p. 74.
470. Ibid., page 76.
471. Dwight. N., pages 188-189., and John Morton (American politician) - Wikipedia
472. Dwight. N., pages 226-231., and Caesar Rodney - Wikipedia.
473. Ibid., page 242.
474. Thomas McKean to John Adams, 8 November 1779
475. Dwight. N., pages 142-143.
476. Ibid., pages 123-125.
477. Ibid., pages 97-117.

478. Ibid., pages 315-318.
479. Limbaugh, Sr., The Americans who Risked Everything, My Father's Speech: The Americans Who Risked Everything – online.
480. Stoll, Ira., Samuel Adams: A Life, Simon and Schuster, 2008, pages 1-6.
481. Ibid., pages 5-6.
482. Walton, Rus, They Signed for Us, Letter from Plymouth Rock, Vol. 3, Issue 6, July, 1981. – www.plymrock.org.

Chapter 18

483. Pennsylvania Charter of Privileges
484. Stone, Frederick D., The Founding of Pennsylvania, 1884, as quoted in Hall, Christian History of the Constitution, pages 268-269. – www.face.net.
485. The Liberty Bell - Independence National Historical Park (U.S. National Park Service)
486. Armitage, David, The Declaration of Independence in Global Perspective. – available on-line.
487. Ibid., p. 1.
488. Ibid., p. 2.
489. 1776 treaty with Indian tribe a sister of Declaration of Independence – online.
490. Loyalist's rebuttal, Thomas Hutchinson, Strictures Upon the Declaration . . . , 1776, selections. Available online.
491. An Answer to the Declaration of the American Congress | American Battlefield Trust. Available online.
492. See https://classroom.monticello.org/media-item/short-review-of-the-declaration/
493. Walton, Rus, Fundamentals for American Christians, Plymouth Rock Foundation, 1978. The author has a mini course of 14 lessons available going through this course – www.plymrock.org
494. DeMar, Gary, So You Think you Want a Revolution? July 31, 2012 - So You Think You Want a Revolution? • Gary DeMar
495. See the list in this article as an example - How the American Revolution Spurred Independence Movements Around the World | HISTORY
496. Manifesto of the Communist Party – online.
497. Titus, Herb, The Declaration of Independence: The Christian Legacy, Titus Publications, 1995, p. 45.
498. Jones, Archie, *Thomas Jefferson, the Man & the Myth,* Plymouth Rock Foundation, 1998, p. 9.
499. John Adams to Abigail Adams, April 26, 1777 – Founders online.